Record Keeping in a Hybrid Environment

CHANDOS
INFORMATION PROFESSIONAL SERIES

Series Editor: Ruth Rikowski
(email: Rikowskigr@aol.com)

Chandos' new series of books are aimed at the busy information professional. They have been specially commissioned to provide the reader with an authoritative view of current thinking. They are designed to provide easy-to-read and (most importantly) practical coverage of topics that are of interest to librarians and other information professionals. If you would like a full listing of current and forthcoming titles, please visit our web site **www.chandospublishing.com** or contact Hannah Grace-Williams on email info@chandospublishing.com or telephone number +44 (0) 1865 884447.

New authors: we are always pleased to receive ideas for new titles; if you would like to write a book for Chandos, please contact Dr Glyn Jones on email gjones@chandospublishing.com or telephone number +44 (0) 1865 884447.

Bulk orders: some organisations buy a number of copies of our books. If you are interested in doing this, we would be pleased to discuss a discount. Please contact Hannah Grace-Williams on email info@chandospublishing.com or telephone number +44 (0) 1865 884447.

Record Keeping in a Hybrid Environment

Managing the creation, use, preservation and disposal of unpublished information objects in context

EDITED BY
ALISTAIR TOUGH
AND
MICHAEL MOSS

Chandos Publishing
Oxford · England

Chandos Publishing (Oxford) Limited
Chandos House
5 & 6 Steadys Lane
Stanton Harcourt
Oxford OX29 5RL
UK
Tel: +44 (0) 1865 884447 Fax: +44 (0) 1865 884448
Email: info@chandospublishing.com
www.chandospublishing.com

First published in Great Britain in 2006

ISBN:
1 84334 142 5 (paperback)
1 84334 186 7 (hardback)
978 1 84334 142 0 (paperback)
978 1 84334 186 4 (hardback)

British Library Cataloguing-in-Publication Data.
A catalogue record for this book is available from the British Library.

Typeset by Domex e-Data Pvt. Ltd.
Printed in the UK and USA.

Printed in the UK by 4edge Limited - www.4edge.co.uk

Contents

Introduction

The target audience for this book is people charged with responsibility for record keeping, particularly those in mid-career. It is the aim of the authors to enable busy practitioners to become familiar with recent developments in theory and practice. Over the last ten to fifteen years there have been a number of important projects that have addressed record keeping. A great many conferences have been held. Standards have been promulgated where none existed before and a great many publications have appeared. Against this backdrop, it has been a challenge for even the most conscientious practising archivist or records manager to keep abreast of developments.

The number of people employed as record-keeping professionals has increased markedly in recent years. Legislation covering freedom of information, data protection and the liabilities of company directors has been a major factor in driving this development. The implications of regulatory change, and their impact on records professionals, are discussed by Claire Johnson and Moira Rankin in Chapter 5. As the demand for skilled personnel has outstripped the supply of formally qualified staff, a significant number of people have found themselves being reassigned by their employers from other responsibilities. A few of these have been supported in acquiring qualifications, usually by distance learning. Most of those who have been 'recycled' into record-keeping roles have had to find their way as best they can. This book should be helpful to them. It is not, however, a substitute for a course of study leading to a recognised qualification.

Record keeping, encompassing archives and records management in the broadest sense, is a relatively new field of study. The boundaries of the field are poorly defined and porous. This is characteristic of emerging disciplines and need not be a cause of professional insecurity. Physics, economics and other long-established academic disciplines went through a similar phase and established their boundaries, and the methods of research that are appropriate within those boundaries, over a prolonged period of development. One of the potential advantages of working in a developing field is that interdisciplinary approaches can prove stimulating and productive. The realisation of this potential is demonstrated *inter alia* in James Currall's chapter on security in the digital domain (Chapter 3) and Seamus Ross's chapter on digital preservation (Chapter 6).

The contributors to this book all have links either to the Humanities Advanced Technology and Information Institute in the University of Glasgow or to Glasgow University Archive Services or both. HATII has among its research fellows and staff people with backgrounds in archaeology, history, librarianship, mathematics, philosophy and statistics, as well as archivists, digital curators and records managers. As a result, HATII seminars are often challenging, innovative and thought-provoking. Within HATII a postgraduate degree for archivists, digital curators and records managers is delivered. Doctoral students are also becoming part of the mix. Those contributors who are based in Glasgow University Archive Services have service delivery responsibilities similar to those of archivists and records managers elsewhere in the British Isles and other parts of the world. The collaboration between academics and practising record-keeping professionals that this book represents is stimulating and fruitful. Collaborative working, however, is not an easy matter. A great many hours of 'off duty' time have been devoted to writing by those whose primary responsibility is service delivery.

Research is an essential activity in developing and defining the emerging record-keeping discipline: it does not have to be limited to those who hold academic appointments. The findings of two innovative research projects are reported in Chapters 7 and 8. Chapter 7, by Rachel Hosker and Lesley Richmond, describes research on appraisal that brings theory and practice into conjunction. Similarly, Chapter 8, by Victoria Peters and Lesley Richmond, reports on research into the use of functional approaches to the description of records. The latter research has recently been extended to allow experimental application of the newly developed techniques to company records. Historical research provides a mode of research that comes naturally to the many archivists who studied history at university. There is some published historical research, for example by Levy and Campbell-Kelly, which has addressed record keeping in ways that provide new insights and theoretical perspectives.[1] Other techniques are likely to prove equally valuable. The methods of the social sciences can be utilised, *inter alia*: to measure the performance of record-keeping systems; to study the realities of professional life (e.g. how do archivists really appraise records?) and thereby identify gaps between rhetoric and reality; and to engage with users and their perceived needs. Ian Anderson deals with user evaluation, in relation to digitisation projects, in Chapter 9. A word of caution may be appropriate here. User studies can be misleading where those participating lack necessary knowledge. For example, users will sometimes indicate that they want archives without provenance but rarely have any conception of what the result might look like.

Case studies too have a potentially valuable role to play. Some published case studies are of limited value. This is particularly true of those written by the staff of IT vendors: a genre in which everything is a success because failures are not acknowledged publicly. An altogether better kind of case study is that advocated by Peter Checkland in the name of the soft systems approach to information systems. The essential steps in a soft systems case study are: the explicit identification of the theoretical basis for the work; the definition of a research methodology; conducting the research project; and reflecting on the findings and how these may modify the theoretical basis and research methodology. Within the emerging discipline of information systems, the followers of the soft systems approach argue that they have indeed helped to define the field of study and to produce new theoretical insights. It is reasonable to suggest that something similar is already beginning to occur in the related field of record keeping and that there is every reason to welcome and encourage this. The work of Azman Mat-Isa may be cited as an instance of this kind of approach. In Chapter 4 he relates the discipline of risk management to the concerns of professional record keepers.

Much of the new thinking on record keeping discussed in this book originates in Australia and Canada. Many of the key ideas are introduced and discussed in the opening chapter. The development of these ideas has not taken place in a vacuum. Corruption has played a role in making good records management a priority for the public sector in Australia. In the published proceedings of a 1994 conference Sue McKemmish acknowledged widespread problems of financial abuse while the Auditor General of Western Australia stated that poor record keeping had been a major factor in a child abuse scandal.[2] In Canada, the University of British Columbia, at least, has benefited from US Department of Defense funds. Meanwhile, the urgent need to rethink the rationale of post-Apartheid archives has brought forth a welter of creative thinking in South Africa.[3]

We in the United Kingdom have contributed relatively little, so far, to advances in theory and practice. In part, paradoxically, this is because we have more and older archives than our colleagues overseas. British academics charged with educating the next generation of records professionals have been so weighed down with the teaching of palaeography and diplomatics that they have struggled to find time to engage in the development of new theoretical perspectives. This is beginning to change. We are very well placed as a metropolitan centre to contribute to new thinking both in the Commonwealth and in the wider English-speaking world. Recent enquiries that relate to Britain's involvement in the war in Iraq have suggested that there is an urgent need to improve record keeping at the heart of the UK government.[4] The increased demand for postgraduate education that focuses on the needs of the twenty-first century is bound to have an impact on the contribution made by British academics and commentators to international debates. In the final chapter a number of themes that must continue to be addressed are discussed. These include the emergence of an audit culture, the challenges of disintermediation and the need to engage with postmodern critiques (and critics) of archives.

We should like to acknowledge the support and encouragement that we have received from Glyn Jones at Chandos Publishing, from the contributors to this book and from other colleagues past and present. Our students have stimulated us with hypotheses and questions to a degree probably greater than they recognise. On behalf of all of the contributors we should like to thank Victoria Peters for compiling the index. It did not prove feasible to circulate drafts of all the chapters to all of the contributors, so it should not be assumed that every opinion expressed here is subscribed to by all of the contributors.

Alistair Tough
Senior Research Fellow, Humanities Advanced Technology and Information Institute, University of Glasgow and Archivist and Records Manager, NHS Greater Glasgow

Michael Moss
Professor of Archive Studies, Humanities Advanced Technology and Information Institute, University of Glasgow

Notes

1. Campbell-Kelly, M., 'Railway clearing house and Victorian data processing', in Bud-Frierman, L. (ed.), *Information Acumen. Understanding and Use of Knowledge in Modern Business* (London and New York, 1994), pp. 51–74; Levy, D., *Scrolling Forward: Making Sense of Documents in the Digital Age* (New York, 2001).

2. Douglas, Janine (ed.), *Total Recall: Managing the Information Environment for Corporate Accountability* (Records Management Association of Australia (WA Branch), 1994), pp. 1–43.
3. Hamilton, C. et al. (eds), *Refiguring the Archive* (Dordrecht and London, 2002).
4. Butler of Brockwell, Lord (Chairman), *Review of Intelligence on Weapons of Mass Destruction*, HCP 898 (London, 2004); Hutton, J.B.E. Baron, *Report of the Inquiry into the Circumstances Surrounding the Death of Dr David Kelly CMG*, HC 247 (London, 2004).

List of abbreviations

ACARM	Association of Commonwealth Archivists and Records Managers
AIIM	Association for Information and Image Management
AIRMIC	Association of Insurance and Risk Managers
ALARM	Association of Local Authority Risk Managers
AMARC	Association for Manuscripts and Archives in Research Collections
ARELDA	Archiving of Electronic Digital Data and Records Project (Switzerland)
ARK	Archival Resource Key
ARMA	Association of Research Managers and Administrators
ASLIB	Association for Information Management
BAC	Business Acceptable Communications model
BRC	Bioinformatics Research Centre, University of Glasgow
CBS	Centraal Bureau voor de Statistieck (Netherlands)
CCLRC	Council for the Central Laboratory of the Research Councils (UK)
CI	content information
CLIC	Community-Led Image Collection
CPD	continuing professional development
CRS	Commonwealth Record Series
CRKM	Clever Recordkeeping Metadata Project (Monash University)
DAC	Digital Archiving Consultancy (UK)
DCC	Digital Curation Centre (UK)
DELOS	Network of Excellence on Digital Libraries
DIRKS	Design and Implementation of Record Keeping Systems
DLI2	Digital Libraries Initiative Phase 2 (of the NSF) (US)
DoD	(US) Department of Defense
DOI	Digital Object Identifier
dpa	Deutsche Presse-Agentur
DPA	Data Protection Act 1998

DTD	document type definition
EAC	Encoded Archival Context
EAD	Encoded Archival Description
ECPA	European Commission on Preservation and Access
EDM	electronic data management
EDMS	electronic document management systems
EDRMS	electronic document and records management system
EIR	Environmental Information Regulations
ERM	electronic records management
ERPANET	Electronic Resource Preservation and Access Network
FAT	function, activity, transaction [analysis]
Fedora	Flexible Extensible Digital Object and Repository Architecture
FoI	Freedom of Information Act 2000
FOI	freedom of information
FoISA	Freedom of Information (Scotland) Act 2002
GASHE	Gateway to the Archives of Scottish Higher Education
GUAS	Glasgow University Archive Services
HATII	Humanities Advanced Technology and Information Institute
HMSO	Her Majesty's Stationery Office
IAR	Information Assets Register
ICT	information and communications technology
IM	information management
InterPARES	International Research on Permanent Authentic Records in Electronic Systems
IPR	intellectual property rights
IRM	Institute of Risk Management
ISAAR(CPF)	International Standard Archival Authority Record for Corporate Bodies, Persons and Families
ISAD(G)	General International Standard Archival Description
ISMS	information security management system
ISO	International Standards Organisation
IT	information technology
JISC	Joint Information Systems Committee (UK)
MLA	Museums, Archives and Libraries Council
MS	Microsoft
MSSI	metadata standards, sets and initiatives
NAA	National Archives of Australia
NAHSTE	Navigational Aids for the History of Science, Technology and the Environment

NARA	National Archives and Records Administration (US)
NeSC	National e-Science Centre (UK)
NINCH	National Initiative for a Networked Cultural Heritage
NISO	National Information Standards Organization (US)
NLNZ	National Library of New Zealand
NSF	National Science Foundation (US)
OAIS	Open Archival Information System
OCLC	Online Computer Library Center
OCR	optical character recognition
OPSI	Office for Public Sector Information
PC	personal computer
PDCA	plan, do, check, act cycle
PDF	portable document format
PDI	preservation description information
PREMIS	Preservation Metadata Implementation Strategies
PSQG	Public Service Quality Group
PURL	Persistent Uniform Resource Locator
RCRG	Records Continuum Research Group (Australia)
RI	representation information
RIPA	Regulation of Investigatory Powers Act 2000
RKMS	Recordkeeping Metadata Scheme (Australia)
RLG	Research Libraries Group
RM	records management
RSLP	Research Support Libraries Programme
SoA	statement of applicability
SOUDAAM	Source-Oriented User-Driven Asset-Aware Model
TNA	The National Archives (UK)
UBC	University of British Columbia
UML	Unified Modelling Language
VERS	Victorian Electronic Records Strategy (Australia)
XML	eXtensible Mark-up Language

List of figures and tables

Figures

Tables

About the contributors

Ian Anderson is Lecturer in New Technologies for the Humanities in the Humanities Advanced Technology and Information Institute, University of Glasgow. He teaches the digital strand of the Institute's MSc in Information Retrieval and Preservation, and lectures on digitisation to postgraduate students in Computing Science and undergraduates in the Faculty of Arts. Ian was one of the principal researchers and authors of the acclaimed *NINCH Guide to Good Practice in the Digital Representation and Management of Cultural Heritage Materials* (Washington, DC, 2002) and has taught digitisation to cultural heritage professionals in the USA, Europe and New Zealand. His current research interests include archival information retrieval and innovative interfaces to online archival finding aids. Ian is Convenor of the Association for History and Computing UK and Secretary General of the International Association for History and Computing. He is also a member of the Executive Council of the American Association for History and Computing and is on the Editorial Board of Programme: Electronic Library and Information Systems.

James Currall is Director of Strategy and Planning in IT Services and also a senior research fellow in the Humanities Advanced Technology and Information Institute (HATII) at the University of Glasgow. In both these roles he contributes to the new MSc in Information Management and Preservation at the University. He has conducted funded research projects on effective records management, information security, middleware technologies and, most recently, into risk and the value of information assets and how these may effectively be used in the construction of sound business cases for information projects. James's background is in statistics but he is more likely to be heard speaking about the future of archiving and the other information professions.

Rachel Hosker qualified in Archives and Records Management in 2000 and then worked on a number of projects for an information management consultancy. She joined Glasgow University Archive

Services as Business Archivist in 2002, managing the business needs of GUAS clients with the provision of a research collection as well as managing the outreach and teaching programme for the department. This includes input on the MSc in Information Management and Preservation course. Rachel has led projects to survey and rescue endangered business archives in Scotland. She is currently Joint Secretary of the Business Records Group of the Society of Archivists and has published work on business archive provision.

Claire Johnson joined the University of Glasgow in 1997 as Senior Records Manager. Since 2003 she has been the University's Freedom of Information Officer. Her research interests include the development of records management for an age of digital governance and the usability of digitally disseminated information. She teaches on several courses at the university and is a member of the editorial board for the *Journal of E-Government*. She is also a member of the university's Centre for Regulatory Studies based in the Faculty of Law and contributed to their publications on regulation. Her previous work experience has included: Unilever, Peabody Housing Trust, University of Liverpool and the Victoria & Albert Museum. She has studied records and information management at the Universities of Loughborough, Liverpool and Liverpool John Moores.

Azman Mat-Isa is Lecturer in the Faculty of Information Management, MARA University of Technology, Malaysia (UiTM). He has a mixed academic background with undergraduate qualification in mathematics and postgraduate qualifications in library science from UiTM and records management from University College London. He is a PhD candidate in the Humanities Advanced Technology and Information Institute, University of Glasgow, researching records management and accountability of governance. He is also exploring the significant relationship between managing records and risk management in underpinning the effective and efficient operations of an organisation.

Michael Moss is Research Professor in Archival Studies in HATII, where he directs the MSc in Information Management and Preservation. From 1974 until 2001 he was archivist of the University of Glasgow. He is a board member of the National Trust for Scotland and has served on many archival bodies. He has written widely and his latest book, with Laurence Brockliss of the University of Oxford, *Advancing with the Army,* which examines the careers and families of British army doctors during the French wars, will be published in the autumn of 2006 by Oxford University Press.

Victoria Peters graduated in Classics from the University of Oxford before obtaining an MA in Archive Studies from University College, London. She subsequently worked in a range of archive repositories including Lambeth Palace Library, London Metropolitan Archives and Warwick University. She joined the University of Glasgow in 2001 as project manager of the Gateway to Archives of Scottish Higher Education (GASHE) project. In 2003, she embarked on a research project at the university to explore a function-based approach to archival description. In 2006, following the project's completion, she embarked on a second research project, exploring the development of flexible and dynamic online finding aids. From 2004, she has taught on the university's MSc in Information Management and Preservation. She is a member of the Working Group on Record Creators' Functions of the Provisional Section on Standards and Best Practices of the International Council on Archives as well as a member of the committee of the Society of Archivists EAD/Data Exchange Group.

Frank Rankin has been Head of the Open Government Unit at the Department for International Development since 2003. A graduate of the Universities of Glasgow and Liverpool, he has worked as an archivist and records manager for Shell International, the Business Archives Council of Scotland, the University of Glasgow and South Lanarkshire Council.

Moira Rankin received her MA in Archives and Records Management at UCL in 1995, having previously graduated with an MA in History from Glasgow and a Diploma in Management from Heriot-Watt University. She has since been employed by the University of Glasgow in a variety of posts and is currently Senior Archivist. She has been involved in generating a million pounds in project and research income for Glasgow University Archive Services and has undertaken consultancy for several external clients.

Lesley Richmond is the Director of Archive Services at the University of Glasgow and a Senior Research Fellow within HATII. She has been involved in major surveys of business archives in the United Kingdom and is a member of the Steering Committee of the International Council on Archives Section on Business and Labour Archives. Her current research interests lie in the selection and appraisal of archives, in developing methodologies in the appraisal of business archives and exploring new types of archival description (function based). She is also concerned to improve access to and use of historical records, especially to the benefit of the record-creating institution, and to improve public understanding of the role of the record-keeping professions.

Seamus Ross, Professor of Humanities Informatics and Digital Curation, is founding Director of HATII (Humanities Advanced Technology and Information Institute) (*http://www.hatii.arts.gla.ac.uk/*) at the University of Glasgow. He is an Associate Director of the Digital Curation Centre (*http://www.dcc.ac.uk/*), a co-principal investigator in the DELOS Digital Libraries Network of Excellence (*http://www.dpc.delos.ac.uk*) and Principal Director of DigitalPreservationEurope (DPE) (*http://www.digitalpreservationeurope.eu*). He was also Principal Director of ERPANET, a European Commission activity to enhance the preservation of digital objects (*http://www.erpanet.org/*), and engaged in the DigiCULT Forum which worked to improve the take-up of cutting-edge research and technology by the cultural heritage sector (*http://www.digicult.info*). Before joining Glasgow he was Head of ICT at the British Academy and a technologist at a company specialising in knowledge engineering. During 2005/6 he was Visiting Fellow at the Oxford Internet Institute and Visiting Scholar at Wolfson College, University of Oxford. Some of his publications are available at *http://eprints.erpanet.org/*.

Alistair Tough is a Senior Research Fellow in the Humanities Advanced Technology and Information Institute in the University of Glasgow, UK. He is also the Archivist and Records Manager of the National Health Service Glasgow and Clyde Board. He has held visiting research fellowships at Michigan, Oxford and Stanford Universities. He served on the British Standards Institution's subcommittee on Records Management, 2000–05. In 1999 and 2000 he was seconded to the Civil Service Department in Tanzania as an adviser to the Public Sector Reform Programme. He has undertaken records management consultancy work in Britain, Ethiopia, Rwanda and Zambia. In 2002 he received the Annual Award of the Records Management Society of Great Britain.

The editors may be contacted as follows:

a.tough@archives.gla.ac.uk

m.moss@hatii.arts.gla.ac.uk

Records and the transition to the digital

Alistair Tough[1]

Introduction

Much of the existing literature of record keeping is oriented to an ideal world where record-keeping professionals enjoy the support of top management, have a clear and comprehensive mandate, possess ample resources and have a securely founded change management strategy. For many, the challenge is to move the real world towards this desirable state of affairs. It would be a mistake, however, to imagine that we need to start with a blank sheet. There are useful tools and methodologies currently available, and there is much in recent theoretical debate that can be of value to the practitioner.

It is often said that technology has made a massive difference to contemporary record keeping. One has only to think of composite documents that incorporate word-processed text, graphics and tables produced using several different software packages to see the truth in this statement. However, it is worth reminding ourselves that important organisational changes began before the widespread use of personal computers. These organisational changes have included decentralisation and delayering. They have often been accompanied by a mindset that sees back office functions as 'waste'. Here it is important to remind ourselves that there are two major traditions of record keeping in the English-speaking world.[2] The Commonwealth tradition, exported from Britain to Australia, India, New Zealand, South Africa and many developing nations in Africa, Asia, the Pacific and the West Indies, is founded on the principle of pre-action aggregation and routing of records. This has been widely implemented via registry systems. The American tradition, in contrast, is based on individual action followed by post-hoc filing. This distinction is particularly significant because most software packages intended for office use are based on an American approach that cuts out 'back office' functions.

One other preliminary observation needs to be introduced here, regarding the distinction between 'routine' and 'creative' work. Shepherd and Yeo suggest that the latter can pose greater challenges for record-keeping systems.[3] There can be little doubt that routine processes generally lend themselves to the kind of systematic approaches favoured by record-keeping professionals. However, any suggestion that creative work will always and necessarily generate difficulties needs to be examined critically. The degree of external regulation and internal discipline can be crucial factors. These points will be developed further below.

Models of record keeping

Models, and graphic representations, are appropriate to the age in which we live – an era that is noticeably less text bound than most of the preceding century. Levy, alongside many others, argues that a wide range of non-text items ('maps, diagrams, pictures, photographs, and all manner of other conventional and well-articulated, nonverbal representations'[4]) can be regarded as documents in the contemporary world. Models can elucidate thinking, not least where abstract concepts are concerned. Models may also help us to work across disciplinary boundaries. Marilyn Strathern[5] reminds us that all models are products of abstraction and possess ritual and symbolic significance. There is a strong case for saying that we should not shy away from the ritual and symbolic aspects of modelling, as they may work for us. In a paper to the Society of Archivists' 2004 conference, James Currall spoke about the excessive confidence that often characterises IT professionals. As he put it, 'computing scientists' key skills [include] thinking all answers to information problems have been developed since the birth of the computer (by them)'.[6] Strathern makes the point that this confidence derives, in part at least, from the fact that they 'possess' ways of representing reality, even of insisting that it must be made to conform to pre-determined schemata of their devising. Similar phenomena can be observed in respect of knowledge managers. One could argue that this phenomenon has an inherent tendency to produce negative consequences, especially where the clients' needs and views are disregarded by those who 'possess' the dominant model. Among record-keeping professionals, two models have dominated discourse: the life cycle and the records continuum.

The life cycle model has been influential among record-keeping professionals since the middle of the twentieth century.[7] It is usually expressed as a progression from record creation, through active use to a semi-current phase and then to a non-current end point where the record may be selected for preservation in an archive or destroyed. In life cycle thinking, it is generally assumed that records are transferred to an archive so that they may be used for historical and cultural purposes after their value for business purposes has been exhausted. The life cycle model is non-linear: time is not expressed in weeks, months or even years but in stages. Nor are places (office of creation, records centre and archive) separated with any great precision. Relationships within the life cycle can be viewed as a continuum in which place and time are linked. Thus office and current, records centre and semi-current and archive and non-current are seen as necessarily linked terms.

The life cycle approach has been challenged by records continuum models. In its earlier versions the records continuum model constituted an empirical response to the evident inadequacies of the life cycle. These included the following:

- Records do not flow in only one direction. Records that have been put aside may experience a new phase of business use. For example, records relating to the design of an aircraft carrier may be little used between the completion of construction and a comprehensive overhaul many years later. Nonetheless, they take on a fresh currency when the overhaul commences.

- Records creation is not the first step required in a comprehensive model. System design is the first, and crucial, stage in a record-keeping system. This fact was not obvious to those who devised the life cycle model because they worked in an apparently stable paper-based environment where the essential design features of record-keeping systems were often taken for granted.

- Some records may be of value for historical and cultural purposes while simultaneously being of value for practical purposes. In other words, the passage of time does not necessarily imply that records cease to be of value for business. For example, records of properly conducted geological surveys have an indefinite life span because the mineralisation of the earth's crust does not alter significantly over the centuries. Similarly, astronomical observations made by previous generations may continue to be of interest to contemporary science.

Frank Upward has offered a variant of the records continuum model that he regards as a 'paradigm shift'. This has been created in response to a series of challenging questions:

> What will recordkeeping and archiving processes be like when the location of the material matters less than its accessibility, when records no longer have to move across clear boundaries in space and time to be seen as part of an archive, and when an understanding that records exist in spacetime, not space and time, is more intuitively grasped by any practitioner? Such a scenario calls for the invention of new rules within a new game, and will result in a significant re-patterning of knowledge.[8]

Working with colleagues, Upward has produced a model with four 'dimensions' and four 'continua' or axes.[9] The dimensions are: create, where records are created as a reflection of individual users' needs; capture, where records are put into a context that makes them comprehensible and usable to immediate colleagues and clients of the creator; organise, where records are further contextualised to make them comprehensible and usable to the larger organisation in which the creator works; and pluralise, where records are mediated to the widest possible audiences. Upward's continua are: identity, linking individuals to successively more distant organisational settings; transactionality, reflecting the classic hierarchy of functional analyses; record-keeping containers, linking documents to archives via intermediate stages; and evidentiality, linking documentary evidence to concepts of corporate and collective memory.

Upward has represented these ideas graphically by means of his 'dartboard' (see Figure 1.1).[10] Throughout his writings Upward has stressed that this model should be read as non-linear and in a dynamic and flexible way, involving a multiplicity of variants. For instance, when records relating to a matter of public controversy are leaked to the press, the dimension 'pluralise' may occur simultaneously with that of 'capture'.[11] He argues that the adoption of a spacetime continuum is at the heart of the 'paradigm shift' involved in this variant of the records continuum. If this is so, at least one question seems to arise.

Why does Upward use a flat, single plane representation centred on record creation to illustrate his thinking? This appears to be implicitly at odds with his assertion:

Figure 1.1 The Upward 'dartboard'

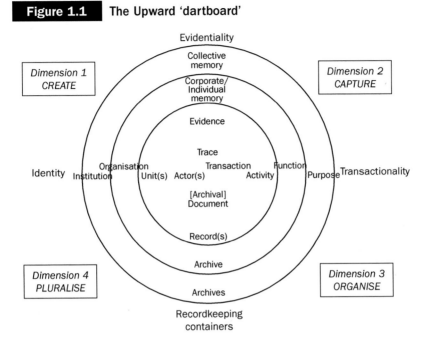

The capacity to imbibe information about recordkeeping practices in agencies will be crucial to the effectiveness of ... archival 'organisations' ... They will have to monitor the distribution and exercise of custodial responsibilities for electronic records *from before the time of their creation*.[12] (my italics)

If the records continuum model is genuinely based on spacetime thinking then an improved multidimensional representation should be possible. The Einstein-Minkowski lightcone model relates space and time to each other through their shared relationship with light (see Figure 1.2).[13]

If we reconstruct Upward's 'dartboard' around the lightcone model, the dimensions (creation, capture, organise and pluralise) are located on progressively wider portions of one cone while his four axes or continua (evidence, transactions, identity and recordkeeping) all meet at the point of creation. If the first dimension (creation) is used as the nodal point in a lightcone model then it becomes logical to create a double lightcone of the kind devised by Minkowski and Einstein on which a further dimension, 'system design', is represented. The continua can be extended into this additional dimension. The record-keeping containers continuum naturally refers to classification schemata and/or file plans in the system

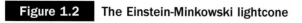

Figure 1.2 The Einstein-Minkowski lightcone

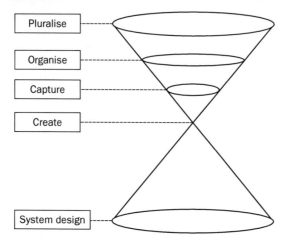

Pluralise

Organise

Capture

Create

System design

Alternative visualisation of the records continuum model, using the Einstein-Minkowski lightcone to represent space-time continuum.

design dimension. The identity continuum deals with the distinction between functions and departmental structures. The evidentiality continuum represents conscious intent (to create and capture records). The transactionality continuum needs to encompass all levels of function, activity, transaction (FAT) analysis to inform system design.

A reconstruction of the records continuum model around the lightcone is intellectually satisfying and can stimulate thinking 'outside the box'. There is scope, however, for alternative approaches to modelling record-keeping systems.

Organisational theory

There was a time when the dominant discourse on organisational theory emphasised hierarchy, rules and top-down management. The work of the sociologist Max Weber on rational bureaucracies may be regarded as representing an advanced variant of such thinking.[14] Hierarchical models were reflected in record-keeping systems. As Martin Campbell-Kelly puts it, 'Victorian data processing was highly routinized and a clerk was often reduced to an automaton'.[15] Graphically the mathematical theory behind industrial age hierarchical thinking can be represented as a simple tree (see Figure 1.3).

Figure 1.3 Classic tree diagram

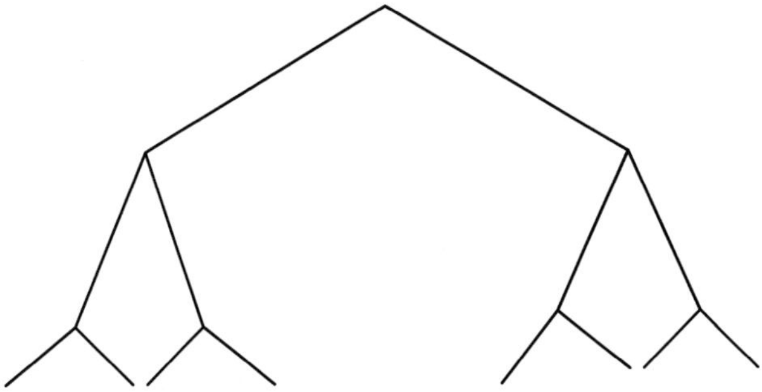

Recent developments in organisational theory emphasise a different approach, with delayering, team working and so forth. Hans Hofman has given a sophisticated account of the impact that these changes have had, and are having, on record keeping.[16] Hofman attributes the changes, in part at least, to the impact of radical innovations in information and communications technology. He raises some pertinent points:

> The loosening of the organizational grip on recordkeeping and the weakening of bureaucratic regimes and rules have their impact on record-creating and subsequently on the forming of archives. Will an archive become a 'collection' of individual approaches of recordkeeping ... Where or how will the organizational needs then be represented?[17]

There is an additional point that many theorists of archive and records management appear to overlook. Human beings are fundamentally different from other living creatures in that we are capable of being aware of theories, of being influenced by them and of supporting, resisting and/or adapting them. Accordingly, our thinking needs to reflect this contrast with the subject matter of the natural sciences. As social creatures we are apt to internalise and/or reject theoretical constructs in conjunction with other people, including colleagues, in ways that reflect our cultural background. The varying ways in which we do this are likely to lead to differences of interpretation within large organisations, even when there appears to be a broad consensus of opinion.

To think that the hierarchical organisational models of the past represent an absolute historical reality is a mistake. It is clear the theories did shape reality in some places and at some times. Nonetheless, there is evidence that they were circumvented. The novelist P.G. Wodehouse wrote an entertaining autobiographical novel set in a bank where soul-destroying routine was decreed by management and evaded by young clerks with a passion for practical jokes, cricket and other diversions.[18] Similarly, contemporary organisational theories do not represent concrete current reality so much as thinking about it. Their proponents often claim that new theories will liberate human potential. Whether the staff called upon to implement them will invariably regard this as being the case is open to doubt. One variant of more complex organisational theory advanced by Dee W. Hock is what he calls the chaordic organisation. On the basis of his experience as Chief Executive Officer of VISA USA and VISA International, Hock argues that chaordic organisations are characterised by the distribution of power and governance, functional subsidiarity, malleability, durability and their capacity to embrace diversity and change.[19] Graphically, the mathematical theory behind chaordic thinking can be represented as a graph (see Figure 1.4). From the perspective of record keeping, what is striking about the chaordic graph is the extent to which it mirrors the design architecture of web-based systems. Perhaps this suggests that organisations (or, at least, some organisations) and their record keeping are changing in parallel.

Figure 1.4   Graph diagram

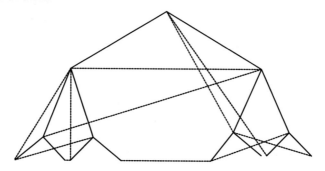

This consideration of organisational theories raises questions about the importation of models from the natural sciences into a human/social context. In particular, there are passages in Upward's writings that suggest that he is seeking to divorce his version of records continuum thinking from its social and human setting and from the context in which it has been formulated. For example:

You do not create a persistent model by basing it on current communication needs or tailoring it to dominant professional perspectives.[20] [And]

The terms (used in the model) are self-defining and not shaped by the need to communicate to an audience of any kind.[21]

The techniques of action research and of soft systems methodology, in particular, have considerable potential as a way forward for research on record-keeping issues. Unlike the commonplace approach to case studies, the soft systems approach requires that the researcher(s) begin by making their theoretical constructs explicit. Research methodologies are then derived from that fundamental framework. These methodologies are applied in real-world situations and, in addition to producing solutions to real-world problems, the findings of the research serve to modify both the worldview and the methodology.[22] This approach is not confined to academia. It is already being used by IT consultants and has the potential to be equally helpful to records management consultants.

DIRKS

DIRKS (Design and Implementation of Record Keeping Systems) is an eight-stage methodology for the managed strategic improvement of record-keeping systems. Some of the stages can be undertaken concurrently. The most up-to-date version of the DIRKS manual is available, along with some supporting materials, from the website of the National Archives of Australia.[23] An excellent guide to using DIRKS is available from the British Standards Institution.[24] In Australian practice, DIRKS is often used in conjunction with the Keyword AAA classification scheme which is dealt with in more detail below. The stages of the DIRKS methodology are:

- **A.** *Preliminary investigation of the organisation's boundaries, mission, decision-making processes, mandate and corporate culture.* In the light of what has been said about organisational theory, one might wish to question whether there will be a single corporate culture. Undertaking individual interviews and PEST (political, economic, social and technological issues) analyses with groups can supplement the annual reports, organisational charts and other formal documentation commonly used in a stage A analysis. This kind of analysis can be used to build a business case for action.

- **B.** *Analysis of business activity including the identification of core functions and the processes by means of which they are delivered.* The great advantage of taking this approach is that it enables solutions tailored to the specific needs of the organisation. A possible drawback is the extent to which this kind of analysis is predicated on 'official', top-down views. Sensitivity to the way in which groups within the organisation may have articulated alternative views on what they do, and how it relates to the wider organisation, may be called for.

- **C.** *Identification of evidential needs and record-keeping requirements.* Essentially this is about meeting the needs of the organisation conceived in formal terms as a single entity. Sensitivity to alternative perspectives may be helpful to the record-keeping professional, not least in avoiding provoking avoidable antagonism.

- **D.** *Assessment of the organisation's existing systems.* This is essentially a records survey conducted against the backdrop of a strong and pre-existing analytical framework. Many record-keeping professionals attempt to undertake system improvement commencing with an assessment of the organisation's existing systems and without undertaking anything approximating to DIRKS stages A to C. Unless the record-keeping professional has been in post long enough to absorb a thoroughgoing knowledge of the organisation, starting at stage D is likely to produce disappointing results.

- **E.** *Identification of strategies for record keeping.* This builds on a gap analysis, comparing the findings of stage D with the desiderata derived from stage C. The four strands of strategy identified in the DIRKS manual are policy (formal orders), design (system specification and technological solutions), standards (particularly in an electronic environment) and the delivery of practical solutions oriented to users' needs. The first three strands are essentially top-down. If strategies that promise to deliver integrated improvement 'across the board' are preferred then policy, design and standards are likely to be emphasised.

- **F.** *Design of a record-keeping system.* This stage too must take the findings of the gap analysis as a starting point because the gap analysis identifies changes that are required. The strategies identified in stage E are turned into a project plan for implementing change. It is important to involve users at this stage. The project plan should have a timescale, specify outputs and indicate the resources to be deployed.

- **G.** *Implementation.* This is about turning the plan produced in stage F into a reality. Staff training and change management are crucial elements. As the DIRKS manual puts it, 'Strategies for better recordkeeping … are likely to require changes in corporate behaviour.'[25] Most writers on change management emphasise the importance of building and maintaining a guiding coalition for change, of changing people's outlooks and attitudes and of undertaking a multi-stage process. Successful change usually involves the delivery of 'quick wins'. These are outcomes that demonstrate that change can work and will be beneficial. According to this way of thinking, there is a strong case for commencing a long-term strategy with an initiative or initiatives that are designed to deliver practical solutions oriented to users' needs. These may encapsulate the elements of policy, design and standards that it is intended to make more general at a later stage.

- **H.** *Review and monitoring.* This may be the final stage in a DIRKS project and/or the first stage of a new one. The objective is to make sure new record-keeping systems continue to work properly and to meet the requirements of the organisation.

A full-blown DIRKS project is avowedly resource intensive. The records management improvement team to be assembled for a 'Rolls-Royce' project should comprise:

- project manager
- record-keeping professionals
- information managers
- information technology specialists
- corporate governance and risk management specialists (including auditors and lawyers)
- business area experts
- staff representatives.

The following observations may prove helpful to practitioners attempting to use DIRKS in real-world settings.

- The DIRKS approach has a tendency to be 'top-down' and can be experienced by some clients as authoritarian and inflexible. This may be unavoidable where risk management is the dominant driver for change. Nonetheless, it can be mitigated where conscious measures are taken to prevent alienation, for example by means of focus groups and other techniques of client engagement.

- Only stage A has to encompass the whole organisation. There are advantages to undertaking stage B across the whole organisation, if resources permit. Everything else can be done by focusing on sub-units.

■ Success breeds success. A strategy that includes 'quick wins' is more likely to build a momentum for change. For example, the experience of the Tanzania Records Management Project was that, after a few ministries had had well-designed and effective new record-keeping systems installed, demand for the services of the project rose sharply.[26]

■ In targeting effort, one can look for priority and/or risk areas. The DIRKS manual does say that one of the options to consider at stage F is 'develop and implement a new records system for high-risk areas of the organisation'.[27] Generally speaking, the most heavily scrutinised and regulated areas and those that are process-driven are least likely to give cause for concern. In contrast, 'creative' areas are likely to be high-risk areas.

■ Risk analysis is not the only basis for selecting areas in which to commence record-keeping system improvement work. It may be better to start by working with colleagues who perceive the need for improvements in their record keeping.

■ There is no need to adopt a heavy-handed approach. Doing so, especially at the outset, can be counterproductive. By offering support to colleagues who want our help, while working within the framework of the DIRKS methodology, record-keeping professionals can begin to make real progress.

Record-keeping metadata

All record-keeping systems are intellectual constructs and metadata is a highly visible aspect of intellectual construction. Metadata is essentially information about information. It is used by information system designers, librarians, IT specialists and knowledge managers as well as by record-keeping professionals. David Haynes, in his excellent introduction to the subject, identifies five main purposes of metadata: resource description; information retrieval; management of information; rights management, ownership and authenticity; and interoperability and e-commerce.[28] Haynes discusses records management as a subset of the management of information, while acknowledging the importance of authenticity in relation to record-keeping systems. It is not practicable to discuss all aspects of metadata in respect of record keeping here. The Pittsburgh Project, however, deserves special mention.

David Bearman and others who were associated with the Functional Requirements for Evidence in Recordkeeping Project at the University of Pittsburgh have argued that it should be possible to base record-keeping systems in an electronic environment on metadata attached to individual records or the records of individual transactions. In other words, an intellectual construct, radically different from conventional classification and filing systems, is both possible and desirable. They propose that records should be encapsulated in or '... inextricably linked to ...'[29] essential metadata that meets the requirements for evidence. These metadata elements include data regarding: registration; identification; discovery and retrieval; rights status; access; use; retention; encoding; rendering; content; source; context; responsibility; and business function. This approach, it is argued, will provide 'granularity' (i.e. much more detailed knowledge of) and control over record-keeping systems and 'make communications received over networks trustworthy for the purposes of conducting business ...'.[30]

Bearman and Sochats's ideal is the record encapsulated in metadata and thereby rendered self-authenticating. They acknowledge, however, that this may prove expensive. As an alternative, they offer the use of 'pointers', i.e. links from individual records to a comprehensive database or library of all conceivably necessary metadata terms. Bearman and Sochats recognise that 'the metadata required ... must be captured by the overall system ... which includes personnel, policy, hardware and software.'[31] They concentrate on ways in which policy can be implemented via hardware and software. They envisage the use of 'clients', i.e. templates, because the data fields in templates can be used to capture key elements of metadata automatically. This is a technique for gaining control that has also been proposed by John McDonald who observes that the spread of workflow-enabled environments, where user interfaces are based on tasks rather than utilities, is inherently favourable to structured record keeping.[32] As McDonald points out, online business delivery lends itself to the classic FAT analyses with which record-keeping professionals are familiar. Workflow systems are generally associated with the handling of very large numbers of essentially similar transactions, for example renewal of insurance premiums and purchases of cinema tickets. In the realm of formal decision-making procedures, Glasgow University's C-DOCS (committee documentation) project represents an implementation, based on the use of templates, which is different from the ordinary workflow system.[33] As early as 1995, Seamus Ross offered a powerful critique of the Pittsburgh Project. He pointed out that the functional requirements used had not been derived from an analysis of real business processes but rather from first principles established by the project. In addition, he argued that implementation would only take place if there was '... evidence that the creation of metadata encapsulated records has corporate value.'[34]

Ten years after Ross delivered his critique, real-world implementations of the Pittsburgh approach, basing entire record-keeping systems on metadata, are still virtually unknown. One possible explanation is the huge effort needed to create and maintain a comprehensive database or library of metadata terms. This is a 'great leap forward' project where intermediate steps are difficult to conceive and consequently quick wins benefiting end users are almost impossible to deliver. Another explanation is that, beyond routine and predictable activities (where it is possible to determine in advance what outcomes are possible), there lies a range of creative work where human intervention in the creation or assignation of metadata may be unavoidable. If the creators and users of records must interact with a large and complex library of metadata terms in respect of every transaction, then it is difficult to see how the Pittsburgh approach can succeed.

In his review of progress in the area of electronic records management during the 1990s, Philip Bantin observes that a range of sets of record-keeping metadata were produced following the pioneering work in Pittsburgh.[35] In addition to those cited by Bantin, MoReq and The National Archives (TNA) guidelines should be mentioned.[36] What most of these specifications have in common is that they address metadata requirements at the level of record-keeping systems as a whole rather than at the item level. It could be argued that where EDRMS have been implemented on the basis of a business classification scheme for the system as a whole, item-level metadata should fulfil the function of indexing. In this case, the metadata elements need to be specified with retrieval in mind.

It might be argued that Bearman and his collaborators overlooked the potential benefits of aggregating related records. We may look to the Create Once Use Many Times Project on record-keeping metadata that is currently under way in Australia for a different orientation.[37] The participants in the Australian project come from the Commonwealth tradition and can be expected to address the issue of pre-action aggregation. In any event, the outcome of the Create Once Use Many Times Project will be of real significance for record-keeping professionals. If, as a result of their work, parts of the Australian public service successfully implement electronic record-keeping systems based on the encapsulation of records in metadata then this could have profound consequences. For the time being, record-keeping professionals need intellectual constructs in which 'metadata can be associated with any level of the file plan and lower levels inherit the attributes of the higher level'.[38] So classification schemes remain a core concern.

Classification

Classification schemes are about putting things together on the basis of shared characteristics, often for purposes of management and/or abstraction. Usually several alternatives are possible, for example sorting books by the authors' names or their subject. Classification schemes for use in relation to current record keeping are generally based on an analysis of the business functions discharged by the organisation in which the scheme is to be used. If metadata alone is not being used to articulate the record-keeping system, file plans and/or directory structures may be derived from the classification scheme.

Functional classification is based on the identification and conceptual modelling of the main functions (both core and support functions) undertaken by an organisation and of the activities of which they are made up. Ideally, top-level terms in a business classification scheme should relate to the fundamental purposes that the organisation exists to achieve. This should orient the record-keeping system to broadly organisational goals rather than narrowly technical ones. The usual approach is to analyse functions, activities and transactions from the top downwards. The full analysis of transactions (processes) depends on decomposing them into the various steps that create record-keeping requirements. There is an alternative approach that uses comprehensive deconstruction of processes to build a business classification scheme from the bottom up, starting with transactions and aggregating these to identify activities and then functions.

The process of undertaking the necessary analysis and constructing a comprehensive business classification scheme 'involves a significant investment in staff time'.[39] The rationale for the effort expended is generally that it yields a scheme that can be utilised repeatedly thereafter. In other words, a full analysis is only justified where reuse of the product is possible. This can be an issue where one-off projects are concerned. Where a recognised project management methodology is used, such as PRINCE,[40] the answer may be to build on the generic forms of project documentation required in addition to, or as an alternative to, purely functional terms.

It is worth mentioning one exemplar of business classification schemes, Keyword AAA.[41] Like DIRKS it is an Australian product. It is a generic scheme intended to cover the shared functions of governmental agencies (such as human resource management) while leaving individual agencies to work up additions that are specific to their own unique functions. Keyword AAA is not as well known as it deserves to be, probably because (unlike DIRKS) it is not freely available. Users must pay for licences. The United Kingdom Parliament at Westminster uses Keyword AAA and the published account of that implementation provides an insight into the methodology involved.[42]

KAAA consists of three parts:

- introductory material, explaining how to use the scheme;
- the business classification scheme, in a hierarchical format based on FAT analysis and using the terms function, activity and transaction;
- a thesaurus of terms that serves as an index and places each term in context by use of the classic terminology of thesaurus building (broader terms, narrower terms, related terms and non-preferred terms).

Keyword AAA is not without its critics. Stephen Bedford has outlined three major areas of comment. First, abstract concepts are a problem for many users, not least where a term in the second level of the hierarchy can have both many broader terms and many narrower terms. Secondly, as a generic thesaurus, Keyword AAA was not really compiled by functional analysis in the pure sense of the term. Thirdly, precisely because it is limited to terms relating to shared functions, it has an inherent tendency to favour central administration over those activities that constitute the true essence of public service.[43]

Functional classification is favoured by records managers with good reason.

- If DIRKS stage A and B analyses have been undertaken then the essential early steps towards functional classification have already been taken.
- Functional classification provides a good basis for security classification and access permissions.
- Functional classification supports classic records management activities (retention and disposal, removal to records centre/off-line storage).

Outside the realm of records management, there are good reasons for senior management to favour functional classification. These include:

- *Fluidity of organisational structures.* While departmental boundaries often change and teams are short-lived, the underlying functions being delivered tend to remain much more stable. Thus functional classification schemes enable the delivery of services to continue during periods of organisational upheaval.

- *More comprehensive retrieval, not least for legal purposes.* A good business classification scheme can make it possible to limit the range of records that must be searched and thereby make the task manageable. Search engines cannot be relied on for this.[44]

- *Secondary internal use.* In many organisations the creators of records are not the only users internal to the organisation. For example, public health specialists make extensive use of clinical records for epidemiological purposes. Thus clinical records, created to manage immediate patient care, have a secondary use within the health service. Records contextualised by functional classification will be more readily understood by staff other than creators.

- *Evidential value is enhanced by linking records to their business context and thereby linking related records to one another.*

Resistance from the creators of records to the introduction of a hierarchical classification scheme is sometimes encountered. This may be due to inherent conservatism or poor presentation. Whatever the background, critics who argue that a three-tier hierarchy is unnecessarily complicated do need to be answered. It may be worth looking for an element of compromise. One way of achieving this is by means of user-focused analysis, possibly utilising soft systems methodology[45] to modify the terminology used at the transactions level to resemble users' perceived needs. This may mean introducing clients' names or subject terminology that would not otherwise be used. In order to maximise support from users, and to reduce confusion, it may be helpful to refrain from using the terms function, activity and transaction in manuals and training. Some users can become fixated on the terminology to the detriment of the purposes that it is intended to achieve. Using an alternative terminology such as levels 1, 2 and 3 may be preferable. Where departments or teams within an organisation have invested heavily in content management software, it may be as well to think carefully before asking them to take up functional classification as well. The two approaches are unlikely to work well together.

Indexing provides an opportunity to organise records on the basis of functional analysis and then to make the system comprehensible to non-specialists by using alternative representations and terms. The use of controlled vocabulary is valuable in this respect and the term 'thesaurus' is widely used by record-keeping professionals, although ISO 2788 'Documentation – guidelines for the establishment and development of monolingual thesauri' is rarely followed.[46] Indexing can help to build users' support by making retrieval demonstrably easier and simpler, so long as the terminology that they use naturally appears in the index.

The international standard for records management – ISO 15489

The international standard[47] has Australian roots. Work on drafting ISO 15489 started with the Australian standard ASA 4390.[48] ASA 4390 in turn was based on DIRKS, a variant of records continuum thinking, and familiarity with business classification schemes of which Keyword AAA may be regarded as an exemplar.

In essence, ISO 15489 is a guidance standard. It sets out the characteristics of record-ness in broad terms (authenticity, reliability, integrity and usability) and provides an approach for creating record-keeping systems that will deliver these desiderata. This is recognisably the DIRKS methodology. Both the standard and DIRKS have been criticised by Gary Johnston, who suggests that they lack adequate testing and quality mechanisms, lack an explicit recognition of the need for systems building and configuration, and take for granted the creation of classification schema.[49] Nonetheless, the standard has made an impact. The nature of that impact, however, varies from place to place and setting to setting. A recent survey of user and non-user experience (undertaken in the context of a planned revision of the standard) produced 421 responses from a possible population of several thousand. These responses included a large number from record-keeping professionals (59 per cent), a substantial number from other information professionals (15 per cent) and some from executives/administrators (11 per cent). These included a significant number of supporters for the rewriting of ISO 15489 to make it a mandatory standard and/or an accreditation-cum-compliance process. The findings of the survey were reported to a meeting of the relevant ISO committee held in Australia in late 2004. This meeting decided not to attempt to rewrite ISO 15489 as a compliance standard. Instead, detailed technical work is being undertaken to produce supporting publications on record-keeping metadata and access. The outcome of the Create Once Use Many Times Project on record-keeping metadata referred to above is likely to have a significant impact on the way in which the international standard develops.[50]

Julie McLeod's ongoing work suggests that most British users of ISO 15489 are focused on benchmarking and profile-raising.[51] Benchmarking largely consists of using the general statements of principle (particularly that records should possess authenticity, reliability, integrity and usability) as a yardstick by which to judge the evidential value of existing systems. Rarely, in the UK, does it involve utilisation of the full DIRKS methodology. Instead work often commences with a gap analysis, leaving out the first two stages of DIRKS. In the case of the Keyword AAA implementation undertaken by the UK Parliament at Westminster, referred to above, a great deal of DIRKS-style analysis must have taken place, but the implementation has not been labelled by those who carried it out as following ISO 15489. Profile-raising involves using the very fact of the existence of an international standard as a lever in achieving greater credibility, management buy-in and resource. This is the curious phenomenon of the standard in being. When the standard is used in this way, what is in it becomes less important than the status implied by its existence.

In the African countries of the Commonwealth, as in Britain, the standard appears to be used primarily for benchmarking and profile-raising, whereas the DIRKS methodology is not much used.[52] Koo Ombati has produced a draft 'national standard' for use by the Kenya National Archives and Documentation Service. The use of the term 'national standard' is significant as it implies a greater authority than that conferred by a procedure manual, although the two have much in common. This draft:

- contains substantial sections devoted to records surveys, records centres and records retention;
- assumes the widespread use of classification schemes and is intended to support and promote this;
- refers to the general statements of principle that appear in ISO 15489;
- makes no reference to any variant of DIRKS methodology.[53]

There is a marked contrast with the North American private sector experience of Mary M. White-Dollman.[54] She reports a 'real-world' implementation of the DIRKS methodology, undertaken in the name of implementing ISO 15489, in the context of a merger between two large energy multinationals. She makes several telling points:

1. It provides an excellent overview of records management concepts that speak (*sic*) to information technologists.
2. Its approach to records management is process driven.
3. IT professionals are typically familiar with process-driven models.

Interestingly, White-Dollman's experience is of dealing with a mainly electronic hybrid record-keeping environment. Ombati's experience, in contrast, is largely of dealing with tangible recording media (he includes diskettes and other removable media but does not address records stored online). The use of ISO 15489 in North America is likely to be influenced by the existence of an alternative in the United States DoD 5015.2-STD standard for electronic records management.[55] This is a compliance standard designed specifically to meet the current record-keeping requirements of the American armed forces. Under the procurement rules of the US Department of Defense, suppliers may be obliged to demonstrate that they comply with DoD 5015.2-STD. Although not intended for wider application, this standard has been adopted by other departments and agencies of the US government and even introduced by the United States Agency for International Development into Uganda.[56]

The distinction between a compliance standard and a guidance standard is not absolute. Performance improvement measurement can provide a way of bridging the apparent divide. The British Standards Institution has published a guide to the development of performance improvement measures that are specific to records management. This includes a substantial range of possible metrics devised by Philip Jones.[57]

Post custodialism

The roles and responsibilities of archives in the digital age are at the heart of the debate over post custodialism. The basic proposition of the post custodialists is fairly simple: in an electronic age, who possesses records is no longer important. This is because records need no longer exist as only one tangible original in one place. They argue that, instead of concentrating on the transfer of records to an archive, archivists should focus on preserving records and making them accessible, even if this means leaving them in the systems that first created them. Post custodialism was born out of real-world experience. Plenty of archives have been asked to accept unintelligible electronic records where crucial metadata is lacking. The post custodial view sits easily with recent freedom of information (FOI) legislation in many countries.[58] The public is now entitled to see many official records long before their transfer to an archive is likely.

While this case may seem persuasive, there is a serious debate around it. A core issue is metadata. Post custodialists, particularly those associated with the RCRG (Records Continuum Research Group) in Australia, argue that record-keeping professionals should be involved in system design. In this role, in addition to addressing the immediate needs and concerns of record creators and immediate users, they should ensure that metadata are captured for the benefit of future users, primarily users with historical and cultural interests. The implication is that the distinction between archivists and records managers will become vestigial.

An opposing view comes from the University of British Columbia (UBC). Duranti and MacNeil argue that adding metadata at the point of creation for the benefit of hypothetical future users is a mistake. Doing so involves tampering with the evidential value of the records because that derives ultimately from the creators' concern with immediate business uses. In addition, any attempt at seeking to serve future users will inevitably privilege some users and thereby necessarily disadvantage others (whose needs we may be unable to predict or even imagine).[59] Duranti and MacNeil posit that metadata other than that needed by the creators must be added when records are transferred to the custody of a disinterested third party. This is the classic fiduciary role of archives. None of this implies that record-keeping professionals should exclude themselves from systems design – just that they should address the business needs of the creators and nothing more.

Interestingly, the National Archives of Australia (NAA) adopted a post custodialist stance in the late 1990s and then changed their minds. Now they insist that all e-records scheduled for archival preservation must be placed in their custody. In the UK too, TNA have adopted a custodial stance, although they do accept that there may be exceptional circumstances. Malcolm Todd states that these are 'where there is a compelling continuing business need for the creating Department to retain access to its material and technical or cost constraints rendering the holding of the material by both [the creating Department and TNA] impracticable. An example might be a complex meteorological or geographic database.'[60]

Todd's references to cost and continuing business acknowledge critical 'real-world' factors. He also recognises by implication that some databases are, by their very nature, not readily split into 'current' and 'historic' portions. To this dichotomy, we may add the concept of secondary internal use, for example the reuse of clinical records for epidemiological purposes. In that case the occurrence and nature of the use is largely predictable (in contrast to tertiary cultural use) and the cooperation of creators is more likely to be forthcoming. User attitudes are a key issue. Where creators question the cost and value of the metadata they are required to supply or create (or some of it), compliance and quality are likely to be problematic.

Notes

1. The author would like to acknowledge the support and the stimulation of thought that has come from many seminars and discussions with colleagues and students in the Humanities Advanced Technology and Information Institute (HATII) in the University of Glasgow. In particular, Professor Michael Moss and Professor Seamus Ross both offered extensive comments on the first draft of this chapter. In addition, the author benefited from a number of discussions with Paul Lihoma and Richard Wato, Commonwealth Professional Fellows at HATII in 2005.
2. Upward, F., 'Records continuum', in McKemmish, S. et al. (eds), *Archives. Recordkeeping in Society* (Wagga Wagga, 2005), particularly pp. 214–18.
3. Shepherd, E. and Yeo, G., *Managing Records. A Handbook of Principles and Practice* (London, 2003), pp. 54–7.
4. Levy, D., *Scrolling Forward. Making Sense of Documents in the Digital Age* (New York, 2001), p. 31.
5. Strathern, Marilyn, *Virtual Society? Get Real!* (2000) (available at *http://virtualsociety.sbs.ox.ac.uk/Grpapers/strathern.htm*, accessed 12 July 2005).
6. Currall, J., 'What's wrong with archivists and records managers?', unpublished paper to Society of Archivists conference, Glasgow, 2 September 2004.
7. Just how widely life cycle thinking had spread can be seen in Baxter, T.W., *Archives in a Growing Society* (National Archives of Rhodesia and Nyasaland, Salisbury, 1963), particularly pp. 1–18.
8. Upward, F., 'Modelling the continuum as paradigm shift in recordkeeping and archiving processes, and beyond – a personal reflection', *Records Management Journal*, 10 (3), 2000, p. 119.
9. For work undertaken by others on the records continuum model see McKemmish, S. et al., 'Describing records in context in the continuum: the Australian Recordkeeping Metadata Schema', *Archivaria*, 48, 1999, pp. 3–42.
10. Acknowledgement is due to Alex Du Toit who first christened this diagram 'Upward's dartboard'.

11. For an instance, see McKemmish, S., 'Traces: document, record, archive, archives', in McKemmish et al., op. cit.

12. Upward, F., 'Structuring the records continuum, part two: structuration theory and recordkeeping', *Archives and Manuscripts*, 25 (1), May 1997 (available at *www.sims.monash.edu.au/research/rcrg/publications/recordscontinuum/fupp2.html*, accessed February 2006).

13. Salgado, Rob (anon.), 'The Einstein-Minkowski Spacetime: introducing the Light Cone' (1995) (available at *www.phy.syr.edu/courses/modules/LIGHTCONE/minkowski.html*, accessed February 2006).

14. Mommsen, W.J., *The Age of Bureaucracy. Perspectives on the Political Sociology of Max Weber* (Oxford, 1974).

15. Campbell-Kelly, M., 'Railway clearing house and Victorian data processing', in Bud-Frierman, L. (ed.), *Information Acumen. Understanding and Use of Knowledge in Modern Business* (London and New York, 1994), pp. 66–7.

16. Hofman, H., 'The archive', in McKemmish et al., op. cit., pp. 131–58. Another stimulating consideration of the consequences of organisational change can be found in Barry, R., 'The changing workplace and the nature of the record', unpublished paper presented to Association of Canadian Archivists annual conference, 1995 (available at *http://www.mybestdocs.com/barry-r-aca1995-wkp-rec.htm*, accessed 22 September 2005).

17. Hofman, op. cit., p. 155.

18. Wodehouse, P.G., *Leave It to Psmith* (London, 1924).

19. Hock, D.W., 'Chaordic organization: out of control and into order', *World Business Academy Perspectives*, 9 (1), 1995, p. 13. I am grateful to Arthur Allison for introducing me to the writings of Hock and the mathematical theories associated with them.

20. Upward, 'Modelling the continuum …', op. cit., p. 125.

21. Ibid., p. 124.

22. Checkland, P. and Holwell, S., *Information, Systems and Information Systems – Making Sense of the Field* (Chichester, 1997), pp. 3–30. I am grateful to Mike Haynes of CSSM who first introduced me to the soft systems approach.

23. Available at *http://naa.gov.au/recordkeeping/dirks/summary.html* (accessed 12 July 2005).

24. McLeod, J., *Effective Records Management – Part 2: Practical Implementation of BS ISO 15489-1*, British Standards Institution, BIP 0025-2:2002 (London, 2002).

25. *DIRKS – Strategic Approach to Managing Business Information. Step A – Preliminary Investigation* (Canberra, National Archives of Australia, 2001) (available at *http://www.naa.gov.au/recordkeeping/dirks/dirksman/dirks.html*, accessed February 2006), p. 8.

26. A summary of the work of the Tanzania Records Management project can be found in: International Records Management Trust, *Records Management Project. Report for the period April to July 2000 and Project Completion Report*, TAN/YR3/QR4 (2000). Requests for copies should be addressed to: IRMT, Haines House, 6th floor, 21 John St, London WC1N 2BP, UK.

27. *DIRKS – Strategic Approach to Managing Business Information. Step F – Design of Recordkeeping System* (Canberra, National Archives of Australia, 2001) (available at *http://www.naa.gov.au/recordkeeping/dirks/dirksman/dirks.html*, accessed February 2006), p. 4.

28. Haynes, D., *Metadata for Information Management and Retrieval* (London, 2004).

29. Bearman, D. and Sochats, K., *Functional Requirements for Evidence in Recordkeeping: the Pittsburgh Project* (n.d.) (available at *www.archimuse .com/papers/nhprc/BACartic.html*, accessed 20 June 2005)

30. Ibid.

31. Ibid.

32. McDonald, J., *The Wild Frontier ... Isn't So Wild Anymore*, paper to Annual Conference of the Records Management Society of Great Britain, Cardiff, 15 April 2002. This conference paper refers back to his seminal article: McDonald, J., 'Managing records in the modern office: taming the wild frontier', *Archivaria*, 39, 1995, pp. 70–9.

33. Currall, J. et al., *No Going Back? Final Report of Effective Records Management Project*, Glasgow University (Glasgow, 2002) (available at *www.gla.ac.uk/InfoStrat/ERM-Final.pdf*, accessed 24 June 2005).

34. Ross, S., *Commentary on Pittsburgh University Recordkeeping Requirements Project*, paper presented to Society of American Archivists Annual Meeting, 1995 (available at *http://eprints.erpanet.org/archive/ 00000060/01/SR_commentary_SAA1995.htm*, accessed 3 November 2005).

35. Bantin, P., *Electronic Records Management – A Review of the Work of a Decade and a Reflection on Future Directions* (2002), pp. 19–21 (available at *http://www.indiana.edu/~libarch/ER/encycloarticle9.doc*, accessed 3 November 2005).

36. *Model Requirements for Management of Electronic Records*, Cornwell Consultants (available at *http://www.cornwell.co.uk/moreq.html*, accessed 25 November 2005), and *Guidelines for Management, Appraisal and Preservation of Electronic Records* (TNA, 1999) (available at *http://www.nationalarchives.gov.uk/electronicrecords/advice/guidelines.htm*, accessed 25 November 2005).

37. *Prototyping of Integrated Systems Environment Supporting Automated Recordkeeping Metadata Capture and Re-use*, Record Continuum Research Group, Monash University, 2005 (available at *http://www.sims.monash. edu.au/research/rcrg/research/crm/firstiteration.html*, accessed 12 July 2005).

38. Haynes, op. cit., p. 105.

39. Jeffrey-Cook, R., 'Developing a fileplan for local government', *Bulletin of the Records Management Society of Great Britain*, 125, 2005, pp. 3–5.

40. Bentley, C., *PRINCE 2: An Outline* (The Stationery Office for the Central Computer and Telecommunications Agency, 1997).

41. *Keyword AAA. A Thesaurus of General Terms* (Sydney, Australia, revised edn 1998, reprinted 2001).

42. Gibbons, P. and Shenton, C., 'Implementing a records management strategy for the UK Parliament: the experience of using Keyword AAA', *Journal of the Society of Archivists*, 24 (2), 2003, pp. 141–57.

43. Bedford, S., *Records Classification Systems*, paper to Records Management Association of Australasia conference, 2005. I am grateful to Tamara Puli for providing me with a copy of this paper.

44. See Tough, A. and Moss, M., 'Metadata, controlled vocabularies and directories ...', *Records Management Journal*, 13 (1), 2003, pp. 24–31 for a discussion of this point.

45. Checkland and Holwell, op. cit., pp. 155–72.
46. International Standards Organisation, *Documentation – Guidelines for the Establishment and Development of Monolingual Thesauri*, ISO 2788-1986 (Geneva, 1986).
47. The international standard consists of two parts, one dealing with general principles and the second with their application. The bibliographical details of the BSI variant are as follows: British Standards Institution, *Information and Documentation – Records management – Part 1: General*, BS ISO 15489-1:2001 and British Standards Institution, *Information and Documentation – Records Management – Part 2: Guidelines*, PD ISO/TR 15489-2 (London, 2001).
48. Standards Australia, *Records Management*, AS 4390.1 – 1996 to AS 4390.6 – 1996 (Sydney, 1996). This standard has been superseded as Australia has adopted ISO 15489.
49. Johnston, G., 'An alternative model for the design and implementation of records management systems', *Bulletin of the Records Management Society of Great Britain*, 126, June 2005, pp. 13–17.
50. The author served on the British Standards Institution's sub-committee on records management, 2000–2005. Much of this section is based on information made available to members of that sub-committee.
51. McLeod, J., 'Assessing the impact of ISO 15489 – a preliminary investigation', *Records Management Journal*, 13 (2), 2003, pp. 70–82.
52. Tough, A.G., 'Records management standards and the good governance agenda in Commonwealth Africa', *Archives and Manuscripts*, 32 (2), 2004, pp. 142–61.
53. Although the draft standard has not been published, some indication of the thinking that lies behind it can be found in the following article: Ombati, K., 'Domesticating ISO 15489 and ISAD(G) at the Kenya National Archives and Documentation Service', *ESARBICA Newsletter*, 2, 2004, p. 5.
54. White-Dollman, Mary M., 'ISO 15489: a tool for records management in mergers', *Information Management*, 38 (5), September/October 2004.
55. United States of America, Department of Defense, *Design Criteria Standard for Electronic Records Management Software Applications*, DoD 5015.2-STD) (Washington, DC, 2002).
56. Tough, op. cit., p. 150.
57. Jones, P.A., *Effective Records Management. Part 3: Performance Management for BS ISO 15489-1*, British Standards Institution, BIP 0025-3:2003 (London, 2003).
58. Tough, A.G., 'The post-custodial/pro-custodial argument from a Records Management perspective', *Journal of the Society of Archivists*, 25 (1), 2004, pp. 23–4.
59. Duranti, L., 'Concepts and principles ...', *Records Management Journal*, 9 (3), 1999, p. 156.
60. Todd, M., *Recordkeeping* (London, TNA, winter 2005), 3 (available at *http://www.nationalarchives.gov.uk/services/pdf/winter2005.pdf*, accessed February 2006).

2

Implementing EDRMS and shaping the record

Frank Rankin

There is often a sharp divergence between the model of electronic records management (ERM) found in government and corporate policies and in professional and vendor literature on the one hand, and the reality of implementation in the real-life world of businesses, public authorities and non-profit organisations on the other. While the Platonic ideal is of robust and complete record-keeping systems which also permit flexible and full data-sharing and enable knowledge management and decision-making, the reality may fall anywhere on a scale from highly effective and popular corporate knowledge system to abject and languishing failure.

This chapter will look at some of the practical issues in the implementation of electronic records management within an organisation and the implications these have – positive and negative – for the corporate record. (This is drawn largely from public sector experience in the UK.) The chapter does not set out to provide definitions or a how-to guide, both of which proliferate elsewhere, but to discuss the choices that face organisations in introducing an ERM solution and how these can affect the nature of the organisational record. It presupposes electronic records management based on fully functional ERM software and architecture rather than attempts to apply records management principles to a relatively uncontrolled electronic environment, such as networked drive storage. It also assumes the implementation of a 'front-end' EDRMS, which captures documents and records at or soon after creation, rather than a back-end ERM approach that captures records as they 'fall off' an electronic document management system.[1]

Some clarification of terms may be useful. Electronic document management systems (EDMS) applications emphasised the flexibility, sharing and retrieval of structured data objects, to improve the sharing of information and its integration into business workflows. And as recently as 2001, a leading practitioner could lament that 'It is a fairly depressing fact ... that many EDM systems have very few, if any, records management features or discipline.'[2]

Electronic records management systems (ERMS) typically will have some document management functionality but focus on the required ability to lock down definitive electronic records that are robust and unchangeable and which have appropriate contextual metadata and effectively managed life cycles. Crudely put, EDMS focuses on informational value while ERMS focuses on the evidential value of documents and records.

UK government departments in most cases are adopting electronic document and records management systems (EDRMS) that combine ERM functionality with the ability to hold a wider range of business information and documents that are not required as part of the formal corporate record but do have to be retrievable and reusable for everyday business needs. Increasingly the market is moving towards EDRMS and the chapter assumes for the most part that this would be the tool being implemented.

Completeness of the record

Devolved paper-based records systems require that the user make an active decision to select a document to become part of the record, and a physical action to print if necessary, punch and place the relevant papers on the correct file. (Centralised registry records systems would place some of these actions in the hands of specialised records staff, but would still depend to a varying extent on instructions or information provided by the record creator.) The paper record is shaped day to day by the decisions of humans. While electronic records management offers the scope to reduce the reliance on individuals, this may not be automatically applied.

Organisations differ in what constitutes a 'complete' record. In highly regulated industries it may be necessary to capture all the recorded information created or received as part of a business process and to retain this as part of an audit trail. More often, employees are given the autonomy to identify which documents need to be captured as records, particularly if there are qualitative decisions to be made, for example in the development of policy or in creating the audit trail for a decision, in deciding which e-mails carry substantive information or instructions or which drafts demonstrate key points in the development of the document.

Electronic systems may influence the 'completeness' of the record in a number of ways.

- *Record-keeping choices may be automated.* For example, organisations covered by Sarbanes-Oxley may avoid disposal risks by taking a policy decision to capture all incoming and outgoing e-mail traffic. This would provide a very complete audit trail, very little of which may be of true evidential or informational value.

- *Record selection may be less narrow.* Where an EDRMS combines the everyday information store for business users with the corporate record (particularly if it has supplanted alternatives such as personal or shared network drives or 'archiving' functions within an e-mail application), it will include significant volumes of relatively ephemeral working documents alongside high-value records in the same electronic repository – often in the same virtual folder. Particularly if the capture of all business documents is mandatory or automated, this represents a potentially colossal increase in the volume of the formal corporate record over the traditional paper file. In this respect the e-record may be more 'complete' than the paper system it supersedes, but quality is another matter.

- *Alternatively, record selection may remain a relatively autonomous task for the employee* – first in deciding which documents are captured to the EDRMS and, where this is a separate step, in deciding which are 'declared' as corporate records.

Depending on the configuration of the EDRMS, most applications will offer opportunities or prompts to the user to designate a document as a final corporate record at the initial point of saving and at future edits or amendments to metadata. Typically, the act of declaring an object as a 'record' prevents further amendments being made to the content of the item itself and in many cases to the associated metadata. Items declared as records may be treated differently in terms of retention/disposal. For example, the users may be permitted to delete 'ordinary' documents but not those designated as records, or designated records may be subject to longer retention periods than documents that are not given record status.

At both decision points (capture and designation as a record) there may be significant divergence in practice between individuals, teams and departments across an organisation. The 'completeness' of the record would remain reliant on the behaviours and values of the organisation.

Volume of retained data is a related issue. Typically in paper filing systems (particularly in devolved, non-registry systems) and in relatively unmanaged electronic storage of documents, very high levels of duplication are found. A single document distributed in hard copy to ten individuals may be kept on ten files. In e-mail form, the same circular may have been forwarded to many more colleagues and the duplication increased, with printed versions placed on file and electronic copies kept in multiple versions in personal and shared network drives as well as hard drives and removable storage. The resulting damaging implications for version control, storage and retrieval costs, disposals management, security and discovery risks are a key part of the argument in favour of EDRMS investment. Duplication should be reduced by the potential to save a document to a single location in a shared corporate fileplan and alert interested parties to its presence and location. EDRM systems may have the functionality to recognise an attempt to duplicate an item already stored in the system and either bar this or at least make the user aware. Thus, regardless of its implications for the range and completeness of the information identified as records, EDRMS should significantly reduce the volume of documents and records held by the organisation. However, for those systems that retain embedded earlier versions of a document, enabling users to revert to those versions or follow the development history of a document, the actual savings in electronic storage volumes may be much smaller than anticipated. Each successive version, although not immediately visible to a browsing user, still takes up server space.

Where EDRMS investments have failed, the show-stopper cited most often by the bruised participants is a lack of user buy-in. Where they were found by users to be inconvenient, where there were real or imagined gaps in reliability or performance, where they were given insufficient impetus by management or could simply be circumvented, EDRM programs have failed simply because users voted with their feet and took their information storage requirements elsewhere, to the detriment of the corporate record.

Appropriate use of all relevant means of mitigation is vital. Those available will depend on a range of cultural and practical factors, but will include some of the following:

- *Building confidence in performance.* This may include investment in ironing out network problems as well as robust user testing of the EDRM system. All off-the-shelf EDRMS products will perform well in a small organisation with a hundred or so users working over a single local area network. But the product's ability to be expanded to a much larger user constituency – its scalability – will be the single most significant technical challenge in medium and large organisations. Where the system has to be used over a distributed network, particularly if the network relies on satellite links to sites overseas, system performance must be tested. Remedial measures such as local caching servers may be necessary to deliver acceptable performance in sites remote from the main server. Where there are performance problems, rapid and honest communication with users should help to avoid some of the frustration and decline in confidence.

- *Removal of alternatives.* Options here depend on how centralised the ICT management (and, indeed, how directive the overall management style) of the organisation is. The lock-down of hard drives and USB ports, the removal of shared and personal network drives, even the banning of portable media such as memory sticks, may be considered. Such moves will see an increase in use of the system, but bad habits that formed in using personal and even shared drives can migrate to use of the ERM as well.[3] Removing from users the ability to create folders at will, as they can in shared network drives, is something of a culture shock. While losing the power to create infinite numbers of sub-folders is a clear benefit for records and information professionals, this will be less apparent to users.

- *Training and guidance.* In most projects this will be the most labour-intensive component, and it has to be relevant and role based. For example, detailed knowledge of the disposals management functionality will only be of interest to the records management team, while details of the audit trail function will primarily be of interest to the internal audit team. Most users will simply want to know how to carry out their everyday tasks. Training focused on the specific needs of the users is likely to be the most cost-effective approach, streaming training to the requirements and needs of the roles the recipients will have to fulfil. No matter how extensive your guidance materials, (some) users will always want more, and will demand specific 'how-to' advice for issues and transactions that never occurred to them in the management of paper records or electronic documents on a shared drive.

- *Compliance and policing.* EDRM systems will typically have a range of pre-defined and bespoke reports that run on the system to allow policing and audit. Establishing that appropriate documents and records are captured, that fileplan allocation is correct and that metadata is complete and accurate will remain key tasks and can be partly automated. However, human audit is also vital to identify where weaknesses are and to correct them through training, guidance or more robust measures where necessary.

- *Performance management.* Where there is sufficient management support, connecting effective use of the EDRM and compliance with IM policies into the performance management system sends a clear signal about the behaviours that the organisation expects. For example, some UK government departments issued directives in the run-up to ERM implementation that all staff should have an EDRM-related objective in their performance goals for that year.

- *Tie EDRM into key business processes.* Where capturing documents to the EDRMS or working with them in that context is an integral part of the workflow processes – from project management tasks to expenses claims – users will be obliged to engage with the system and will also begin to see gains for their own immediate business tasks.

Control of items outside the EDRMS

Most organisations will continue to hold information sources outside the EDRMS. These will include items prohibited because of intellectual property issues (see below), items precluded through cost-effective use of media (for example, videos or sound recordings that would take up prohibitively large files if digitised), and paper-based documents whose format precludes cost-effective scanning, e.g. occasional large-format plans or drawings, or voluminous legacy paper filing. To avoid critical gaps in the record these will still have to be controlled, potentially within the EDRMS using protocols for capturing surrogate data, to signpost items that cannot be held on the system. Thus the EDRMS can effectively become a registry system for physical documents also. Effective and easy-to-access scanning services for the capture of items still received in paper form will usually be necessary. While the inward flow of paper can be controlled on the supplier side in contractual arrangements, it will be much more difficult to place such limits on customers, consumers or partners. Most EDRMS are unlikely to be able to hold dynamic systems such as relational databases (although occasional 'snapshots' may be captured to the EDRMS to provide a record).[4] Such assets may also need to be managed through surrogate metadata.

A key cultural challenge may be the breaking down of proprietary instincts, the initial horror among users that others in the organisation can see – and even work with – 'their' documents. Because they can create and access documents at their desktop – in contrast to walking to the corporate files – there is a tendency to consider electronic files on a personal or shared drive as 'their' documents. In part, such attitudes are a by-product of the evolution of computers through the 1980s and 1990s, away from mainframes to freestanding personal computers (the language is interesting) before the move back towards networks. These attitudes must be challenged but, occasionally, the concerns of the users are sound. The eradication of silos is often cited as a business driver for EDRM,[5] but sometimes silos are good and useful. For example, it may be necessary to deal separately with records and information that should not be available to the user constituency as a whole, such as sensitive personal information or internal investigations of fraud or misconduct.

Intellectual property rights and digital rights management are complex areas and can be a barrier to EDRMS use. The storage of an externally generated copyright object on a shared electronic storage system (such as an EDRMS) without the copyright holder's permission is an offence in Europe. In reality, many organisations will be breaching the law in any case without EDRMS where staff, without realising the implications, capture publications e-mailed to them or downloaded from websites onto shared network drives. Placing a printed copyright report on a paper file raises no such difficulty. The advent of EDRMS increases the risks of discovery and prosecution. Users need good support and advice – which may include copyright agreements with key partners, e-library services or off-line storage with metadata signposts from the ERM – if relevant copyright materials are not to be omitted from the record.

ERM and EDRM systems (it is likely to be absent from purely EDM systems) have retention and disposal functionality that will permit the automated disposal of time-expired records. As well as the labour savings and the increase in accuracy and completeness in the application of retention schedules, this potentially represents a shift in the shape of the archival record. With electronic records the selection for permanent retention of a genuinely random record – and therefore a more statistically effective representation of the whole – becomes relatively straightforward. (There is the danger here that a risk-averse organisation may also, by the simple changing of a figure in the EDRMS, extend the retention period of records 'just in case', and without seeing the costs of indefinite retention. The records manager may have to call on all his or her skills of persuasion to avoid this.[6])

Archivists therefore should no longer see the accidental survival of records – most often particular instance records – simply because they were stored away and forgotten. On the other hand, the accidental losses of records – a flood in the record store back in 1999 or a fire in a branch office – should no longer be an issue. With paper-based records systems, off-site duplication of vital records is a well-established technique, but it is impossibly costly to apply to the entirety of the corporate files in all but the best-resourced organisations. The balance becomes a matter of risk management. With EDRMS, the whole corporate record should be subject to regular back-up and therefore far more resilient than previously. Conversely, this represents a lot of informational and evidential eggs in one electronic basket – the business continuity processes have to be robust and tested.

In preparing for the future migration and preservation of electronic records, a major tool is the ability to limit the range of types of file formats that will be permitted and supported. Most EDRM systems will allow the administrator to pre-define a list of MIME types that will be permitted. Where users try to save electronic documents of non-supported file formats, they will either be refused or be prompted to save the document in a new rendition that is in a supported format. There is a balance to be struck between steering users towards a limited set of industry standard formats to ease future management challenges, and presenting barriers to users with genuine business requirements for specific file formats.

Quality of the record

The creation of records rich in contextual metadata – the concept of the 'self-documenting record'[7] – is frequently emphasised as a key potential gain from EDRM for the records professional. EDRMS will capture and create a wide range of metadata on the documents and records they contain, both system-defined metadata on the history, location and properties of the electronic object and user/organisation-defined data on the content and context of the document: what MacNeil categorises as the 'metadata of the electronic system' and the 'metadata of the records'.[8] The holy grail of the records professional, namely ensuring the integrity of the documents and records for which he or she is responsible, can be made explicit in the electronic environment. The auditable metadata captured and created with an EDRMS provides (without wishing to stray into the post custodial versus pro custodial debate) a hitherto unparalleled custodial history at the individual record level.

This systems metadata, recording precise data on the time and source of capture of an e-document together with an audit trail of any subsequent actions carried out upon it, is the bedrock of a reliable e-record-keeping system. The traditional practice of registration of paper documents has been abandoned by all but a few organisations in the Anglophone world because it is laborious and represents a significant overhead. A well-implemented EDRMS represents what can be seen as a renaissance for registration.[9] Only through this process can there be any confidence that an e-record has not been tampered with after the fact.

Quite apart from the records management requirements for accurate and appropriate metadata, the implementation of EDRMS forces organisations to take metadata seriously to enable data sharing and retrieval. Where, in a local shared drive, users from within a small team may be expected to have shared knowledge of the content and source of documents, even with fairly meaningless or ambiguous titles, once such documents are shared corporately, this becomes a barrier to the reuse of information and introduces risks of misinterpretation. Organisations will have to define naming conventions and may even have to agree meanings of terms in common use where the precise definition is ambiguous.[10]

Most EDRM and EDM packages can integrate with taxonomy systems that will automatically search the textual content of a document (at the point of capture), compare the text with a business-defined thesaurus of terms and subjects, and allocate appropriate keywords. This automation can certainly enrich the searchable metadata in a cost-effective manner. Where left to the user, it is questionable how often individuals would have the skills or inclination to allocate keywords to any but the most significant documents.

Some sources stress that 'metadata entry should be as automated as possible'[11] and that users will resist any burden of metadata entry. There is a counter-argument for users being prompted to assume ownership of the records they create and capture by at least reviewing some metadata. The use of default values and the use of document properties (the title of a word-processed document, the sender of an e-mail) as potential metadata can reduce the business overhead and the burden on the user. The use of templates for specific documents can offer further control of the metadata captured. These will typically be defined for generic administrative documents, such as minutes, memoranda, orders and payments, and for key business documents, such as board papers, outcome reports and project proposals. The flagging of key document types also opens up the potential for 'horizontal' appraisal and selection of records for permanent preservation. The identification and acquisition of, say, all final project reports or all quarterly divisional reports can be achieved simply and quickly.

Metadata describing the context and content of e-documents is vital. In the paper environment, files are held physically by the users who know them; they can provide context and interpretation. In the corporate electronic environment brought by EDRMS, this control is weakened. Other users can access those documents directly without recourse to the creators and 'owners' and 'there is a real danger of misinterpretation'.[12] Retrieval of an individual document by text or metadata search is standard within EDM and EDRM systems. Unless the user chooses to look for the context provided by the file, that document may have to stand alone. The increasingly corporate nature of information holding generates the need to be consistent in what has to be captured as metadata, but, more simply, may even require new rules on nomenclature. Allison cites the example of BP finding that the company had 35 different meanings for what constituted a sale.[13] What records are called and the very language used within them will evolve through the implementation of EDRMS, as organisations seek to build common terminology and naming conventions.

The structure within which the record is stored and retrieved – the fileplan and folder – will also be critical to the context and control of electronic records. At the time of writing, EDRM systems generally remain wedded to the hierarchical structure of classes and folders. Arguably the key single records management task in preparing for EDRM implementation is the development of a fileplan or business classification scheme which adequately reflects the business activities and record-keeping requirements of the organisation and still presents a logical and usable structure for the allocation and retrieval of records and documents. Decisions made in the development of the fileplan will affect the structure of the record, but may also influence the completeness and accuracy. A meaningful and clear fileplan will ease the task of users capturing records to the correct class and folder.

Fileplan structures may be based on a functional appraisal of the organisation (mapped on business functions, activities and tasks), on organisational structure (divisions, departments, units) or possibly a hybrid, with functionally based upper levels and lower levels based on organisational structure. Purely functional fileplans reduce the need for change in the face of management structures (functions and activities tend to change less often) and are less reliant on detailed knowledge of how the organisation is managed. (Of course, it still requires a grasp of what the organisation does.) Organisational fileplans are more readily recognisable by users and give a greater sense of 'ownership'. Hybrid options attempt to compromise, providing some of the benefits of both, and certainly this approach is recommended by the UK's National Archives.

In the UK, The National Archives have directed that government ERM systems should have a single layer of folders (that is to say, no sub-folders) in their fileplan and the selection for preservation will still be based on the folder.

More ambitious records managers may have their sights set on less structured systems where document-level metadata is used to retrieve and manage life cycle. Certainly there is no logical reason why ERM should not be based on individually managed records where such management tasks as security, retrieval and disposal are controlled by specifically applied metadata. And, of course, the 'folder' within an EDRMS does not really exist as a physical entity or location – it is only another item of metadata which groups documents and records. The bespoke folder based on a specific project, subject, document or record type, or time period – recognisable to users and convenient for browsing – could be created virtually through saved searches, giving multiple, user-defined views of the record as opposed to the single view presented by paper files and electronic directory structures based on pre-defined folders.

At the time of writing, abandoning electronic folders presents a serious problem for many EDRMS products: systems are not designed for managing unstructured repositories of hundreds of thousands of documents. This approach also places greater reliance on the accuracy of metadata allocated at the point of creation (with great difficulty of retrieval where this fails) and represents a potentially increased workload of records management tasks, for example where review for disposal has to be carried out against individual records rather than folders.

The traditional paper file brings together everything on a given case or subject. Within a functional fileplan, these data may be spread across separate functional headings but brought together by metadata, such as case number, project reference, budget code, etc. Appraisal and archival selection can become horizontal (selecting specific document types) as well as vertical. Where a disposal schedule is applied vertically, perhaps based on the high-level functions in a functionally based fileplan, there is a potential problem with documents on a single case having different disposal periods. Documents on a single project or topic could come up for disposal or review at different periods – financial documents after seven years, general correspondence after three, strategic plans after ten. Therefore if appraisal is left to the point of disposal, the records may be inconsistent or incomplete.

Benefits realisation will be key in most organisations to measuring the return on investment for EDRM implementation. Benefits analysis will tend to focus on immediate business gains for the organisation, particularly in terms of cost-savings and business process efficiencies. Records could simply fall off the agenda. Effective advocacy could see records concerns included in the balance sheet. Setting measurable targets for the quality of the record, such as the completeness of contextual and provenance audit information and the accuracy of metadata in a target proportion of records, creates a significant benchmark for the records management team to meet but also gives a highly visible commitment to such concerns and will mean that a wider range of individuals will have a vested interest in getting record keeping right.

Where organisations are moving to networked drives, which may be specific to teams or individuals or to a corporate ERM with wide-ranging access rights, new security models may be necessary. Security may need to use a range of complementary approaches – roles-based, group-based or security classification based – to meet legitimate needs for restricting access. The concomitant risks of over-setting security, with the resultant loss of shared information, must be set alongside the risk to the corporate record if business users are dissatisfied with the security placed on their information and opt out of the ERM. Since sensitive documents will typically include some of the most business-critical information in the corporate record, clearly a solution that omits this material will damage the record. Sometimes this may be unavoidable and may have to be dealt with in a hybrid solution. Within the UK government, many ICT systems, including ERM solutions, may only be approved for holding material up to the security level of 'Restricted'. This means that higher levels of security classification ('Confidential', 'Secret', etc.) may have to be retained on paper files that form a significant part of the corporate record.

An additional new pressure for ordinary users is the greater potential oversight that EDRMS brings. A line manager can review the work of a particular section or colleague from his or her own desktop without the user realising. For those organisations that previously had robust paper-based RM programmes, the visit of the records staff to audit the paper files would be advertised and visible. Not so the EDRMS audit. For all these reasons, there are potential new pressures on staff to get it right when creating and capturing e-records. While there is a danger of overstating the 'Big Brother' component – and indeed overly heavy-handed 'policing' of the EDRMS may be a disincentive to staff to create and capture documents in the first place – the increased visibility of documents and records and the clear allocation of responsibilities provided by metadata and audit trails should see improvements in the accuracy and quality of e-records. On the other hand, initiatives to encourage the use of EDRMS can backfire to the detriment of record quality. One government department in the UK set a numerical target for numbers of documents to be saved into the EDRMS by each member of staff. The result was a large volume of low-value, duplicated and nonsensical documents. Qualitative targets are more difficult to set and police but will ultimately be more successful.

The loss of the relative stability and changelessness of paper-based information is the principal challenge and the only genuinely new issue presented to records professionals by EDRM. E-documents may be presented in a number of different renditions – MS Word to Adobe Acrobat PDF as a simple example. Both policies and systems configurations will have to be clear on what constitutes the record. Self-modifying documents as simple as a letter produced in MS Word with an automated date field create problems for identifying the final record.[14] Means of securing field codes or automatically updating have to be tested as part of configuring the selected EDRMS to the needs of the business.

The existence of EDRMS may also affect the way information is created and distributed. For example, intranet content will probably be refined as reference documents previously shared through that platform can be made available through the EDRM; the intranet can be more focused as a communication tool rather than a repository for policies, guidance and forms.

From business case to business change – delivering ERM that delivers the record

In 1999 the UK government set a target for all its departments to manage all newly created records electronically by the end of 2004.[15] This might have appeared to be a gift to long-serving, long-suffering public sector records managers who had for some time urged employers to make such investments. But by the end of 2005 only a minority of departments had successfully implemented EDRM, the majority having made significant progress but still being some way from completion. Even with such an unarguable external business driver and top-level commitment, this demonstrates how significant a task ERM implementation is in a complex organisation.

The tone and main thrust of the business case for ERM investment will, like that for investment in record keeping generally, rely heavily on the nature and culture of the employing organisation – the need to maintain a view of the 'overall strategic objective'.[16] Moreover, each organisation's 'journey' into EDRM will be unique, based on the management and record-keeping culture.[17] The transition to EDRM is a unique opportunity to express the importance of information management in general and of record keeping in particular, visibly and unambiguously for the whole organisation.

This can be achieved most clearly in the adoption (or reiteration) of corporate information- and records-management policies. But there are other opportunities as well.

The statement of requirements is the opportunity in the procurement process for all stakeholders – business owners, ICT managers, security specialists, records and information managers, users and customers – to define precisely what they need. Critical issues to include from the record-keeping perspective, which may well be overlooked by ICT professionals and others more concerned with immediate business issues, include:

- the functionality to 'lock down' definitive records;
- the selection of acceptable file formats. There is an opportunity here for the business to review the range of file formats created and used. ICT colleagues may welcome the opportunity to rationalise the software in use and supported by collating and applying a restricted list of acceptable file formats. Such a list can take into account the needs of migration where long-term retention will be an issue. On the other hand, ruling out file formats that the organisation uses may lead to gaps in the record, as users who are recalcitrant, have specific business needs for specific file formats or cannot avoid receiving weird and wonderful file formats from customers and stakeholders are obliged to find alternative storage for these formats.

EDRMS projects can be highly vulnerable to scope creep – the gradual (or not so gradual) widening of the purpose and aims of the project. Classic examples are to bolt on to an ERM project changes to the desktop, further software roll-outs or significant re-engineering of business processes. Senior management may also wish to see hard cost-savings, including job cuts, as an integral element of the project aims. Such widening of the scope can dilute or even crush the ERM objectives themselves. Where such impetus cannot be resisted, ensuring that further resources – people, money and time – are provided to meet the new objectives is critical if the records management improvements are not to be obscured.

Implementation can also be distracted by the temptation to carry out significant business process re-engineering as part of the ERM implementation.[18] Carrying out the absolute minimum necessary to allow operating units of the organisation to carry on with their work while integrating with EDRM will reduce both the time cost of carrying out the re-engineering and avoid the resistance you are likely to encounter. Negative feelings towards revisiting business processes can colour attitudes to the EDRMS itself. More positively, by giving users the tools, they are very likely to begin to change business processes themselves once they have experience of using EDRM and confidence. This increases their feeling of ownership and provides a range of good-news 'wins' once the system is rolled out. A very simple example from a UK government department involved payment authorisation documents previously sent as e-mail attachments or in paper form to be 'signed off' by the authorising colleague. EDRMS now allows the document to be placed in an accessible folder to which users are directed to edit the appropriate authorisation document and approve it by locking it down as a record. This was not a complex workflow, but the process is faster and avoids the retention of multiple – and contradictory – versions, and the application of the EDRM tool was at the initiative of ordinary users rather than coming from the IT or records management teams.

Record-keeping professionals make assumptions and assertions about the importance of issues of 'record-ness' that our users and employers do not. Even where management pays lip service to the value of information as an asset and of record keeping for audit and accountability, this may not translate into the necessary decisions and choices to get it right. Allies within the organisation are necessary. Natural supporters may be found among colleagues in Internal Audit whose needs for robust audit trails chime neatly with the themes and principles espoused by archivists and records managers. Similar coalitions can be built with company secretaries or their equivalent legal sections and those teams responsible for compliance and quality control.

A corporate EDRM programme goes far beyond a mere RM, IM or even ICT project. It is, first and foremost, a programme of change management. Selecting and acquiring a solution is relatively easy; the complicated part is fitting the EDRMS to the organisation and the organisation to EDRM. The skills and knowledge of ICT professionals are vital: beyond the technical problems of network architecture, systems and integration and roll-out, they are usually highly skilled in project management, a gap in the skill set of many records and information professionals. ICT colleagues will also be vital in testing compatibility with the network and testing 'touch points' with other systems, where the ERM system will have to inter-operate in workflows with packages including project management, management information systems, accounting packages, customer relations management, enterprise content management and geographical information systems. Failure in any of this connectivity will damage the integrity of the record and the confidence of the user.

Any survey of EDRM products will be outdated before publication. However, emergent standards (TNA, MoReq, DoD) have done much to provide a benchmark for purchasers and vendors and have forced the software houses to be clear in their aims, certainly for that part of the industry active in the UK. There is much guidance in the literature of checklists of questions for vendors – on standards compliance, import and compatibility, integration with paper retention/disposal, format capture, OCR, indexing attributes and metadata, search facilities, controlled vocabularies and integration with other IT infrastructure.[19] Good vendors with extensive experience of ERM increasingly have high awareness of record-keeping priorities. They may even be in a position to identify records issues, challenges and solutions that records managers – often too close to the problems in their own organisations – do not pick up on.

That said, care has to be taken, particularly regarding the over-optimistic claims of software producers and vendors. Good and honest communication with vendors and consultants can bring creative solutions to bear on some of the most challenging ERM problems. Ensuring that you are speaking a common language as far as possible is also vital to managing relationships between records managers, archivists, IT professionals, information scientists and librarians, project managers, management and customers.

Periods of transition have historically been dangerous times for the preservation of the record. Society and the information management community are in a transitional phase in that we have a full range of technologies for the rapid handling and distribution of digital information but we are still realising the full implications of this and developing the protocols, policies, legislation and behaviours to cope with many issues, record keeping and digital preservation not least. Organisations will necessarily pass through a transitional period while EDRMS is rolled out and the issues raised will include the following:

- the need to handle hybrid information and record systems – paper, unmanaged digital (on hard drives and networked drives) and managed digital.[20] The hybrid management of electronic and paper records is likely to be a long-term requirement for many organisations as well as a transitional one;

- the need for clarity on the precise point at which the electronic record takes over from the paper;

- interim protocols for working between sections of the organisation at differing points of ERM implementation; for example, how do two departments share business documents if one has access to EDRM while the other does not yet have access?

- transfer of legacy records – in most cases back-scanning of paper-based legacy records is unlikely to be cost-effective or business critical, though some users will expect and demand it.

Conclusion

Even the best EDRMS does not represent a magic bullet. Where there is no pre-existing RM discipline, EDRMS implementation will not automatically create it.[21] Furthermore, EDRMS products have not yet addressed all the issues, particularly in terms of long-term preservation: 'Migration and software obsolescence are just two issues that EDRM systems have not resolved.'[22]

The form of the record after the advent of electronic records management will not be universally consistent. Depending on the needs, priorities and choices of the organisation, the corporate record could be much smaller or much larger than before. The quality of the record could be significantly enhanced or irreparably devalued. The act of record keeping could be heavily controlled and centralised or dramatically democratised and devolved. The outcome depends on the culture of the organisation, the business needs, and the support and compliance of managers and users.

EDRMS simultaneously pushes record-keeping responsibilities into the hands and onto the desktops of colleagues all across the organisation and provides unprecedented tools for applying effective records management automatically across a corporate system. Effective EDRM systems will significantly shape the record in ways beyond the deliberate aims of automation. Perhaps future reviews of records contents of the organisations we work for now will find less duplication (and contradiction) between records, more accurate and robust information, and clear linkages and metadata providing authorship, context and integrity – if our generation gets it right.

Notes

1. Howard, Stephen, 'Hybrid records management – a local government perspective', *Records Management Bulletin*, 110, October 2002, p. 5.
2. Allison, Dik, 'The application of records management disciplines into electronic data management', *Records Management Bulletin*, 103, June 2001, p. 9.
3. Gregory, Keith, 'Implementing an electronic records management system – a public sector case study', *Records Management Journal*, 15 (2), 2005, p. 84.
4. Johnston, Gary P. and Bowen, David V., 'The benefits of electronic records management: a general review of published and some unpublished cases', *Records Management Journal*, 15 (13), 2005, p. 135.
5. For example, Gregory, op. cit., p. 89.
6. Johnston and Bowen, op. cit., p. 139.
7. Hedstrom, Margaret, 'How do archivists make electronic archives usable and accessible?', *Archives and Manuscripts*, 26 (1), 1998, p. 14.
8. MacNeil, Heather, *Trusting Records* (Dordrecht, 2004), p. 96.
9. Horsman, Peter, 'The intelligent management of hybrid systems', *Records Management Bulletin*, 97, June 2000, p. 17.
10. Allison, op. cit., p. 11.
11. Maguire, Rachael, 'Lessons learned from implementing an electronic records management system', *Records Management Journal*, 15 (13), 2005, p. 11.
12. Allison, op. cit., p. 11.
13. Ibid.
14. For example, ibid., p. 13.
15. HM Stationery Office, *Modernising Government*, Cm. 4310 (London, 1999), Section 5.
16. Wiggins, Bob, 'Making the case for electronic records management: a Churchillian viewpoint', *Records Management Bulletin*, 110, October 2002, p. 21.
17. For example, see Gregory, op. cit., and Smyth, Zoe A., 'Implementing EDRM: has it provided the benefits expected', *Records Management Journal*, 15 (3), 2005.

18. Johnston and Bowen, op. cit., p. 136.
19. For example, see Wilson, John, 'Ten questions to ask vendors of EDM systems', *Records Management Bulletin*, 93, October 1999, p. 3.
20. Howard, op. cit.
21. For example, see Maguire, op. cit., and Smyth, op. cit.
22. Ryan, David, 'The future of managing electronic records', *Records Management Journal*, 15 (3), 2005, p. 129.

3

Security and the digital domain

James Currall

Introduction – what is security about?

Security does not sound a very exciting topic for this book, which is showing you new and challenging ways to view your business and how you conduct it. Security means many different things in different contexts. Most of the time, what it is about is protection of people or objects. In our context, security is about protection of information. Two questions arise from the notion of protection of information:

- Why is protection necessary?

and

- What are we protecting it from?

The first question concerns the fact that information has value. If it did not, there would be little point in keeping it. That value is not always value in a strictly financial sense, although the cost of recovering or recreating information may be a significant issue. Archivists have traditionally defined four main types of record value, namely: administrative/informational, legal/evidential, compliance/regulatory and historical. Security is about protecting these as much as anything else. Additionally, a great deal of information is about people, and in many cultures and circumstances people have a right to expect that at least some of the information about them is treated as confidential. Confidentiality implies protection.

The second question concerns the fact that there are threats to information, an aspect that we will return to at intervals in this chapter.

If one is to protect something, one has to identify what the threats are so as to take appropriate steps to mitigate them. This chapter is essentially about what the threats are and the steps that can be taken in relation to them. If you have been an archivist or records manager for some time, you will probably have a fairly shrewd idea as to how to deal with many of these issues in a world of physical manifestations of information (books, manuscripts, ledgers, minute books, maps, plans and such like). You may be rather less clear about how to deal with these matters in a world of digital manifestations (bits, bytes, computer files, databases and networks). One of the tasks of this chapter is to make the connection between the two worlds, so that you can use and build upon what you already know as the balance of your work moves from physical towards digital, as it probably will.

Security – the what and the who

It is convenient to split the varied aspects of information security into two groups: those concerned with ensuring that the information itself remains undamaged and genuine, and those concerned with ensuring that those who can access the information have a right to do so. In concept, these matters are no different in the world of digital representation from what they are in the world of physical representation. The differences are differences of degree, how they manifest themselves, and how those responsible for managing information assets can minimise the threats to their security.

What – ensuring that it is the right stuff

There are three areas of information management in which security plays a role, ensuring that the actual information that you manage is safe and secure: authenticity, integrity and availability. Digital assets are not directly perceived by human senses; they can only be viewed and manipulated rather indirectly through complex processes that cannot be fully understood by the end user. A great deal is taken on trust in our interactions with computers, and the possibility of fraud and duplicity is always with us. In addition, the concept of an original is problematic in the digital world, where copies can be identical to each other in all respects and the process of simply viewing a digital object may make several copies along the way.

In the digital world, it is every bit as important as in the paper world that we know that the information we manage is authentic, that its integrity is guaranteed, and that people can gain access to it when they need to. This presents considerable challenges to the archivist and records manager who will have to learn new skills and cultivate new partnerships to deal with them.

Who – ensuring that it is the right person

There are two elements to information access control or ensuring that the right people have access to the right thing. The first is identifying who the person wishing to access information is and the second is whether or not they should have access to the information resource. The first is termed authentication and the second authorisation. In digital information security this distinction is very important.

IT personnel have long realised that access to computers, rooms and information should be based on individuals, but what has taken rather longer to acknowledge is that we have access to information as a result of roles that we occupy rather than directly as a result of who we are as individuals:

- lecturer or teacher, student or pupil, employee, parent, Member of Parliament, etc.;
- resident of X, member of club Y or society Z.

A single individual may have many intersecting roles and to what information they have access is the sum of what each role entitles them to. A separation of authentication from authorisation makes it much easier to model and manage the linkages between people and information resources.

Some aspects of ensuring that only the right people have access to information are common to both paper and digital worlds. Physical security falls into this category. Information may be made available to selected people by keeping doors, filing cabinets and drawers locked and not leaving information lying around where anyone passing by can see it.

In some situations security is assumed in the digital world because of mistaken beliefs or understanding of the situation. An example is that many people assume e-mail to be secure because they send it off, it usually reaches the person they sent it to and they are unaware of anyone else seeing it. In fact, e-mail is sent across the Internet as 'plain text', that is as a sequence of characters that could be read by anyone along the way. Information on the Internet is put into the system and bounces its way from place to place until it arrives at its destination. If I set up a suitable monitoring program, I can watch very large amounts of information go past that are not destined for me. E-mail is thus similar in many ways to putting a postcard in the mail; it can be read by many people as it makes its way from you to me. There are techniques that can be used to put e-mail into the digital equivalent of 'sealed envelopes', but this strong encryption is rarely used and confidential reports and references fly around the Internet unprotected. People have started to understand that a floppy disk or CD, while needing a computer to reveal its secrets, will yield them to anyone who gets hold of it.

Although obvious if you think about it, paper manifestations of information are only available to people who are present in the same place at the same time. This is not true of digital manifestations on computers that are attached to networks. Computers and networks make information potentially available to everyone, everywhere, all the time. This opens up the number of people who might gain access to your information (whether or not you want them to). Much of computer security is about trying to make sure that people around the globe do not obtain unauthorised access. In recent years this has become increasingly difficult. If you really do not want unauthorised people to access your information, do not connect the computers containing it to a network. Instead, transfer information to and from them using removable media such as tapes, floppy discs, memory sticks and CDs.

The nature of the threat

Traditionally, records managers and archivists know a lot about the threats to physical manifestations of information. In many ways the types of threat are the same in the digital and physical worlds and any of the following can happen to both physical and digital manifestations. The main differences are: how likely each of them is, where the threat comes from and how it may be reduced.

- *Getting into the wrong hands – confidentiality*. When information gets into the hands of people who have no right to have it, this can have serious consequences, with the possibility of your organisation being sued or facing charges under privacy or data protection legislation and, even if the consequences are less serious, embarrassment or loss of commercial advantage may result.

- *Being damaged – integrity.* Damage, whether accidental or deliberate, is potentially serious. It may be costly to put right, may be undetected until it is too late and may lead to further security problems.

- *Becoming out of date – integrity/relevance.* Information that is out of date may be misleading, resulting in extra work or other unnecessary cost, and may be damaging to the organisation, its workforce, customers or reputation. After all, who can have confidence in an organisation that does not manage its information resources?

- *Being unavailable or irretrievably lost – availability.* The unavailability of information will almost certainly reduce efficiency of operation and affect the quality of decision-making. More importantly, it may result in damage or lead to a loss of reputation.

- *Not being what it says it is – authenticity.* Clearly, if information is to be useful, those making use of it must be able to have confidence that it is what it purports to be.

Information security management is concerned with the preservation of confidentiality, integrity, availability, relevance and authenticity. The objectives are to ensure that: information is accessible only to those authorised to have access to it; the accuracy and completeness of information and processing methods are safeguarded; authorised users have access to information and associated assets when required; people are seeing the correct version; and the information object is what it appears to be.
Information is particularly vulnerable during:

- *creation* – poor practice in naming, capture of appropriate metadata and 'filing';

- *storage* – failure to ensure that information is not overwritten, is adequately backed up, etc. and protection from on-site and off-site attackers;

- *access* – ensuring that the appropriate people have access to the information to view and to alter it;

- *transport* – information is particularly vulnerable when it is beyond the confines of the organisation.

Additional risk arises through keeping information for too long. There need to be suitable processes for proper destruction. In the digital world getting rid of information can be a very difficult thing to do.

Technical threats

Information security is not all about technical threats. In fact, security is not a technical issue, but use of technology can represent a threat to information security and technologies are often required to implement security solutions. In this section we are going to put the technical threats under the microscope because it is an area with which many archives and records management professionals are uncomfortable. It has probably not been included as part of their training and the landscape changes with each passing day.

The information architecture

The information architecture of most organisations has a number of elements.

First, there is the 'personal' machine on your desk that provides your primary instrument of access to digital information. This machine is at least partly managed by you – you have responsibility for many aspects of how it operates, although in many organisations other aspects are managed by technical support staff. Unlike a standard office telephone, which operates in a set way as it was manufactured to do, your computer will operate as the programs that are loaded on to it tell it to. This means that, if a program is loaded on to your machine (in addition to those that are normally there) that instructs it to send copies of every keystroke that you type to my computer in Glasgow, that is exactly what it will do. For this reason you need to take the management of your computer very seriously. Remember that, if you are authorised to access and manage certain information, then to all intents and purposes so is your computer (whether or not you told it to and whether or not you are actually present). Poor use of individual computers has the potential to compromise the whole of your digital record-keeping or archiving systems.

The second element is the array of servers that provide you with a variety of services: printing, web interfaces, filestore, electronic document and/or records system (EDMS/EDRMS), backups and so on. These machines are generally managed by specialists who know what they are doing, but cannot be guaranteed to know what you think they are doing or want them to do. These people will ensure that these machines are well managed to minimise the threats that they know about and wish to control. You cannot assume that this includes all the threats that are important to you. An example might serve to illustrate the difference in perspective. Most servers have some arrangements in place for backup. Suppose you accidentally delete a digital object on the file server that you use. You might naturally assume that those running the server can simply go to the backup and retrieve the object for you. This may not be the case. Those managing the server are making backups to deal with one major eventuality – disk failure. If a disk fails, what they want to do is to get a new one and recreate the filestore exactly as it was before. It is often easier for backup systems that have this objective to store material in such a way that the only restoration possible is to recreate a new disk by overwriting everything, rather than by finding and restoring every object individually. The result would be that they would be unable to satisfy your requirement without buying an additional disk, restoring the whole backup on to it and then looking for your object to copy to your storage space on the old disk. They are unlikely to wish to do this unless someone's life depended on it. Some threats are related to how these servers are managed.

The third element is the network that connects the computers in your organisation. Again this is likely to be managed by professionals, but remember that its purpose is to make it as easy as possible for information to get from one machine to another (although there will be some controls). The network frequently cannot distinguish between information that should be travelling from machine to machine and that which should not. A rogue program that gets on to your machine might easily be able to travel to everyone else's. Some of the threats to information security lie on machines (and with people using them) attached to your organisation's network.

The fourth element is the connection of your organisation's network to the global network or Internet. In many ways this is the Wild West, where the law of the jungle applies (to mix metaphors). It is likely that there will be some sort of gateway between the two, but, in order to allow useful information in, the controls are unlikely to be draconian. The rest of the computing world is attached to the Internet and that is where many of the threats that we are discussing lie or originate.

Threats to confidentiality

From a technical perspective, the key to confidentiality is access control mechanisms. In a sense this is no different from the paper world where you lock confidential papers away in filing cabinets and drawers and behind locked office and building doors. You allow people past these controls using keys and, increasingly, swipe cards and other tokens. The major threats to digital information result from having inadequate access control mechanisms and through people being able to bypass the access control mechanisms as a consequence of security compromise elsewhere in the system. You need to be concerned with the design of access control at a logical level, cooperating with systems designers and support staff. You need also to be concerned with access control at an operational level, cooperating with the systems support staff to ensure that they manage system security appropriately.

Technical measures that are required to counter these threats to confidentiality are: secure systems, secure authentication methods and an authorisation process and system that matches your needs.

Failure to destroy completely information that is no longer required or relevant is another important threat to confidentiality. Typically information resides in: local copies on individuals' machines or on shared file servers, backup copies of individual and shared filestore, copies in the filestore of other people (both within and outside the organisation) to whom the information has been distributed, and finally in the backup systems of these other people. Little wonder that it is very difficult to actually destroy *all copies* of a digital object. To make matters worse, when you delete a digital object on your computer, it is not actually removed. What happens is that the directory entry for the item is removed. One of the functions of this entry is to point to where it can be found on the disk. There are easily obtainable tools that can restore deleted digital objects. The main determinant of success is how much disk activity has taken place between deletion and the attempt at restoration.

The measures needed to deal with this threat to confidentiality are really organisational rather than technical: clear distribution policies, clear destruction policies, single sources rather than copies that have to be updated individually, shared originals on file servers rather than individual copies in personal space, carefully worked-out destruction processes and a shared understanding between archivist, records managers and technologists about types of backup and the needs of record keeping and destruction.

Threats to integrity

The threats under this heading are those that affect computer systems generally, causing widespread disruption rather than being targeted at a specific piece of information. As computer applications have become more sophisticated and the users have become more demanding in relation to seamless integration of one type of activity with another, so it has become easier to embed instructions within e-mail messages, documents, spreadsheets, etc. This class of threat seeks to execute code using mechanisms that under normal circumstances are intended to support this ease of use. In general, the objective is to allow unauthorised activity or access to computer systems rather than to specific digital objects. A general heading for the software that constitutes this type of threat is malware. Malware can be classified on the basis of how it is executed, how the code is distributed and/or what it does:

- *Viruses*. Self-replicating programs that spread by inserting copies of themselves into other programs or documents, they are frequently distributed via e-mail or other standard person-to-person communication mechanisms. The infection routine of the virus arranges that, when the host program is run or the document opened, the viral code is run as well. Normally, the host program or document operates as normal after infection by the virus. Some viruses overwrite other programs with copies of themselves, which destroys them altogether.

- *Worms*. Similar to viruses but they are stand-alone programs and thus do not require host documents to spread themselves. They usually modify the operating system of their host machine so that they are started as part of the startup process. To spread, worms either exploit some vulnerability of the host operating system or use some kind of bogus incentive to trick users into running them.

- *Trojans*. Named after the classical Wooden Horse of Troy, these programs present themselves as an appealing prospect such as a screensaver, greetings card or useful free program. While they may do what they claim, they also carry out other tasks, which may result in third parties being able to take control of your computer at will (including having access to all your digital objects), or use your filestore for the distribution of copyright or illegal material. Trojan horses cannot replicate themselves, in contrast to viruses or worms. To complicate matters, some trojan horses can spread or activate other types of malware, such as viruses.

Viruses and worms often act as carriers for other types of malware, such as:

- *Spyware*. Collects and sends information about your browsing behaviour to other parties without your knowledge.

- *Keyloggers.* Copy the sequence of keystrokes that you make when using your computer into a computer file. This file may then be inspected directly by a hacker or e-mailed to another party without your knowledge. Keyloggers are primarily used to collect credit card details and passwords, which are then used by unauthorised people.
- *Backdoors.* Are pieces of software that allow access to your computer system, bypassing the normal authentication procedures.

Innocent documents from people that you know may contain malicious code put there by any of the mechanisms. If your record system contains documents 'infected' in this way, opening them could destroy the record system or at the very least spread the 'infection' or other malady to the computers of anyone accessing it.

Technical measures are needed to deal with these threats: effective, up-to-date virus detection software (new viruses appear on a daily basis), up-to-date operating system and applications software patches to deal with security loopholes that are discovered from time to time and may be exploited by the above mechanisms, and regular checking of the integrity of computers, software and user files.

This is the area where individual users need to recognise that they have a role. The mechanisms used to distribute malicious code often make use of 'social engineering' – spurious incentives to download or open a digital object – and also make use of the fact that people are either lazy or ignorant in relation to managing and maintaining their computers properly. Some of this maintenance can be, and in many organisations is, automated, but it cannot all be. Resisting 'scams' that introduce malicious code is entirely down to individual responsibility.

Threats to availability

Information availability is often not seen as a security issue, but if information is kept securely it should be available when it is required. From a technical perspective, there are four types of problem that affect availability of information.

Perhaps the most obvious problem is system malfunction. We have all experienced unavailability as a result of our computers, networks or file servers breaking down. Often the loss of access is temporary and thus simply inconvenient but, if the right precautions have not been taken, the unavailability may be permanent and very large-scale.

The second problem is human error. One might not regard this as a technical matter, but human error frequently occurs as a result of unfamiliarity with systems, poor understanding of what systems are really doing, poor system design or high levels of system complexity. It may be very easy to delete important information without realising fully what the result of a particular action is.

The third problem is caused by the fact that digital information is only 'available' via the use of computer programs and not directly via the senses. Possessing the digital object containing the information is not enough, as you also need a program that can access the information and render it in such a way that you can understand it. In a world of rapid technological change, those designing and selling software are constantly changing the formats in which they store information and the way that their programs operate.

The final problem is related to the nature of the medium on which digital representations of information are stored. There are several aspects to this problem. With paper-based representations of information, a visual inspection will reveal that degradation is taking place. In the digital realm it is often not possible to detect problems visually and it is only when one comes to 'read' the medium via computer software that one discovers that there is a problem. If a paper document starts to degrade, it may happen relatively slowly and most of the information is still readable; the loss of 'availability' is very gradual and can be arrested at any time. In the digital domain, the corruption of a single byte of a large digital object might make it completely unreadable. Most digital media types (tapes, floppy disks, hard disks, CDs, DVDs, etc.) have a relatively short usable life by comparison with paper. These aspects, taken together, mean that information stored in a digital form can be very vulnerable to loss, unless managed very carefully.

Any of the problems outlined have the potential to destroy individual objects or whole systems. Careful management of digital information assets and programs to access them is the key to countering the threat to availability. A crucial component of this is to have a well thought out backup strategy, which ensures that there is an adequate number of copies stored securely in more than one location, that backup copies are taken at suitable intervals, and that this is driven by the needs of records and/or archival management and permits full destruction where needed. A second component is to put in place processes to detect problems with digital objects and carry out appropriate remedial action. It is no use waiting until you need to use a particular digital object and discovering that it is unreadable. By that time, the unreadable object may well have been faithfully backed up, replacing the uncorrupted version on all media. Technologies that may be appropriate as *part of* such processes include digital signatures, checksums and hashes,[1] all of which can be used to detect whether objects have suffered any change or degradation. A third component is to ensure that you know what programs produced your digital assets and the formats they are stored in. The National Archives in the UK have established a resource called PRONOM, which contains technical information about the structure of digital object formats and the software products that support them, and is available on the Internet.[2] It is often helpful to select a more robust format that can be read by many different programs rather than a proprietary one that can only be read by current software from one supplier.

Threats to relevance

In the digital world it is now fairly frequent for colleagues to have been working with different versions of a document and as a result have wasted effort or been seriously misled. This problem is not confined to the world of digital representation, but the speed and ease with which information can be changed in the digital realm does increase the likelihood of working with an out-of-date copy or out-of-date information. In spite of this, many documents have no version information that would allow someone to distinguish the current version from any previous or future one.

As with many of the threats that we have considered in this section, there is no substitute for good management practices, but there are technical measures that can help. The problem can be reduced by ensuring that systems are designed such that they share information and all participants draw a particular piece from the same source rather than each keeping a separate copy. There are technologies and techniques for achieving this across many types of system but a fuller discussion of these is beyond the scope of this chapter. At a practical level, storing documents or other digital objects in shared file space on servers rather than sending copies around by e-mail can go a long way to reducing proliferation.

In addition, there are technologies, often in the form of EDM or EDRM systems, that handle revision and allow individuals to 'check out' a document for editing and check it back in once they have finished. This approach keeps track of changes and allows the recovery of any previous version and details of what particular changes were made, when and by whom. Surprisingly, the overhead in terms of file space required to achieve this is very modest. I have a dozen versions of a recent document available at a cost of less than twice the file space required by the final version alone.

Threats to authenticity

Under this heading, we are concerned primarily with the substitution of one version of a digital object for another in order to falsify the record. We will not concern ourselves with issues concerning whether or not what was accepted by the archivist or records manager was the genuine article in the first place. The approach to dealing with that aspect is no different from the one you might take with paper accessions.

The ease with which digital objects may be modified means that, without appropriate processes in place, they may leave no readily discernable trace. This is a major issue in terms of being able to establish the authenticity of digital objects.[3] As in the paper world, there is no substitute for good custodianship. In terms of the technical measures that may be employed to aid archivists and records managers in the maintenance of authenticity, there is one area that deserves mention – digital signatures.[4]

The traditional concept of a signature is:

> any mark made with the intention of authenticating the marked document. (American Bar Association)

A digital signature is designed to serve similar purposes to a traditional handwritten signature:

- authentication (establishing the identity of the author);
- integrity (that the signed document, or other object, is unchanged); and
- non-repudiation (the author cannot deny the transaction).

Digital signatures are produced from a combination of something unique to the person signing (a person's 'private key') and something unique to the document being signed (a digital digest of its contents). Each signature is therefore unique to the document to which it relates. Moreover, a person may have as many 'keys' as are required to generate different signatures for different purposes. Traditional handwritten signatures are impossible to steal but easy to forge. Unlike traditional signatures, digital signatures are almost impossible to forge but the keys used in signing may, if not properly looked after, be stolen or misused. A useful analogy is with seals that were used widely until the late nineteenth century to authenticate documents (Currall and Moss, 2000; Currall, 2002). There were personal seals and seals associated with offices (or roles) held by individuals and with institutions. In the case of seals they were also difficult to forge but could be stolen or misused.

A digital signature does not look like a traditional signature and is in fact a small incomprehensible digital object. An example is given below:

```
-----BEGIN PGP SIGNATURE-----
Version: PGPfreeware 6.0.2i
iQA/AwUAOVMeDypYUiSnnmBwEQLh6QCePfQXRriaPoHaZifx
YqSAn+0QwjIAn3lh
TxSvy2tQZSlvEPkFi/5dl6bq=u9gB
-----END PGP SIGNATURE-----
```

In the world of paper, documents are viewed directly by the human observer. In the digital world all 'objects' are streams of bytes that have meaning only when interpreted by a 'program'. Similarly you do not require any tools to make traditional signatures (except a pen). To verify a traditional signature, you need to have some sort of knowledge about what the signature ought to be/look like. It is relatively easy to detect alterations to paper documents, so long as you are looking at originals and not photocopies. You do, however, require tools to create and verify digital signatures and to detect alterations to those digital documents, in addition to contextual knowledge such as who the document should be signed by and what their signature is like.

Finally, it is important to emphasise that digital signatures are distinct from computer graphic images produced by scanning handwritten signatures. These graphic images may easily be copied from document to document, so they are not useful or valid in terms of asserting identity or integrity. Digital signatures on the other hand provide for increased confidence in digital information exchange in the areas of identity and integrity. The most common use of digitally signed objects is the set of signed certificates installed in your web browser that permit secure connections to be established between your browser and the web servers of e-retailers such as Amazon.com or the online sales sites of airlines.

Like any other device, digital signatures are only as useful as the process that surrounds their issue, distribution, use and revocation. With appropriate processes (including traditional processes such as registration in an associated volume, multiple witnesses and the participation of the most senior executives), digital signatures can carry the same sort of authority that seals do. Without such processes, they have little value.

Risk

Earlier discussion has focused on a wide range of possible threats to digital information. It is now time to try to put these into some sort of perspective. There are three elements to this: first, the principles of most of the things that have been discussed are no different in kind from those that you deal with in respect of physical information manifestations; secondly, you can make life much easier by ensuring that, as archivists and records managers, you establish good understanding and working relationships with those who provide technical support for your operations and, finally, it is necessary to undertake a risk analysis before rushing to action.

What is risk?

So what is risk and how is it analysed? The list of threats above is *not* a list of risks. Writing them down in the form of '100 reasons why you should not be able to sleep for worrying' is not a risk analysis. A risk has three elements: a contingency, a consequence or impact (with some measure of how big) *and* a likelihood of occurrence. As I sit here writing, a possible risk occurs to me. A large passenger jet could come crashing into my house. This is a contingency. The impact of that would be disastrous for me and my family. So why am I not worried and trying to do something about it? Clearly, the answer is that the likelihood is so low that this contingency becomes relatively unimportant to me. People are often rather perplexed when they say 'we must do something about X because we might get sued' or 'we must do something about Y because it is a legal requirement'[5] and I say 'so what?' I am interested in taking action only if there is a real risk. The e-mail server has failed three times in the last six months and the supplier says he can no longer get parts to fix it, so next time it fails it fails for good – this gives a manager all three elements and they can take appropriate action as a result.

There are a number of difficulties with risk in general and in the digital domain in particular. An example is that people do not take risks seriously until the contingency actually occurs. They then overreact and rush around doing things. Gradually the memory fades away, leading to an unwillingness to act. Think about what happens after a rail or air crash. Many of the consequences are rather remote unless you have actually experienced the outcome concerned and therefore it is difficult to understand the impact. The assessment of likelihood can also be difficult, particularly in relation to new legislation for which there is no case law and when it is difficult to know how many people will exercise new rights. Likelihood is also notoriously difficult to assess for 'rare' events (such as multiple failure of nuclear reactor safety systems). In computer security, many security problems do not happen often enough to get a good estimate of likelihood, and for the most part our systems are too good for our rhetoric. This leads to people relying on them, leaving things until the last minute and having no plans for the eventuality of failure.

Security is about reducing risk:

- risk to the individual:
  - loss of a day's/week's/month's work;
  - impersonation;
- risk to the organisation:
  - reputation;
  - litigation;
  - the work of members;
  - financial loss;
  - fraud.

Security is also about controlling risk. We cannot control risk if we have not identified the risks and evaluated them in terms of impact and likelihood. In other areas of risk management, the establishment of a formal risk register, together with processes to ensure that it is reviewed and revised at regular intervals, is undertaken. This is rapidly becoming the norm in information management and is a part of the developing standards discussed in the next section. The threats discussed earlier need to be assessed in your situation and approaches to tackling them identified and prioritised. There are essentially four ways to deal with risks:

- *treat* – control the risk by taking appropriate steps to make it less likely or to lessen the impact;

- *take* – accept the risk and its consequences (especially if there is nothing feasible and/or affordable that can be done about the risk);

- *terminate* – avoid the risk by not doing the activity any more;

- *transfer* – make the risk someone else's problem (e.g. by insurance, outsourcing, etc.).

This section has introduced only the bare bones of risk and hinted at how to go about tackling it. What you now need is solid guidance and fortunately you do not have to make all this up from scratch; there are templates, standards and guidelines to help you and we will deal with these in the next section.[6]

Information security and organisations

As archivists and records managers, what are the real risks that you are trying to guard against? Both in relation to your work and to that of the organisation that you serve, the fundamental high-level risks are of being unable to get on with your business and spending a lot of time sorting out compromised information. As professionals, you are also trying to guard your organisation from compliance failure, litigation and corporate amnesia while also enabling the organisation to assert its legal and other rights.

Organisations require policies and practices recognising that information security is not just about computers and networks; it needs to cover most areas of work practice. This will become clearer in the discussion of the standards in this area. Organisational policy frameworks need to recognise the need for a good understanding of the issues surrounding security and serious commitment at all levels. There needs to be a risk-based approach to managing the security. Security measures need to be easy to use and to provide access to information according to multiple cross-classified roles in the organisation. It is clear that whatever you do will provide more inconvenience to the legitimate users of information than to those who might seek to disrupt your information environment. It is just the same as the security measures in your house or car which make life much more difficult for you than for potential thieves.

One size does not fit all. You need different levels of security for different purposes. Think for a moment about a bank. The security measures to restrict access at the front door (during banking hours) are very limited. It is much more difficult to get behind the counter and there are security systems to ensure that only employees do that. To get into the vaults, where the things of real value lie, there are further layers of security involving multiple keys, time locks and so on. We need to ensure that the measures deployed are proportionate, bearing in mind that it is sometimes cheaper and more effective to accept risk rather than try to eliminate it. If we take a suitably balanced approach, people will find it easier to accept higher levels of security for the really important matters.

What we are seeking to do is to strike a balance:

- ease of use *with* protection of information;
- cost of protection *with* risks posed by inadequate protection;
- privacy of information access *with* monitoring for aberrant behaviour;
- automatic protection *with* user understanding and behavioural change.

Standards for information security

Information security is an important matter for all organisations and the subject of international standards. The current standard started off as a British Standard (BS 7799) but has now become an International Standard (ISO/IEC 17799:2005 and ISO/IEC 27001:2005).[7] The standard is in two parts.

ISO/IEC 17799:2005 – Information Technology – Security Techniques – Code of practice for information security management

This part can be viewed as a comprehensive list of best practice in security matters. It consists of 132 specific security controls under eleven major headings or Control Areas:

- Security Policy
- Organisational Security
- Asset Management
- Human Resource Security
- Physical and Environmental Security
- Communications and Operations Management
- Access Control

- Information Systems Acquisition, Development and Maintenance
- Information Security Incident Management
- Business Continuity Management
- Compliance.

In assessing and applying the controls, it needs to be borne in mind that they do not all apply to all organisations, but identifying that some of them are not relevant is part of the task. What you can see from the list is that ISO/IEC 17799:2000 is very wide-ranging and is not focused purely on 'techie' matters.

ISO/IEC 27001:2005 – Information Technology – Security Techniques – Information security management systems – Requirements

This part is a specification for information security management systems (ISMS), a framework within which an organisation can monitor and manage all aspects of information security to control risk. It is against this that certification to the Standard can take place for organisations that require certification. The steps in the process are:

1. Define an information security policy.
2. Define the scope of the information security management system (ISMS).
3. Perform a security risk assessment.
4. Manage the identified risks.
5. Select controls to be implemented and applied.
6. Prepare a 'statement of applicability' (SoA).

The implementation and operation of an ISMS is based around a PDCA (Plan, Do, Check, Act) cycle:

Plan	– understand security requirements, establish policies, carry out risk analysis.
Do	– deal with risks and implement and operate controls.
Check	– monitor and review performance and the ISMS itself.
Act	– identify and implement improvements, deal with new issues and apply lessons learnt.

Many organisations, and perhaps more importantly their insurers, are now demanding that their business partners have certification against standards such as ISO/IEC 27001 and its predecessor BS 7799-2 as a condition of doing business with them in order to defend themselves against poor information management practices in others that might impact on their own business.

Conclusions

The principles of information security in the digital world are essentially the same as in the physical world. This means that, as a practising archivist or records manager, you are already well versed in them. The practice, however, is rather different. There is really only one feasible approach to dealing with the new situation and that is to form a close partnership with professionals in the IT domain, such that they understand what you are trying to do and you understand what is practically possible. You should be aiming for innovation as a result of partnership, rather than a simple supplier–consumer relationship.

From your side, you need to understand the threats, where they come from, what they mean and the effects that they can have. In addition, you need to understand both the role that technology can play in providing solutions and also the problems that technology brings with it.

A systematic approach must start with a thorough analysis of the threats facing your holdings and the risks both of taking steps and of not taking steps to counter them.

From the IT side, it is essential that you operate on relatively secure machines, both individual workstations and the server and network infrastructure that supports them. You should not underestimate the role that every person who uses a computer has in ensuring that their machine does not fall prey to a range of types of malware. Your IT professionals should be able to take care of the server and network infrastructure, but their job will be made difficult if individuals indulge in practices that open up security vulnerabilities.

As is the case in the world of physical information manifestations,in the digital world much of security is about good management and processes, and there is a clear need to establish good practices that are proportionate to the risks involved. People will circumvent procedures that are unnecessarily cumbersome and the net result of over-burdensome procedures may be poorer rather than greater security.

Things will go wrong. So you need to plan on that basis and have appropriate tools to monitor the situation and to recover from problems. Every aspect of security discussed in this chapter needs the support of good record keeping, so that you know what has been done, how, when, by whom and to what.

Notes

1. Digital signatures are discussed in the section on 'Threats to authenticity'.

   A checksum is a simple way to check the integrity of information by detecting errors. It works by adding up the basic components of a message, typically the bytes, and storing the resulting value. Later, the same operation can be performed on the information and the result compared with the original checksum, and (assuming that the sums match) conclude that the message was probably not corrupted. The simplest form of checksum, which simply adds up the bytes in the data, cannot detect a number of types of errors. In particular, such a checksum is not changed by reordering or multiple errors that cancel each other out.

   A hash function takes a sequence of characters of any length as input and produces a short fixed-length sequence of characters as output, sometimes termed a message digest or a digital fingerprint. If the same hash function is used, the same result will be produced for a particular input sequence, but a radically different result if the input sequence has changed in any way. Hash functions are less vulnerable to the problems indicated for checksums. Common hash functions are MD5 and SHA-1.

2. The first version of PRONOM was developed by the National Archives digital preservation department in March 2002. Its genesis lies in the need to have ready access to reliable technical information about the nature of the electronic records now being stored in digital archives. Digital information is encoded into a form that can only be processed and rendered comprehensible by very specific combinations of hardware and software. The accessibility of that information is therefore highly vulnerable in today's rapidly evolving technological environment. PRONOM holds the technical information about the structure of the formats, and the software products that support them. It was developed to provide this function, initially as an internal resource for National Archives staff, but is now on the Internet at: *http://www.nationalarchives.gov.uk/pronom/*.

3. The InterPARES project has been doing some interesting work applying diplomatics to the digital world (*http://www.interpares.org/*).

4. A good, non-technical account of digital signatures and the context of their potential use can be found in Clifford Lynch's article 'Authenticity in a digital environment: an exploratory analysis of the central role of trust' (Washington, DC, 2000) (available at *http://www.clir.org/pubs/reports/pub92/lynch.html*, accessed February 2006).

5. There is usually a good reason for the legal requirement and the risk may be better specified in terms of that more direct consequence than in terms of breaking the law.

6. The ERPANET Risk Assessment Tool (*http://www.erpanet.org/guidance/docs/ERPANETRiskTool.pdf*) is one useful resource, as is the DIRKS guidance on risk assessment in Appendix 11 of the DIRKS documentation (*http://www.naa.gov.au/recordkeeping/dirks/dirksman/dirks_A11_risk.html*).
7. Documents relating to the standard can be purchased from the BSI (*http://www.bsi-global.com/*) or ISO (*http://www.iso.org/*) or Standards Direct (*http://www.standarddirect.org/*), and many consultancies have websites via which ISO/IEC 17799:2000 and BS 7799-2:2002 or ISO/IEC 27001:2005 advice, guidance, information and service can be obtained (e.g. *http://www.gammassl.co.uk/bs7799/, http://wwwinduction.to/iso17799/*).

4

Risk management and managing records

Azman Mat-Isa

It may appear obvious to many readers of this book that effective risk management must depend to some extent on the availability of appropriate records. What may be less obvious is that effective risk management itself generates records and that ensuring that the right records of the risk management process are created and managed is an integral element of both good records management and good risk management.

Perceptions of risk influence decisions and behaviour. Organisations, in both the public and private sectors, need to perceive risks in order to reduce uncertainty and to achieve economic operation and longevity of the organisation. Risk refers to the uncertainty that surrounds future events and outcomes. It is the expression of the likelihood and impact of an event with the potential to influence the achievement of an organisation's objectives.[1] The success of risk management is partly dependent on the accuracy of records in organisations, as every judgement made must be based on reliable information. In an age when compliance and legislation are of increasing concern, it is essential for organisations to comply with regulations and, if they do not, to be able to explain why.

Risk does not end when a particular business process or transaction has been completed, but may remain as a long-term threat to the organisation. Furthermore, some records will remain forever as archives, thus presenting endless risk, particularly to public organisations. The implementation of the Freedom of Information Act 2000 where users have rights to access relevant records is a wake-up call to the public sector to ensure that they are prepared for any consequences. Indeed, they are directly accountable to the members of the public, and therefore a balance between risk and the types of records to keep is crucial to ensure that they can operate as economically as possible.[2]

To ensure the effectiveness of risk management, an organisation must have a risk management strategy that is designed in line with the organisation's goals. The application of the strategy should be embedded into the organisation's business systems, including strategy and policy setting processes, to ensure that risk management is an intrinsic part of the way business is conducted.[3] Sampson suggests that, in order to function effectively, future records managers need a wider range of business management skills and a high level of technical expertise in a number of areas, including information technologies, changing regulatory and legal issues and requirements, and evolving information needs of the organisation.[4] Although it will be a long and time-consuming process, providing up-to-date academic and training programmes is certainly a useful way to train multi-skilled records managers.

What is risk management?

Traditionally, risk management is about controlling loss and the financial status of an organisation, and is implicitly linked to the insurance industry.[5] During the 1960s, companies began to employ risk managers because of the increasing cost of insurance. Thompson states that during this time multinational companies decided that corporate managers and overseas insurance brokers needed to manage risk internationally.[6] However, at this stage one of the key barriers faced by organisations was the lack of risk management experience. Such qualifications as existed were tailored to insurance managers. The change in emphasis from insurance management to risk management was slow and poorly received by senior management due to the continuing focus on insurance controls.

In the 1970s, corporate mergers and acquisitions resulted in new and unexpected risks, as the underlying nature of the business of corporations changed after merger or acquisition. Organisations quickly moved beyond buying insurance as the only risk control solution and adopted alternative methods, such as loss prevention, loss control and operational risk management. Then, in the 1990s, risk management expanded further to cover areas such as industrial safety, hazard analysis and environmental planning in response to tightening controls and external pressures. Thompson also insists that risk management now relates to the harm that may be suffered by any type of facility or activity because of an unforeseen (or indeed predicted) event, and it has been accepted as part of management science.[7] One of the key drivers for risk management is the necessity to comply with international legislation and expected standards of corporate governance that require organisations to demonstrate greater accountability and transparency in their dealings. Organisations have recognised the need to respond to the effects of competition and economic change by reviewing their overall cost of business. Risk management has also become an integrated part of strategic corporate governance to ensure the integrity and accountability of organisations while at the same time pursuing organisational goals.[8]

Sampson defines risk management as a business management function or process that analyses the costs, risks and benefits of alternatives in order to determine the most desirable or appropriate course of action.[9] Risk management is about making decisions that contribute to the achievement of an organisation's objectives at the individual activity level and in functional areas. It assists with decisions such as: the reconciliation of science-based evidence and other factors; costs with benefits and expectations in investing limited public resources; and the governance and control structures needed to support due diligence, responsible risk taking, innovation and accountability.[10] Risk management should be a continuous and developing process, which runs across the organisation's strategy and its implementation. It should address methodically all the risks surrounding the organisation's activities past, present and, in particular, future.

The United Kingdom HM Treasury's Orange Book (2004) states that risk management is not a linear process; rather it is the balancing of a number of interwoven elements that interact with each other and which have to be in balance with each other to be effective. Specific risks cannot be addressed in isolation from one another as the management of one risk may impact on another. Similarly, Meulbroek (2002) also states that risk management will not achieve its full potential and benefits if it is conducted by various individual departments across an organisation, because it tends to be tactical rather than strategic. Tactical risk management has limited objectives, usually the hedging of specific contracts or of other explicit future commitments of the firm; strategic risk management addresses the broader question of how risk affects the value of the entire business. Meulbroek further elaborates that incorporating more risks results in an integrated risk management system that must embrace all risks that affect value. Operational risk, product market risk, input risk, tax risk, regulatory risk, legal risk and financial risk compose the broad classes of risks faced by most organisations, risks that in aggregate form the overall risk exposure of the firm.

The management of risk at strategic, programme and operational levels needs to be integrated so that the levels of activity support each other. The hierarchy of risk model (Figure 4.1) suggests that the higher

Figure 4.1 Hierarchy of risk

Uncertainty

Strategic — Strategic decisions

Programme — Decisions transferring strategy into action

Project and operational — Decisions required for implementation

(© Strategy Unit, UK, 2002)

the hierarchy, the higher the level of uncertainty. Understandably, it is the nature of the tasks that determines the level of uncertainty. The project and operational level has the lowest uncertainty level. Decisions made by project and operational managers are based on statistical data, hence uncertainty depends mainly on the accuracy and reliability of the data used. The programme level is exposed to a higher level of uncertainty, not least because there are choices of alternative methods or mechanisms that can be used to implement the strategic decisions made by the top management. Meanwhile the strategic level, usually at the level of the board of directors, focuses on decisions that determine the direction and sustainability of the organisation. Records are essential to these decision-making processes. Records at the operational level are used by middle management, while, in turn, key elements of such records will then be used by the board of directors.

As risk is unavoidable, every organisation needs to take action to manage risk in a way that can be justified as tolerable. Risk is not limited to internal threats. It is essential to be sensitive to any changes in the external environment and to the actions of competitors. It is undeniable that the assessment of all these risks is dependent on the accuracy of the information available, which is the product of systematic and comprehensive record-keeping and monitoring procedures.

Elements of risk management

Risk management processes consist of a series of activities to achieve organisational goals. The Association of Insurance and Risk Managers (AIRMIC), the Association of Local Authority Risk Managers (ALARM) and the Institute of Risk Management (IRM) provide an explicit model of risk management processes (Figure 4.2).[11] It is a cyclical process,

Figure 4.2 The risk management process

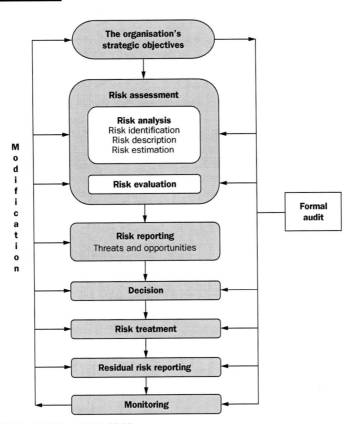

(© AIRMIC, ALARM and IRM, 2002)

which allows modification of every part of the process over time to meet the organisational goals. A formal audit process will provide a check for ongoing risk management activities. AIRMIC, ALARM and IRM advocate that risk management protects and adds value to the organisation and its stakeholders by:

- providing a framework for an organisation that enables future activity to take place in a consistent and controlled manner;

- improving decision-making, planning and prioritisation by the comprehensive and structured understanding of business activity, volatility and project opportunity/threat;

- contributing to more efficient use/allocation of capital and resources within the organisation;

- reducing volatility in the non-essential areas of the business;
- protecting and enhancing assets and company image;
- developing and supporting people and the organisation's knowledge base;
- optimising operational efficiency.

The most crucial part of risk management is risk assessment, which consists of two major activities, namely risk analysis and risk evaluation. In risk analysis, the process of identifying risk is the trigger for subsequent activities. AIRMIC, ALARM and IRM state:

> Risk identification sets out to identify an organisation's exposure to uncertainty. This requires an intimate knowledge of the organisation, the market in which it operates, the legal, social, political and cultural environment in which it exists, as well as the development of a sound understanding of its strategic and operational objectives, including factors critical to its success and the threats and opportunities related to the achievement of these objectives. Risk identification should be approached in a methodical way to ensure that all significant activities within the organisation have been identified and all the risks flowing from these activities defined.

In essence, risk management is a continuous process, and therefore risk assessment should be documented in a way that records the stages of the process. The Orange Book[12] states that documenting risk assessment creates a risk profile for the organisation which:

1. facilitates identification of risk priorities (in particular identifying the most significant risk issues with which senior management should concern themselves);
2. captures the reasons for decisions made about what is and is not tolerable exposure;
3. facilitates recording of the way in which it is decided to address risk;
4. allows all those concerned with risk management to see the overall risk profile and how their areas of particular responsibility fit into it; and
5. facilitates review and monitoring of risk.

Theoretically, it is complicated enough but practically it is far more complicated to secure pertinent and accurate records that will support a precise methodical assessment to identify risks across an organisation. Risk description and risk estimation are the output of risk identification, which will then be used in risk evaluation to compare the eliminated risks against risk criteria that the organisation has established. Subsequent activities of risk management are risk reporting, decision-making, risk treatment, residual risk reporting and monitoring, depending on the ability of the risk management team to assess and make a judgement based on the information available, both from internal and external resources. General perceptions cannot be used as the basis for identifying risk as they are not necessarily accurate. Decisions on the types of risk present must be based on empirical and methodical assessments of available records. Lion and Meertens reveal that risk avoiders selected more positive information than risk takers, contrary to the general assumption that, as risk avoiders focus on the worst outcomes, they would prefer negative information about risk.[13] Risk takers, on the other hand, would prefer positive information about the risk. However, the trend of information seeking differs under different circumstances, hence systematic and methodical assessment is deemed necessary to determine the types of records required.

Mehr and Hedges, both economists, state that the process of analysing an organisation's present exposure is usually called risk analysis.[14] It needs to be done economically and effectively. It is folly to waste time and other resources in accumulating information that is not needed to accomplish the objectives. From the information and records management perspective, risk analysis would not achieve its goals in the absence of accurate records. Managing records must be given priority and adequately supported if risk management is to succeed. As Simons rightfully pointed out, as a company grows, the money invested in such systems (information systems) should grow commensurately.[15] It may seem wasteful at the time, especially since success makes risk seem so remote, but it is money well spent. Unfortunately, many managers do not learn this lesson until it is too late. Radner insists that, although managers in a firm have many different functions, one of the most important is that of processing information.[16] He further states that information processing is a huge decision-making machine that takes signals from the environment and transforms them into the actions to be taken by the 'real workers'. The most effective way to make risk management central to an organisation is to make the process integral to the organisation's decision-making process, that is central to all organisational activities, especially records management. The records manager has an important role in ensuring the availability of accurate and authentic information to underpin the decision-making process.

The roles of records management in risk management

Nevertheless, a records management team often faces difficulties in convincing senior management of the importance of their role. Problems and difficulties of managing records cannot be solved individually; instead concerted organisational efforts must be made to attain maximum benefits. Today, the contribution of records management seems to be more explicitly recognised. The collapses of Enron and WorldCom have had a significant impact on the future of records management through the coming into force of the Sarbanes-Oxley (SOX) Act 2002, which is not limited to American companies but touches all publicly owned businesses across the world that trade with the United States. Boards of directors and senior management have now realised that documentation of business activities and records retention are essential requirements of the Act. The SOX Act requires good corporate governance and accountability and the integrity of financial and accounting systems in public organisations. These requirements can only be fulfilled if the records and information that reside in the systems are authentic and reliable.

In the wake of the SOX Act, CEOs are much more likely to regard records management as an essential function, one that they must initiate, fund and manage. The Act contains a number of important provisions, including mandated retention requirements for certain types of records.[17] The findings of surveys and models of business solutions by leading IT consultants prove these claims. A survey undertaken by Gartner entitled 'Corporate governance spending disrupts software purchases' reveals that records management and enterprise content management are regarded as the technologies that can contribute most to corporate governance.[18] For records and information management professionals, this is not a surprise as they have for long insisted that good record keeping is fundamental for effective and efficient administration. The problem was (and maybe is), according to Stephens, that many corporate executives were inclined to regard records management as a discretionary endeavour, one unrelated to the overall success of the business and therefore unworthy of serious management attention.

The root of today's problems is mainly a consequence of electronic forms of information. With complicated information systems across organisations, information is always at managers' fingertips. The birth of various types of information management systems, such as electronic document management, knowledge management, integrated document management, content management and enterprise content management systems, has sidelined the fundamental ingredient, that is records management. Colledge and Cliff assert that suppliers and industry analysts should both accept some of the blame for the confusion in the marketplace and the loss of recognition of the importance of records management.[19] Good record-keeping practices have been neglected, thus exposing organisations to risks from various quarters. Records are not given proper retention periods, thus making monitoring and control of record movements ineffective. The need to integrate record-keeping requirements into information systems is imperative if another Enron-like collapse is to be avoided.

Meanwhile, Sampson, who viewed risk management from the records management perspective, argues that:

> Risk analysis of records involves defining the records, assigning responsibility for the activities, identifying potential hazards, and analysing and classifying vital records. It is a strategic approach to activity development that promotes its cost-effectiveness. It weighs the cost, benefits, and risks of various record-keeping practices against the relative value of various record groups. It balances the costs of re-creation of records versus protection, and costs of preservations through backup systems or insurance versus the costs of loss prevention through facility modifications. It also balances the costs of recovery against the costs of recreating information lost or total loss of information. Such analysis identifies those practices that will provide the most flexibility within the legal, ethical, and practical constraints.[20]

In the case of Enron, an accounting firm, Arthur Andersen, was found guilty by a US District Court in Texas of destroying Enron-related documents that Andersen knew (or could reasonably have anticipated) would be relevant to a Security Exchange Commission investigation.[21] Records were prematurely destroyed. Under the Sarbanes-Oxley Act, there are serious penalties for destroying records prematurely. Under the Act, the board of directors is accountable for any action and business operation performed. Moss, in Chapter 10 of this book, points out that risk cannot be delegated through an organisation, as those who are fiduciarily accountable for its management have to take responsibility for any failure. It is no longer possible for them to claim that they are unaware of wrongdoings by their officials.

Indeed, a holistic business management approach is desperately required to resolve such concerns. Oracle, one of the leading business solution vendors, has produced a compliance architecture model as an option for a business solution that they claim can ensure adequacy and compliance with the SOX Act (Figure 4.3).[22]

The model by Oracle suggests that a holistic and orchestrated approach is required for a business to succeed. Specifically, the relationship between records management and risk management is explicitly shown. Records management is an integral part of enterprise content management that underpins business process management,

Figure 4.3   Oracle Compliance Management Architecture – comprehensive, sustainable compliance

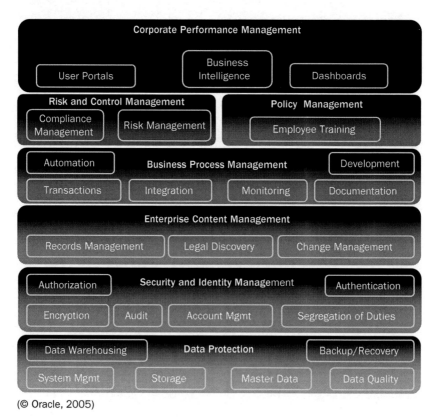

(© Oracle, 2005)

which in turn underpins risk management and control. Under enterprise content management, alongside records management are legal discovery and change management. Rationally, decisions to keep or not to keep records must take into account the legal needs, which accords with the risk management objective of minimising risk, as records can be used in self-defence or to challenge others. The accuracy and integrity of records is highly dependent on the security and controls of the systems to ensure that they cannot be tampered with. In addition, electronic records are constantly under threat as software and hardware will deteriorate or become obsolete over time. There is no single digital preservation solution that fits all circumstances, thus an organisation must initiate suitable preservation methods for the safekeeping of their electronic records. It is undeniable that this model and the findings of Gartner's survey suggest a significant role for records management by ensuring accuracy and adequacy of records not only to underpin risk management but more importantly to ensure that organisational goals can be achieved.[23]

Sampson, who explores the relationship between these two fields, is firmly categorical that the main contribution of records management to risk management is through records retention schedules.[24] These allocate suitable retention period to records, taking into account perceived threats of litigation. Egbuji states that it will be very costly for an organisation to retain and maintain all its records.[25] It is not only the cost of keeping the records that matters, but more importantly the risks that are associated with them. The function of records management is not just about keeping records but also destroying them as well, so as to achieve the economic efficiency that determines the sustainability of an organisation. Hence, the organisation needs to institute a record protection activity that will use such resources as are available to identify and secure valuable and sensitive records for as long as they remain valuable and sensitive. Employees cannot be blamed for destroying records according to the retention schedule as the responsibility rests with the board of directors of the organisation.

Davies contends that many companies have lost their 'corporate memory' and have found themselves repeating errors made in the past.[26] There is a growing awareness of the value of knowledge and experience and of the need to capture it for the company to use when the people in whom it resides have left its employment. Although Davies advocates knowledge management to ensure the capture of the 'corporate memory', the underlying activity is records management that plays an essential role in capturing memory by documenting all necessary components of 'corporate memory'. Tombs strongly advocates the effectiveness and contribution of knowledge management systems.[27] He asserts that records management has proved its usefulness because it reflects the real world all of the time and it is remarkably stable, as it does not constantly reinvent itself as a delivery mechanism. Furthermore, he suggests that time has shown the significance of the contribution of traditional records management to the efficiency and effectiveness of an organisation, whereas knowledge management is yet to prove its potential. An influential scholar in the field of knowledge management, Malhotra admits knowledge management systems often unravel and themselves become constraints in adapting and evolving such systems in business environments characterised by a high degree of uncertainty and radical discontinuous change.[28] It is, therefore, very complicated and time consuming to recognise the changes that have taken place at any particular time, even with an audit trail in place, as information systems usually only display the most up-to-date records. Knowing the processes or changes that occurred to a particular record is certainly helpful for risk management teams to identify appropriate decisions or actions.

Risk management assists the identification of critical business functions, which, in turn, identifies the level of importance and related risks. Reed suggests that not all processes generate records, and it is the role of records management working within a risk management framework to identify how far each process should be recorded.[29] However, this role cannot be accomplished in the absence of commitment from managers across an organisation. In addition, identifying critical business functions and keeping their records are two separate tasks that require different professional qualifications. As risk management is the responsibility of individual departmental managers, then it is their responsibility to identify critical business functions, and together with a records manager they should be able to determine adequate metadata, particularly contextual metadata, to ensure their records remain intact over time.

Sampson claims:

> Risk management of records enables a proactive approach to potential adversities, rather than a knee-jerk reaction in a crisis.
> Risk analysis should ask these questions:
>
> — What records truly merit protection because of their content and value?
>
> — What are the risks if the information is available, if it is not available, or if it falls into wrong hands?

— What is the likelihood of litigation or investigation, and for how long?

— Will there be sufficient evidence for a defence or to file a claim?[30]

A record retention schedule is an essential tool that facilitates the systematic destruction of records. However, producing the schedule requires a comprehensive effort to ensure that records first fulfil their business and legal requirements prior to their destruction. Developing a records retention schedule requires legal advice and expertise to weigh the costs, litigation risks and benefits of retention time periods to determine the most reasonable retention period for individual record categories. It is, however, usually costly for an organisation to take legal advice. Alternatively, an internal audit and risk management committee can be formed to ensure adequacy and compliance with all regulations. Retaining records as long as possible for no reason is a strategy based on the assumption that the records will be more helpful than harmful to the company. Some organisations may prefer not to keep certain records as their continuing existence may present legal risks. Even if there is a risk, if it would not cost more than the cost required for keeping those records, these classes of records would normally be kept for a shorter period of time to meet their business functions. In such a situation, risk is tolerable.[31]

Notes

1. Treasury Board of Canada Secretariat (2001) (available at *http://www .tbs-sct.gc.ca/pubs_pol/dcgpubs/riskmanagement/rmf-cgr01-1_e.asp*, accessed 15 September 2005).
2. It may be more economic to destroy records where the cost of keeping them is more than the cost of tolerable risks, particularly if the probability of the risk occurring is small.
3. HM Treasury, *The Orange Book: Management of Risk – Principles and Concepts* (London, 2004) (available at *http://www.ogc.gov.uk/sdtoolkit/ reference/ogc_library/related/orange-book.pdf*, accessed 6 October 2005).
4. Sampson, K.L., *Value Added Records Management: Protecting Corporate Assets, Reducing Business Risks* (Westport, CT, 1992). Karen L. Sampson heads Scenarios by Sampson, a consulting firm in Parker, Colorado. Formerly manager of records and administration for a major airline and earlier a consultant associated with other firms, she has published widely on business practices. Her experience enables her to act as an advocate for the significant contributions of records management alongside risk management.

5. Mehr, Robert Irwin and Hedges, Bob, *Risk Management: Concepts and Applications* (Homewood, IL, 1974), and Meulbroek, L., 'The promise and challenge of integrated risk management', in *Risk Management and Insurance Review*, 5 (1), 2002, pp. 55–66. Mehr, a professor of finance, claimed that he was the first to advocate risk management in 1955, when he first published a book on risk management in the insurance industry. This is not a surprise as insurance companies are constantly exposed to the uncertainty of potential claims. Hence, a comprehensive and systematic method for assessing risks is essential to reduce uncertainty and increase competitive edge in the business.

6. Thompson, D., 'Risk management: a brief history', *Journal of Banking and Financial Services*, 117 (3), June–July 2003, pp. 30–2.

7. Ibid.

8. Organisation for Economic Cooperation and Development (OECD), *Governance of the 21st Century* (Paris, 2001) and *Principles of Corporate Governance* (Paris, 2004).

9. Sampson, op. cit.

10. Treasury Board of Canada Secretariat, *Integrated Risk Management* (Ottawa, 2001) (available at *http://www.tbs-sct.gc.ca/pubs_pol/dcgpubs/riskmanagement/rmf-cgr01-1_e.asp*, accessed 15 September 2005).

11. Association of Insurance and Risk Managers, Association of Local Authority Risk Managers and Institute of Risk Management, *A Risk Management Standard* (London, 2002) (available at *http://www.theirm.org/publications/documents/Risk_Management_Standard_030820.pdf*, visited February 2006).

12. HM Treasury, op. cit.

13. Lion, R. and Meertens, R.M., 'Security or opportunity: the influence of risk-taking tendency on risk information preference', *Journal of Risk Research*, 8 (4), June 2005, pp. 283–94.

14. Mehr and Hedges, op. cit.

15. Simons, R., 'How risky is your company?', *Harvard Business Review*, 77 (3), May/June 1999, pp. 85–94.

16. Radner, R., 'Hierarchy: the economics of managing', *Journal of Economics Literature*, 30, September 1992, pp. 1382–415.

17. Stephens, D.O., 'The Sarbanes-Oxley Act: records management implications', *Records Management Journal*, 15 (2), 2005, pp. 98–103.

18. Getronics, *Reduce Risks and Improve Productivity through Efficient Record-keeping* (2005) (available at *http://www.getronics.com/NR/rdonlyres/ebfkvw637k5qvlyv7etcfnfjbnsougp2tf2xyojkr2zgibw7bh5alaqciam332zatbphify6mes7dxrw6m4tbx7odud/wp_gartner_records_management_reduce_risk.pdf*, accessed 17 September 2005).

19. Colledge, G. and Cliff, M., 'The implications of the Sarbanes-Oxley Act: it's time to take records management seriously', *KMWorld*, 12 (8), 2003 (available at *http://www.kmworld.com/publications/whitepapers/Records/colledge&cliff.pdf*, accessed 19 September 2005).

20. Sampson, op. cit., p. 169.

21. Watzke, G., 'The Arthur Andersen reversal: sound records management still required' (available at *http://www.ironmountain.com/resources/resource.asp?svc1_code=1&resource_key=986*, accessed 19 September 2005).

22. Oracle (2005) 'Information enables compliance at every level: Oracle compliance architecture', (available at *http://www.oracle.com/solutions/corporate_governance/corp_gov_c14507-01.pdf*, accessed 23 September 2005).

23. See 19 above.

24. Sampson, op. cit.

25. Egbuji, A., 'Risk management of organisational records', *Records Management Journal*, 9 (2), August 1999, pp. 93–116.

26. Davies, A., *A Strategic Approach to Corporate Governance* (Aldershot, 1999).

27. Tombs, K., 'Knowledge management is dead: long live records management', *Records Management Journal*, 14 (2), 2004, pp. 90–3.

28. Malhotra, Y., 'Why knowledge management systems fail? Enablers and constraints of knowledge management in human enterprises', *American Society for Information Science and Technology Monograph Series*, 2004, pp. 87–112.

29. Reed, B., 'Metadata: core record or core business?', *Archives and Manuscripts*, 25 (2), 1997, pp. 218–41.

30. Sampson, op. cit., p. 169.

31. The author is grateful to Prof. Michael Moss, Prof. Seamus Ross, Dr James Currall, Alistair Tough and Lesley Richmond for their comments.

5

Records professionals in a multimedia age: turning lead into gold?

Claire Johnson and Moira Rankin

Introduction

This chapter considers the changing legislative and regulatory environment in which records professionals work and pays particular attention to the United Kingdom. Recent changes are placed in context and their implications and impact evaluated. One observable consequence has been a rapid increase in demand for the services of records professionals. Another consequence has been the diversion of records professionals away from core activities and towards answering enquiries that are regarded as 'freedom of information' or 'data protection' requests.

As Chapter 10 explores, the function of the archive is basically twofold – to provide access for anyone with valid information requirements and to preserve information appropriate to meet those needs. Issues can arise where the two are seen to be in conflict; most often the clashes come in the middle ground of selection, retention and appraisal. In the later twentieth century a crisis of confidence emerged that archivists/records managers have not yet resolved. It is no urban myth that archivists are occasionally asked if they can turn lead into gold. How often do we actually tell people what we do these days? Do we still need to or should we just agree that we are like librarians? We are not always getting our message across even to our own colleagues and managers, so it is not surprising that the majority of the public have no clue what we do and that some even fleetingly believe we are alchemists conjuring a valuable product out of a base element.

The problems are further being compounded in the digital age by the perceived need to influence records creation to ensure long-term survival. Although there are instances of good practice, this need has not yet been successfully addressed by records professionals in a way that captures the attention of those with real power. This chapter discusses the challenges we face. Who are archivists and records managers in the digital age? How best can we harness technology to perform a full range of tasks with confidence, verve and vigour? To be able to answer these questions we must first explore the dynamics of organisations in the digital age, drawing out the issues that affect those who create, use, convey and have custody of information.

Relationships between record creators and custodians in most modern organisations are complex and this is reflected in the administrative processes that support these relationships. The functions and activities of corporate life established over the second half of the twentieth century are now more fluid than in previous decades, and accompanying technological innovation brings with it a range of challenges and potential conflicts for several key groups – record creators, senior managers, information systems managers, records managers and archivists.

Digital information systems present new challenges to provide evidence of integrity, security and authenticity that are distinct from, but not independent of, the intellectual attributes of the record. The emergence of BS ISO 15489:2001[1] has provided practitioners with a recognisable quality standard to use in their daily work and as a promotional tool to help demonstrate to senior managers their unique contributions to business practice. It defines the attributes of many information management activities and the characteristics of a record such as authenticity. Though these issues may not yet be of immediate or conscious concern to the average citizen, they are of fundamental concern to records professionals, the ICT community and the historian. Any discussion about the development of archival practice, its theoretical underpinning and practical understanding of systems as well as technologies requires new approaches to interacting with all stakeholders.

In Ann Pederson's article[2] she states that in modern society we are all called to be record keepers but few are conscious of it.

> As recordkeeping is one of the most ubiquitous aspects of modern society, almost every process we undertake – working, studying, shopping, driving, dining, communicating by email

or telephone – generates or involves some form of record. Furthermore, we all participate in this recordkeeping and so are de facto recordkeepers, though few of us are aware of this role.[3]

Although it can be argued that this is not new, the point remains that the digital age could bring the best opportunity for records professionals to fully engage with stakeholders. The digital environment offers new opportunities for delivering continuity of care in corporate record keeping that were much more difficult to achieve in the analogue systems. Delivering this requires a holistic perspective on information management.

Archivists and records managers in the digital age

The subtle differences in the traditional definitions of archives and records management can be confusing to the untrained eye:

Archives management
> n. ~ The general oversight of a program to appraise, acquire, arrange and describe, preserve, authenticate, and provide access to permanently valuable records.

Records management
> n. ~ The systematic and administrative control of records throughout their life cycle to ensure efficiency and economy in their creation, use, handling, control, maintenance, and disposition.[4]

The vast majority of Pederson's unconscious record keepers[5] are unaware of these differences and would not be at all interested in whether or not we have convinced our parent organisations of the value of heritage and/or corporate efficiency and compliance skills. Many skills are common to both the archivist and the records manager (see Table 5.1 below) but the terminology is different depending on the audience. As noted by Frank Rankin in his 2002 report on Scottish archival training, the skill and knowledge demands on the twenty-first century archivist or records manager are continually expanding.[6] This makes it fundamentally important that we understand and communicate clearly among ourselves so that we can communicate confidently with others.

The fundamental linking point for archivists and records managers is record keeping. What connects librarians and museum curators to records professionals oriented to historical and cultural matters is making value judgements about which items to make accessible and preserve. However, our task is far more complex and we rarely make this argument at budget allocation time. We first have to decide whether a piece of information is a record; we have to decide if it is of value to a range of potential users from creators and auditors to architects and historians. A librarian does not first have to decide whether the main outputs of their work are books or web resources – the publisher has already made that decision for them in judging the work worthy of publication. Although management of web resources is bringing new challenges for the library community, they are still making the same fundamental decision as to whether this published resource is of value to their users. The inevitable comparisons to museums and libraries are simply not valid when it comes to the basic processing of records in any media. Initiatives like Logjam in the North West of England may be starting to make a difference at least in the mindset of funding bodies.[7] Another point of reference is an article by Hector MacQueen, chair of the body that advises the Scottish Executive on records issues, which identifies the widening gap between records professionals and museum/ library professionals as a result of freedom of information legislation.[8] The fact remains that we need to communicate clearly who we are and what we do if we are to remain a valid profession in the digital age. Managers try to pigeon-hole us as something else and all too often we concede for a peaceful life.

In training archivists and records managers in the UK there has been a tendency to concentrate on managing the physical form of the record at a fixed stage in the continuum rather than developing the skills needed to manage informational content regardless of age, stage and form. Michael Cook has indicated that this is a stubbornness arising through tradition in most European nations and that there are lessons to be learned from the developing world in their approaches to information management education.[9] However, there are signs that archival education in the UK and elsewhere is changing. Literature for the new University of Glasgow MSc course advertises the view that 'The course will provide an understanding of contemporary information and records management issues against the background of historical needs and goals of information and record users.'[10] It is too soon to assess the success of this statement but the employability of graduates is a significant measure of its success.

A challenge to define the skill set of the archivist and records manager was issued by James Currall at the 2004 Society of Archivists Conference in Glasgow,[11] on which occasion he asked what in particular do we contribute to help individuals (record creators and decision makers) make sense of the digital information age? It is primarily in managing, facilitating and mediating informational content that our skills lie, as Table 5.1 demonstrates. To be successful, communicating this to users, managers and the other information professions is essential.

Table 5.1 Skill and partnership matrix for the archivist and the records manager*

Skill set/ knowledge base	Partnership	Sample task	
		Archivist	Records manager
Access provision	1. User communities 2. Format managers (e.g. Conservators, ICT, Estates Dept)	Designs finding aids to enhance accessibility and usability of archives.	Designs filing systems to enhance accessibility and usability of records.
Acquisition management	1. Depositors 2. Legal advisors	Ensures an accession register is fully maintained and accurate. Ensures deposit agreements are complete and appropriate.	Ensures transfer receipt log is fully maintained and accurate. Ensures transfer agreements are complete and appropriate.
Control of information	1. User communities 2. Legal advisors	Creates collection policies and appraisal schemes to promote consistent and controlled application of selection criteria.	Creates business classification schemes and retention schedules to consistently control information.

Table 5.1	Skill and partnership matrix for the archivist and the records manager* (cont'd)		

| Skill set/ knowledge base | Partnership | Sample task | |
		Archivist	Records manager
Disaster planning	1. Format managers 2. Estates	Plans to prevent disasters or minimise corporate, national or local memory loss in the event of a disaster.	Plans to prevent disasters or minimise vital records loss in the event of a disaster.
Education and training provision	1. User communities 2. Teaching and learning professions	Delivers a range of education and training opportunities to stakeholder communities.	Delivers a range of education and training opportunities to stakeholder communities.
Ethics	1. User communities 2. Employers	Professionally obliged to abide by codes of conduct.	Professionally obliged to abide by codes of conduct.**
Management	1. Employers 2. Other management professionals (e.g. HR, Finance, Estates)	Understands and applies the principles of good resource management.	Understands and applies the principles of good resource management.
Publicity	1. User communities 2. Media relations professionals	Demonstrates the value of archival services through a carefully selected mix of advertising tools.	Demonstrates the value of records management services through a carefully selected mix of advertising tools.
Quality assurance	1. Standards bodies 2. Quality assurance professionals	Strives to meet recognised professional standards in all aspects of work, e.g. BS 5454, ISAD(G).	Strives to meet recognised professional standards in all aspects of work, e.g. BS ISO 15489, MoReq.

Table 5.1	Skill and partnership matrix for the archivist and the records manager* *(cont'd)*

Skill set/ knowledge base	Partnership	Sample task	
		Archivist	Records manager
Risk assessment	1. Legal advisors 2. Insurance/risk professionals 3. User communities 4. Format managers	Balances risk of destruction of information and cost of preservation/con-servation against future research needs.	Helps the organisation to balance risk of destruction of records against corporate compliance responsibilities.
Security management	1. Format managers 2. Security professionals	Creates a suitable balance of security and user friendliness for physical access to the archive collections.	Helps others to create a suitable balance of security and user friendliness in their filing equipment.
User needs analysis (market research)	1. User communities 2. Market research professionals	Creates a range of services based on user demands.	Creates a range of services based on user demands.
Value appraisal	1. User communities 2. Risk assessment professionals 3. Legal advisors	Appraises the value of documents to decide whether they are records that meet a variety of research and corporate memory needs.	Appraises the value of documents to decide whether they are records that meet a variety of compliance and corporate efficiency needs.

* The skills and knowledge may be applied equally in the digital or the analogue information sectors.
** For example, *http://www.rms-gb.org.uk/resources/140*, accessed February 2006, and *http://www.archives.org.uk/membership/codeofconduct.html*, accessed February 2006.

There is an obvious parallel in the professional partnerships we have had in the analogue and the digital world. In a recent article Helen Forde is generally positive about access and preservation in the twenty-first century but she warned of the dangers in assuming that access will inevitably be supported by preservation. In both the analogue and the digital order, the divide between the smaller and specialist repositories and the nationals is not diminishing and may even be increasing. Forde succinctly puts it, 'What is possible for those in the vanguard is not easily replicated for the rearguard.'[12] The issues with preservation and access can be all too apparent in dealings with funding bodies. There have been instances of bids for cataloguing being funded while linked bids for conservation are turned down. It may be that this is finally changing with the new emphasis put on preservation and conservation by the Wellcome Trust's Research Resources in Medical History grant scheme signalling a renewed interest in preservation over access. However, the National Council on Archives have signalled that archive services in 2006 are generally at crisis point with chronic underfunding,[13] so it remains to be seen whether their public petition will have any impact.

Archivists have long relied on the skills of conservators in managing the analogue form. The current fashion for access over preservation means that many archivists are managing tasks traditionally associated with professional conservators. The development and implementation of preservation policies, conservation assessments and the regulation of environmental conditions are something for which few archivists are formally trained and yet many are doing it and learning as they go. It could be argued that, by defending our own territory and ensuring our own survival thus far, the role of the professional conservator has been downplayed and eroded. The archive and records management profession is now facing the danger that the managers of the form, the ICT profession, are sidelining us in the same way. There would appear to be only two ways to overcome this danger. The first option is to concentrate on content management and forge strong, mutually beneficial partnerships with all the other managers of content and form. The other is to radically rethink archive and records management education to ensure that all the required skills in content and form management are learned by archivists and records managers. This would take at least a two-year full-time course of learning which has not seemed a popular choice in the UK,[14] although it has long been in place in Canada.[15] Both of these options require a clear definition of the professional roles in relation to the other stakeholder professions. Given the pre-existing dominance of the ICT profession in the digital order, the pragmatic and realistic approach for the twenty-first century would seem to be a concentration on managing informational content and developing strong professional dialogues and partnerships. As records professionals, we should ideally be self-confident enough to assert and share our knowledge and skills with other groups. Archivists and records managers can never hope to have the expertise of ICT people, so productive ways to collaborate need to be developed.

The corporate information environment

The effective use of corporate information, especially digital corporate information, is complex and only the major issues can be addressed in this short chapter. These are, to a great extent, already familiar to the records professional, as they relate to the establishment of trust between the creator and user. The established information content skills are directly transferable to the digital domain while those dependent on managing the format are still being developed in collaboration with other disciplines. The diplomatic of digital information and the search for the attributes of the authentic record in digital systems have been at the heart of the InterPARES project at UBC[16] since 1999.

Effective record keeping can only be at best a tool for business efficiency and effectiveness. It does not deliver accountability in itself, despite the occasional hyperbole of record-keeping professionals. Accountability is a by-product of getting both the governance structure and record keeping right. This is explored in detail by Anthony Willis's article on corporate governance and the role that records management can play in delivering improved organisational accountability.[17]

There are a number of questions for which no one can fully provide answers yet:

- Is the future to be dictated entirely by the compliance agenda? We can only assume that it will and plan for even greater regulatory intervention in the information world while hoping to keep it all under control.
- How is a balance achieved between the need to keep information appropriately (i.e. only that which meets the terms of legally and administratively necessary retention) and the increased capacity to retain more digital information than ever before?
- How can we hope to cover every contingency in the records continuum?[18] The assertions of the records continuum theorists seek to give credence to

the integration of the responsibilities of archivists and records managers within the digital domain, but is this really so?

- Are the questions being raised by historians about the functional analysis approach to macro-appraisal going to make us think again about such approaches? This begs the supplementary question – do digital records give us the opportunity to engage stakeholders in appraisal? Initiatives such as that outlined in Chapter 8 by Peters and Richmond indicate a possible way forward.

All we can be certain of is that the next decade will be crucial in determining the power of each stakeholder group in relation to shaping the digital order. Michael Power[19] discusses the contemporary challenges of increased compliance requirements in tandem with improving organisational effectiveness.

The role of record creators

Information professionals need to be engaged with 'corporate life' by demonstrating the value of their role through their understanding of business requirements and the specific advice they can offer to those responsible for the production and dissemination of corporate information. The digital domain demands that the responsibilities of each party are well understood and that decisions about contextual information and the appropriate retention are made as consistently as possible. Creators should be considered as key players in the record-keeping environment and together with decision-makers have to be convinced of the necessity for our involvement at the planning stage of information creation.

As our streamlined, or just flattened and under-resourced, organisations ask their employees to move beyond basic motivation to more complex levels of commitment, then ensuring effective (rather than just efficient) use of ICT infrastructure places more demands on everyone. For example, the pre-definition of structured information in an electronic document and records management (EDRM) system requires a much more complex engagement with the content of organisational information outputs (records, creation systems and resources) and understanding of technological deliverables than a paper-based filing system ever did.[20]

Archivists and records managers need to become better informed about the business and technological dynamics that affect the expectations and daily needs of record creators and decision-makers. At present, information professionals do not always have a well-integrated role in the activities of other employees as either a provider of advice about efficient/effective working or as the recognised custodian of those records deemed worthy of permanent preservation. Those parties such as auditors, statisticians, lawyers and regulatory authorities, who have a role in interpreting or ascribing the value of information assets, are increasingly considered as agents necessary to the appropriate management of information. The value of information needed to support decision-making is multifaceted and dependent on the perspective and priorities of those assessing it – literally 'value, like beauty, is in the eye of the beholder'[21] – so it can be measured in more than just financial terms. Only once the value of an information resource is understood can it be regarded as an organisational asset.[22] Records creators and decision-makers are necessarily key players in this process and need to be engaged in this discussion if a robust information resource is to be created and maintained.

Is it only in highly regulated sectors (such as financial services or pharmaceuticals) or in other types of high-cost product liability environments that comprehensive information management is most frequently justified, afforded or achieved?

Regulation and accountability

The range of regulations that affect the management of organisational information has increased in both volume and complexity in the last couple of decades. There has also been an expansion in the concept of the 'information rights' of an individual to access information (e.g. about themselves through Privacy and Data Protection Acts, about the working of the public sector through Freedom of Information Acts, environmental information regulations or human rights legislation[23]). Individuals now expect personal privacy to be protected through the secure and appropriate capture, retention and disposal of information.[24] The sanctions when this fails may be financial but the lasting consequence may come from the adverse effect on organisational reputation or corporate image.

The recent emergence in the UK of the Reuse of Public Sector Information Regulations, which came into force on 1 July 2005 implementing a European directive, means that individuals now have extended rights to use information created as part of routine public sector business. The Office of Public Sector Information, formerly HMSO and now merged with The National Archives, provides online access to UK legislation and the management of Crown copyright.[25]

As with much UK legislation, the inspiration for establishing rights of access to information often emerges from European Union law. The Data Protection Acts 1984 and 1998 and the Reuse of Public Sector Information Regulations 2005 are based on EU directives but the Freedom of Information Acts are domestic primary legislation that have followed the EU's initiatives in providing access to its own documents. The EU laws that provide rights of access to information are surveyed in Philip Coppel's work on information rights.[26]

The relative costs of compliance mean that risk assessment methodologies may need to be utilised to assess business priorities and make best use of limited resources (see Chapters 3 and 10 in this volume). In order to balance the requirements of compliance and integrate with routine business processes many players need to contribute and ownership is required from senior decision-makers. Senior executive officers also need to be kept informed about the risks and costs associated with non-compliance. This requires both the consistent identification of liability from business activities (and record creation is just one such activity) and a high level of trust between operational units through their compliance with policies and practice that are put in place by their governance structure. The assessment of how well an organisation is meeting the compliance agenda by embedding it into business processes is a function of many strategic players within an organisation. It may be that, as a consequence of the increased burden of regulation, senior managers are required to use some risk assessment methodology in order to establish at what point the effort and cost of compliance outweigh the sanctions for non-compliance.

The impact of selected legislation and regulation

The regulatory and legislative bodies rarely take into account the impact of their actions on the record-keeping environments, although records management codes of practice were issued to accompany both Freedom of Information Acts in the UK.[27] The impact of some of the most recent government intervention is discussed in this section. The constantly evolving regulatory environment of the early twenty-first century means this will only stand as a snapshot of the position in late 2005. The separation of underlying issues from the basic legislative requirements is an attempt to highlight the key issues for information professionals.

Meeting the requirements of regulatory compliance is a mandatory strand of professional practice and in addition to the legislation itself there may be additional codes of best practice, codes of conduct and ethics and articulated expectations of stakeholders about accepted behaviours.

Freedom of Information Act 2000 and Freedom of Information (Scotland) Act 2002[28] (FoI and FoISA)

In Scotland, and perhaps in the UK as a whole, freedom of information (FoI) legislation is seen by many practitioners as the main tool for developing both archive and records management policies in the public sector. However, in practice FoI compliance has sometimes been delivered at the expense of comprehensive or continued implementation of a records mangement programme. Staff may have been taken away from archives and records management roles to ensure the enquiries are being answered within the allotted 20 days. Records management efficiency gains from pre-January 2005 are now beginning to be lost while organisations decide how much impact FoI is really going to have. It is hoped that the risks of this approach have been carefully considered and that ground can be made up before audits of records management code compliance are undertaken or before an Information Commissioner has cause to undertake a full investigation.

It seems likely that the practice of information audit and the creation of information asset registers are likely to increase as FoI becomes more firmly embedded. These are already widely used in British government departments but they are not yet much used in the wider public sector as part of the proactive release of information.[29]

In November 2005 the Scottish Executive launched a consultation to review the workings of the FoISA. The investigation will focus on the operation of the Act and in particular the fees structure and the prohibitions on disclosure of information. The effect that FoI has on the information landscape is hard to judge at present. Although many believe it heralds a new level of organisational accountability and good information practice, those working in mature FoI environments such as Canada or Australia are less ebullient about the long-term benefits. It certainly seems possible to use FoI as a tool for more effective organisational communication but the media and politicians will want to set the agenda for what is revealed.

Data Protection Act 1998

As with similar European legislation, the UK Act was a result of a recognition that the growing commercial value in the marketing and sales activities of international business required there to be explicit protection of an individual's rights to privacy of personal data. This was initially (in the 1984 Act) confined to digital personal data and was thus heavily influenced by the ICT profession. The 1998 Act extended rights to cover all structured filing systems and has meant a re-evaluation of the work of archivists and records managers. Since September 2005 the Code of Practice for Archivists and Record Managers under section 51(4) of the Data Protection Act 1998 has been open for revision.[30] The range of organisations that have made contributions has been extremely wide-ranging. The Code still defines the professional roles in separate terms depending on whether the reader is a records manager or an archivist and effectively this means some of the same processes and practices are defined using different language or only mentioned as activities for one or other professional, for example 'appraisal' only appears as an activity for archivists. This serves to reinforce the differences, making it more complicated for those practitioners who are trying to operate an integrated and consistent approach to managing records regardless of their stage in the life cycle.[31]

Regulation of Investigatory Powers Act 2000[32] (RIPA)

RIPA sets out legislation on the interception of communications in the UK. The powers are set out in Chapter II of Part I of the Act, sections 21 to 25. These give law enforcement and other public authorities the ability to require service providers to hand over information about the use of their networks. The government have indicated that, for the types of information covered, these powers should replace the previous arrangements under section 29(3) of the Data Protection Act (DPA), which allowed law enforcement authorities to request that information be handed over to them. RIPA legislates for interception and surveillance in a way that should be compatible with the Human Rights Act while access to personal data will continue to be under the Data Protection Act 1998.

Access to Environmental Information Regulations 2004,[33] Access to Environmental Information (Scotland) Regulations 2004[34]

Under freedom of information legislation, the Freedom of Information (Scotland) Act 2002, section 62, and Freedom of Information Act 2000, section 74, public authorities are under a new requirement to disclose environmental information. This entitlement came into effect on 1 January 2005 alongside the freedom of information legislation and provides a similar access regime by confirming that the culture of public sector organisations (and some private companies that provide public services such as those in the waste, transport and energy sectors) be made more open. They seek to develop the 'right to know' culture in the public sector, and fundamentally change it from one that has previously provided information on a 'need to know' basis. Under this regime environmental information is made available proactively and on request, as soon as possible within 20 working days. Unless one of the exceptions set out in the Regulations applies, this may be extended to two months in circumstances where the information is voluminous or particularly complex. Information must be released unless there are 'compelling and substantive reasons to withhold it'. It is permitted to make a reasonable charge for the supply of the information. If a request for information is refused, reasons must be given in writing and a procedure must be available to review decisions.

Reuse of Public Sector Information Regulations 2005[35]

This instrument implements the EU Directive on the reuse of public sector information (2003/98/EC) and establishes a minimum set of rules governing the reuse and the practical means of facilitating reuse of existing documents held by UK public sector bodies.

Therefore pubic sector records managers need to become more skilled in 'information audit'[36] activities. The development of an 'Information Asset Register' to uphold the requirements identified in the Regulations will become increasingly important. Asset Lists are explicitly mentioned in the 'Guide to Best Practice'[37] which accompanies the regulations. The Regulations provide for public sector bodies to charge a commercial rate for the reuse of documents where appropriate. This will be particularly applicable to public sector bodies that are required to operate in a commercial manner in order to cover their costs, e.g. Ordnance Survey, but potentially introduces an additional role for the records manager to contribute to or adopt as part of their responsibilities.

An example of how non-European legislation can impact on the record keeper can be seen in the commercial world through the Public Company Accounting Reform and Investor Protection Act 2002 (this is more usually referred to as the Sarbanes-Oxley Act or SOX).[38] For any organisation with significant commercial connections in the USA the

Sarbanes-Oxley Act has not only relevance to the records professional but also the cost of compliance has huge financial implications for the organisation. Unlike regulation affecting the public sector, with regulation that affects commercial bodies the costs associated with compliance can be passed on to the customer (in whole or in part).

The Act came as a result of the large corporate financial scandals involving Enron, WorldCom, Global Crossing and Arthur Andersen. It became effective on 1 July 2004, for *all* publicly traded companies. The Act was sponsored by US Senator Paul Sarbanes and US Representative Michael Oxley, and many commentators acknowledge that it represents the biggest change to US federal securities laws in recent times.

The provisions of the Sarbanes-Oxley Act (SOX) detail criminal and civil penalties for non-compliance, certification of internal auditing and increased financial disclosure. It affects public US companies and non-US companies with a US presence. SOX is all about *corporate governance* and financial disclosure. It seeks to protect investors by improving the accuracy and reliability of corporate disclosures made pursuant to the securities laws. The Act radically redesigns federal regulation of public company corporate governance and reporting obligations and significantly tightens accountability standards for directors and officers, auditors, securities analysts and legal counsel.

A recent article by David O. Stephens[39] identifies the impact of the Sarbanes-Oxley Act on corporate culture. More particularly it introduces the experience of records managers in the USA since the introduction of the Act in the financial accounting systems of publicly held companies following the corporate scandals of accounting practice at the turn of the current century. As is indicated throughout this book (see particuarly Chapter 3 by Currall in this volume), the existence of legislation does not in itself guarantee that trustworthiness or reliability will be achieved.

Strategic imperatives for record-keeping professionals

Outside central government, the motivation for senior managers in the public sector to invest in archives and records management frequently depends on the communication skills of the individuals in their employ. They must personally convince their managers of the benefits in terms of the risks of non-compliance, corporate heritage exploitation value or other cost benefits. Archivists and records managers need to demonstrate how they are useful to the functioning of the organisation that they work for. Senior managers should not be expected to be familiar with the skills of these information professionals.

To date, the compliance agenda has been the biggest strategic imperative for senior managers but it is not often clear to them what the records professionals' role should be. The risks and potential penalties for non-compliance with explicit record-keeping legislation such as freedom of information or data protection cannot be seen to outweigh the costs of investing the amounts required to bring archive and record processes into the twenty-first century. The main risk is in terms of the embarrassment of individuals or organisations, as was commented on in the Bichard Inquiry,[40] which made reference to record keeping and understanding of the implications of the Data Protection Act in Humberside and Cambridgeshire police services following the murder of two schoolgirls in Soham, Cambridgeshire.

Records professionals need assistance on several fronts to overcome such disinterest in their work. First, there needs to be an even greater indication from the legislature that records issues are important, and secondly they need a lobbying body to make sound arguments, which thereafter only need reinforcing by the individual professional. Another issue is undoubtedly in the recruitment of more confident, outgoing communicators to the archive and records management courses and thus to the next generation of professionals. Progress is slowly being made on these issues – for example, the JISC-funded 'espida' project[41] at the University of Glasgow, which seeks to define the criteria to convince senior managers of the value of investing in digital preservation.

Collaborate and regenerate

Records managers must have significant and authoritative input into developing and maintaining the file plans or business classification schemes that underpin current record-keeping systems. Otherwise the skills we have built up in the paper order will become redundant. The skills are outlined in Table 5.1. Many of these skills would also be claimed by other professions. It is obvious that records managers need to understand these processes. Archivists cannot be complacent either, if they want to ensure the preservation of the outputs of such systems in the future. The profession needs to speak the language of the technical world and, if that means redefining our own professional terminology to match theirs, then that may be an inevitable compromise. It is certainly essential to enter into a dialogue with the ICT profession if we want to reclaim the definition of the term 'to archive'. To them, as indeed to the majority of the rest of the world, the term 'to archive' still means to put it somewhere and forget about it. Initiatives like Archives Awareness Campaigns[42] and popular family history television series like the BBC's *Who Do You Think You Are?* are bound to raise the profile, but will the public ever automatically understand the subtle differences between the definitions put forward by Richard Pearce-Moses?[43]

Professionalism in the digital age

What defines a records professional in the digital age?

Is record keeping a profession, a trade or a combination of both? The Oxford English Dictionary asserts that a profession is considered as a 'socially superior' occupation to a trade or a handicraft. A growing trend to professionalism in the sense of facilitating and giving professional advice rather than actually carrying out tasks for others seems to be the norm.

Are archivists still historians or historiographers first and record keepers second? Are they still sitting waiting to gain privileged access to write the definitive history of their employer? Should archivists be deciding what the historians of the future might want to use? The last ten years have seen a general shift away from the historian archivist writing the history and making appraisal decisions to the professional archivist advising on sources and facilitating historians to influence appraisal decisions. The UK national repositories with their requirement of staff based at least in part on their archival qualifications rather than on academic historical knowledge have been a major influence on the redefinition of the skills required to be an archivist.

Are records managers still primarily records centre operators waiting to receive the output of their parent bodies? The answer to this is a resounding no, especially in a digital world where the records centre is at best a single server where only a limited number of software packages were used to create the objects. At worst the records centre would be made up of hundreds of servers and thousands of different types of object. Without knowing how and why it was created, it may be impossible for us even to open it to make a judgement as to its value to the parent organisation or the wider society.[44] The days of the records professional as a passive curator are certainly numbered.

Access to research and literature

The trend for publishing research and professional discourse in archives and records management is increasing. Until fairly recently it was more or less possible for the conscientious English-speaking archivist or records manager to read all the professional literature as it was published. In the last two or three years much more has been published on a wider range of subjects. Much is concerned with enhancing the usability of current information, meeting the scrutiny of enquiry regimes (RIPA, DPA, FOI and the like) and establishing the long-term value of the digital record.

New dynamics have become apparent that challenge the archivist's function as custodian of textual artefacts that constitute part of the collective memory of our society. There are, for example, emerging areas of study that explore the culture and politics of archives[45] and the impact of postmodernism[46] on archival science (especially on appraisal). In addition, a new theoretical underpinning for records management is also emerging; a recent article by Zawiyah M. Yusof and Robert W. Chell[47] both provides a survey of its immediate origins and gives a perspective on where the future direction might lie.

Although the emergence of this literature is greatly beneficial to the profession, it could also serve to confuse or deter the overworked practitioner. The resolution of this challenge may require greater individual discipline. Easier access to searchable abstracts would also be useful. Indeed, this book is intended to deliver an overview of recent developments for the benefit of the practising records professional. Online developments, for example on the Society of Archivists website, look promising but much is yet to be done to eradicate the inequality of literature availability. The frequency with which some basic questions are asked on professional mail lists (e.g. JISC listservs) is testament to disenfranchisement of this kind.

Overall, the growth in literature would imply that there is a need for increased specialisation in response to an impossibly big 'ask' in terms of all the knowledge and skills a records professional *may* need in a multimedia environment.

The role of professional bodies and advocacy groups

The role of our professional bodies in regulating conduct and promoting good practice in continuous professional development has been widely debated in recent years. We are now in a 'chicken and egg' situation where we need wider professional recognition of our value to society but members cannot ourselves agree to any enforcement of professional CPD standards. Perhaps the pilot study being conducted by the Society of Archivists in 2006 will help to form sensible opinions.[48]

To take a positive stance, the summary of missions and memberships of the UK's most influential records bodies shows that there are certainly a lot of groups working for the benefit of records and records professionals (see Appendix 5.1). There are positive signs of collaboration between the groups, for example the Archives Awareness Campaign and the Data Protection guide for records professionals. However, there is a danger of conveying mixed and confusing messages to stakeholders. It is easy to find the websites of all the professional bodies and advocacy groups and be unsure which or any to trust. More particularly the danger of diluting and spreading limited resources too thinly should not be underestimated. It is right and proper that there are many journals, websites, newsletters and other publications covering records issues but is there any scope for collaboratively reassessing and redefining them for the twenty-first century? Clarity of understanding in who speaks for us, who stands alongside us and who to work with is essential to begin to decide how best to go forward in the future. Following the example of the conservation groups who joined to become the Institute of Conservation[49] in 2004 could give a louder voice to our relatively small number and be the difference in taking us forward with confidence. However, serious tensions will have to be addressed before this will be feasible. These include a tension between the administrative and cultural roles fulfilled by records professionals. There is also a serious issue about the definition of professionalism.

Standards organisations

As with regulatory intervention in the work of the records professional described earlier, the number of standards issued in the multimedia environment has made the work both easier and harder. There are fewer differences in the cataloguing practices than there used to be but keeping up to date with the standards is becoming ever more challenging. The majority of archivists have come to terms with the strengths and shortcomings of the International Council on Archives General International Standard Achival Description (ISAD(G)) version 2 and many are now conversant with the second International Standard Archival Authority Record (ISAAR), but the next thing to get to grips with is likely to be a standard for creating function and activity based access points. In this, the work done in creating the international standard for records management, ISO 15489, should be valuable.

At a basic level, ISO 15489 provides a means to apply a business analysis of the functional activities in any type of organisation. It covers the assessment of current systems, taking a strategic overview of systems architecture and identifying corporate options and the development of policies and procedures within the organisation. It also provides a mechanism for assessing the impact of the records management programme and performance measurement.

Conclusion

In this time of professional reassessment and readjustment it is possibly inevitable that more questions have been raised in this chapter than have been answered. As Richard Cox states, 'The archivist's responsibility is to know what the organization does at all levels and across all units, not the other way around. If archivists are to appraise records, for example, they must comprehend the full range of an organization's functions and related activities, and identify those that are critical.'[50] Therefore, the fundamental issue remains one of communication. One of the most important challenges is to understand and meet the needs of decision-makers so that our professional perspectives are influential in strategic decision-making. John A. Kargbo explained our purpose succinctly when he wrote: 'the central underlying rationale (of archives management) is to facilitate communication'.[51] Archivists and records managers are finally making steps to improve communication among ourselves and to decide what our messages should be. This is only the first stage after which we then need to communicate those messages clearly to others, and finally we need greater confidence in our dialogue with all our fellow professionals and stakeholders. If we re-evaluate and reassess now, it may actually be possible for the lead to become gold.

Appendix 5.1 Major professional bodies and advocacy groups with an interest in records issues

- ARMA International is a not-for-profit association serving more than 10,000 information management professionals in the United States,

Canada and over 30 other nations. ARMA International members include records and information managers, archivists, corporate librarians, imaging specialists, legal professionals, knowledge managers, consultants, and educators.

- ASLIB stimulates awareness of the benefits of good management of information resources and its value. It represents and lobbies for the interests of the information sector on matters and networks which are of national and international importance. It provides a range of information-related products and services to meet the needs of the information society.

- The Association for Manuscripts and Archives in Research Collections (AMARC) promotes the accessibility, preservation and study of manuscripts and archives in libraries and other research collections in Great Britain and Ireland. It brings together curators, researchers and all who share a scholarly interest in this field.

- ACARM provides a link for archival institutions, archivists and records managers across the Commonwealth. What makes this link especially important is the common heritage of legal and administrative systems, and hence of record-keeping practices, which the countries of the Commonwealth share with each other. ACARM is a valuable vehicle for sharing solutions.

- The British Records Association aims to encourage and assist with the preservation, care, use and publication of historical records. (The Scottish Records Association has similar aims.)

- The ECPA was established in 1994 by a group of scholars, librarians and archivists. It aims to raise public awareness of this issue and to impress the urgency of the situation on policy-makers, funding agents and users. The ECPA acts as a European platform for discussion and cooperation of heritage organisations in areas of preservation and access.

- The International Council on Archives is a decentralised organisation governed by a General Assembly and administered by an Executive Committee. Its branches provide archivists with a regional forum in all parts of the world (except North America); its sections bring together archivists and archival institutions interested in particular areas of professional interest; its committees and working groups are engaging the contribution of experts to specific problems.

- The Museums, Libraries and Archives Council (MLA) is the national development agency working for and on behalf of museums, libraries and archives and advising government on policy and priorities for the sector. The MLA's roles are to provide strategic leadership, to act as a powerful advocate, to develop capacity and to promote innovation and change.

- The National Council on Archives was established in 1988 to bring together the major bodies and organisations, including service providers, users, depositors and policy-makers, across the UK concerned with archives and their use. It aims to develop consensus on matters of mutual concern and provide an authoritative common voice for the archival community. (The Archives Council Wales and Scottish Council on Archives have similar aims.)

- Research Libraries Group is an international, not-for-profit membership organisation of over 150 universities, libraries, archives, historical societies and other institutions with collections for research and learning. The RLG supports researchers and learners worldwide by expanding access to research materials held in libraries, archives and museums. The RLG currently has ongoing projects relating to online access to research resources, global resource sharing and digital preservation.

- The Records Management Society of Great Britain recognises the ever-increasing number of people working in the fields of records and information management. This site is intended as a reference site and single point of contact for discussion and the exchange of ideas.

- The Society of Archivists is the recognised professional body for archivists, archive conservators and records managers. The principal aims of the Society are to promote the care and preservation of archives and the better administration of archive repositories, to advance the training of its members and to encourage relevant research and publication.

Source: Archives Portal on the National Archives website December 2005: *http://www.portal.nationalarchives.gov.uk/portal/*.

Appendix 5.2 Features of key 'information rights' and 'information management' legislation

- *Regulation of Investigatory Powers Act 2000[52] (RIPA).* The RIPA powers only apply to communications data, in other words data about the use of networks.[53] The Act divides communications data into three, rather unclear, types: these seem to mean:

1. information about individual users (e.g. the name of the owner of an account);

2. information about use of the system (e.g. times when a user logged in);

3. information about communications (e.g. the time and to and from headers of an e-mail, or web servers (not pages) accessed by a particular user).

The content of e-mails, the full URLs browsed and any other information such as the content of filestore is not covered by these RIPA powers. In addition to the law enforcement and national security agencies, a large number of other authorities can now use the RIPA powers. A full list of the authorities and the types of data each is entitled to demand is contained in an appendix to the *Regulation of Investigatory Powers (Communications Data) Order 2003 [2]*.[54] The appendix also identifies the rank of the person within the authority who is required to authorise the demand for information.

■ *Access to Environmental Information Regulations 2004,*[55] *Access to Environmental Information (Scotland) Regulations 2004.*[56] The regulations implementing EC Directive 2003/4/EC on public access are also aimed at enabling the UK to fulfil its obligations under the Aarhus Convention[57] and replace existing regulations in place in the UK since 1992.

The Environmental Information Regulations (EIRs) apply to any information which –

1. relates to the environment;

2. is held by a relevant person in an accessible form and otherwise than for the purposes of any judicial or legislative functions.

The Regulations define environmental information as being any information that relates to:

– the state of any water or air, the state of any flora or fauna, the state of any soil or the state of any natural site or other land;

– any activities or measures (including activities giving rise to noise or any other nuisance) which adversely affect anything mentioned above or are likely adversely to affect anything so mentioned;

- any activities or administrative or other measures (including any environmental management programmes) which are designed to protect anything so mentioned.

■ *Reuse of Public Sector Information Regulations 2005.* The main purpose of the Regulations is to establish a framework that provides for:

 - the ready identification of public sector documents that are available for reuse;

 - documents are generally available for reuse at marginal cost;

 - public sector bodies to deal with applications to reuse in a timely, open and transparent manner;

 - a fair, consistent and non-discriminatory process;

 - encouraging the sharing of best practice across the public sector.

There are some specific exclusions to documents held by the following bodies:[58]

 3. These Regulations do not apply to documents held by –

  (i) public service broadcasters and their subsidiaries,

  (ii) educational and research establishments,

  (iii) cultural establishments, (such as museums, libraries, archives, orchestras, and opera, ballet and theatre establishments).

■ *Public Company Accounting Reform and Investor Protection Act 2002 (this is more usually referred to as the 'Sarbanes-Oxley Act' or 'SOX').* The Act gives prominence to records management as an instrument to help ensure internal controls of the audit process and is a starting point for improving the trustworthiness of audit reports.

'Internal control'[59] is the process, effected by an entity's board of directors, management and other personnel, designed to provide reasonable assurance regarding the achievement of objectives in three categories:

- effectiveness and efficiency of operations

- reliability of financial reporting

- compliance with laws and regulations.

The Act states that reliable record-keeping systems are a precondition for compliance with some parts of the Act. Records creation processes and retention decision-making are also covered in the Act.

In order to achieve certification status companies are required to fulfil extensive disclosures, controls and protocols to ensure that information required to be disclosed to the issuer (i.e. the US Securities and Exchange Commission[60]) is recorded, processed and reported appropriately as specified in the Commission's rules and forms. In addition all companies have to submit an annual report of the effectiveness of their internal accounting controls to the US Securities and Exchange Commission.

The criminal penalties for failure to comply with Sarbanes-Oxley certification are between 10 and 20 years imprisonment. This is only slightly less than the penalties for air piracy (20–25 years).[61]

Notes

1. British Standards Institution, *Information and Documentation – Records Management – Part 1: General* (BS ISO 15489-1, London, 2001), *Information and Documentation – Records Management – Part 2: Guidelines* (PD ISO/TR 15489-2, London, 2001). Effective records management (parts 1–3).
2. Pederson, Ann, 'Professing archives – a very human enterprise', in McKemmish, S. et al. (eds), *Archives. Recordkeeping in Society* (Wagga Wagga, 2005), pp. 51–74.
3. Ibid., p. 51.
4. Pearce-Moses, Richard, *A Glossary of Archival and Records Terminology* (Chicago, 2005) (available at *http://www.archivists.org/glossary/index.asp*, accessed February 2006).
5. Pederson, op. cit., pp. 51–74.
6. Rankin, Frank, *Scottish Postgraduate Training Project Report* (Glasgow, 2002) (available at *http://www.archives.gla.ac.uk/hostsite/spat.pdf*, accessed February 2006), p. 51.
7. Logjam Audit of Uncatalogued Collections in the North West website, *http://www.northwestarchives.org.uk/logjam.htm* (accessed February 2006).
8. MacQueen, Hector L., 'Reform of archives legislation: a Scots perspective', *Journal of the Society of Archivists*, 26 (2), October 2005, p. 209.
9. Cook, Michael, *The Management of Information from Archives*, 2nd edn (Aldershot, 1999), p. 36.
10. University of Glasgow Information Management & Preservation Postgraduate Course brochure 2005–6, *http://www.hatii.arts.gla.ac.uk/imp/index.htm*.
11. 'What's Wrong with Archivists and Records Managers?', paper to Society of Archivists conference, Glasgow, 2 September 2004. This covered how archivists and records managers can enhance strategic initiatives with their professional expertise.
12. Forde, Helen, 'Access and preservation in the 21st century', *JSA*, 26 (2), 2005, pp. 193–200.

13. The National Council on Archives website, *http://www.ncaonline.org.uk/announcements/save_the_countrys_memory/*.

14. Rankin, op. cit., pp. 50–1.

15. University of British Columbia Master of Archival Studies Degree, *http://www.slais.ubc.ca/PROGRAMS/mas.htm* (accessed February 2006).

16. InterPARES Project (International Research on Permanent Authentic Records in Electronic Systems), *http://www.interpares.org/*.

17. See: Willis, Anthony, 'Corporate governance and management of information and records', *Records Management Journal*, 15 (2), 2005, pp. 86–97.

18. Upward, Frank, 'The records continuum', in McKemmish, S. et al. (eds), *Archives. Recordkeeping in Society* (Wagga Wagga, 2005), pp. 197–222.

19. Power, Michael, *The Audit Society: Rituals of Verification* (Oxford, 1997).

20. See Chapter 1 in this volume.

21. Badendoch, D. et al., 'The value of information', in Feeney, Mary and Grieves, Maureen (eds), *The Value and Impact of Information* (London, 1994), p. 16.

22. The espida project at the University of Glasgow is working on the assessment of information as an intangible asset. The project website is: *http://www.gla.ac.uk/espida/* (accessed February 2006).

23. The impact of the Human Rights Act 1998 is not yet clear in the field of information management but as case law is tested the requirements for information managers will become established. The European Convention on Human Rights, *http://www.humanrights.coe.int/*, and the UK law are available at *http://www.opsi.gov.uk/acts/acts1998/19980042.htm* (accessed February 2006). See also Reed, Robert J. and Murdoch, Jim, *A Guide to Human Rights Law in Scotland* (Edinburgh, 2001).

24. Coppel, Philip, *Information Rights* (London, 2004). This is a comprehensive textbook for practitioners, which covers not only freedom of information legislation but also domestic rights of access (for example to local government and health records as well as public records).

25. *http://www.opsi.gov.uk/* (accessed February 2006).

26. Coppel, op. cit., Chapter 3, 'Rights of access under European Union law', pp. 83–97.

27. The Lord Chancellor's Code of Practice on records management, *http://www.foi.gov.uk/codemanrec.htm* (accessed February 2006); the Scottish Executive's Code of Practice on records management, *http://www.scotland.gov.uk/Topics/Government/FOI/18022/13383* (accessed February 2006).

28. The text of the Acts and commentaries on the provisions can be found in Coppel, op. cit.

29. Henczel, S., *The Information Audit – A Practical Guide* (Munich, 2001).

30. Codes of Practice on the Data Protection Act 1998, *http://www.archives.org.uk/professionalissues/revisedcodeofpractice.html* (accessed February 2006).

31. Other Codes under the Act, *http://www.ico.gov.uk/eventual.aspx?id=437* (accessed March, 2006), cover employment practices and other aspects of compliance with the Act.

32. *http://www.opsi.gov.uk/acts/acts2000/20000023.htm*, RIP(S). Scottish Codes of Practice were approved in March 2003 and can be found on *http://www.scotland.gov.uk*.

33. The Environmental Information Regulations 2004 (SI 2004 No. 3391).

34. *http://www.hmso.gov.uk/legislation/scotland/ssi2004/20040520.htm* (accessed February 2006).

35. Statutory Instrument 2005 No. 1515 (for more information, see the Office for Public Sector Information (OPSI) (available at *http://www.opsi.gov.uk/si/si2005/20051515.htm*, accessed February 2006).

36. The Office for Public Sector Information (OPSI), incorporating Her Majesty's Stationery Office (HMSO), has the policy lead for the Information Asset Register (IAR), which is used widely across central government as a way of identifying and accessing asset lists.

37. *http://www.opsi.gov.uk/si/em2005/uksiem_20051515_en.pdf*.

38. (The) Sarbanes-Oxley Act 2002 (available at *http://www.ereinsure.com/docs/SOX404eRewhitepaper.pdf*).

39. Stephens, David O., 'The Sarbanes-Oxley Act records management implications', *Record Management Journal*, 15 (2), 2005, pp. 98–103.

40. Bichard, Sir Michael, *The Bichard Inquiry – An Independent Inquiry Arising from the Soham Murders* (HC 653, London, June 2004) (available at *http://www.bichardinquiry.org.uk/*, accessed February 2006).

41. *http://www.gla.ac.uk/espida/*

42. *http://www.mla.gov.uk/*

43. See Pearce-Moses, op. cit.

44. This is explored further by Cox, Richard J., *Archives and Archivists in the Information Age* (New York, 2005). See 'Why records professionals need to explain themselves', pp. 91–117.

45. For example, Tyacke, Sarah, 'Archives in a wider world: the culture and politics of archives', *Archivaria*, 52, Fall 2001, pp. 1–25; or Harris, Verne, 'On (archival) odyssey(s)', *Archivaria*, 51 Spring 2001, pp. 2–13.

46. Cook, Terry, 'Archival science and postmodernism: new formulations for old concepts', *Archival Science*, 1, 2001, pp. 3–27; or McNeil, Heather, 'Trusting records in a postmodern world', *Archivaria*, 51, Spring 2001, pp. 36–47.

47. Yusof, Zawiyah M. and Chell, Robert W., 'Towards a theoretical construct for records management', *Records Management Journal*, 12 (2), 2002, pp. 55–64.

48. Society of Archivists Pilot CPD Scheme website, *http://archives.org.uk/content.asp?id=589*.

49. Institute of Conservation website, *http://www.instituteofconservation.org.uk/*.

50. Cox, op. cit., p. 16.

51. Kargbo, John A., 'Archives management in Sierra Leone', *Journal of the Society of Archivists*, 26 (2), 2005, pp. 243–50.

52. *http://www.opsi.gov.uk/acts/acts2000/20000023.htm*. RIP(S)A Scottish Codes of Practice were approved in March 2003 and can be found on *www.scotland.gov.uk*, accessed February 2006.

53. Updates on the application of the Regulations can be found on the Home Office website: *http://security.homeoffice.gov.uk/surveillance/ripa-updates/*, accessed February 2006.

54. *http://www.opsi.gov.uk/acts/acts2000/sch2*, accessed February 2006.

55. *The Environmental Information ... Regulation No. 3391*, op. cit.

56. *http://www.hmso.gov.uk/legislation/scotland/ssi2004/20040520.htm*, accessed February 2006.

57. *http://europa.eu.int/comm/environment/aarhus/,* accessed February 2006.

58. *http://www.opsi.gov.uk/si/em2005/uksiem_20051515_en.pdf,* accessed February 2006.

59. As defined by COSO, *www.coso.org/publications/executive_summary_integrated_framework htm,* accessed February. *2006.*

60. US Securities and Exchange Commission, available at *http://www.sec.gov/,* accessed February 2006.

61. Quoted in a presentation by PriceWaterhouseCoopers, available at: *www.erpanet.org/events/2004/antwerpen/presentations/erpaWorkshop-Antwerpen_Drift.pdf,* accessed February 2006.

6

Approaching digital preservation holistically

Seamus Ross

Introduction

The pervasiveness of information and communication technology (ICT) has transformed the way we create, access, use and need to manage digital entities. The dependence by companies and public sector institutions on ICT is producing a massive reservoir of material waiting to be assessed for disposal or retention, which in some cases may mean bringing it into memory institutions. The quantities and diversity of the material pose obstacles even to its assessment by archivists, records managers and other information curators. The cultural and scientific heritage of the contemporary world that comes to be held in our memory institutions will provide historians with raw materials for interpreting the twenty-first century. These assets, moreover, serve as sustainable and renewable resources to be exploited in an ever-increasing diversity of ways. Users will expect to be able to do this. In their digital guise these materials provide core resources for enabling education, supporting lifelong learning, underpinning the development of new products by creative industries and improvements in our quality of life.

E-commerce and e-government initiatives continue to raise awareness of the need for reliable and trustworthy information sources. Cunningham and Phillips argued that '[k]eeping information in electronic formats available for e-governance and e-democracy is a public good, just as health services, education and bridges are'.[1] Our trust in the accountability of e-government and its success, therefore, depends upon the institution of transparent, secure and workable digital curation mechanisms within public sector environments. Delivering this vision depends upon the survival of digital data in accessible, usable, reliable and authentic forms. As a result, curation and preservation impacts on the working practices of public bodies, memory organisations, researchers and business sectors including, to mention only five, aerospace, entertainment, finance, pharmaceuticals and publishing. Long-term access to digital materials depends upon the active intervention by archivists, records managers and other digital curators. The notion that individuals or organisations can just keep everything and some piece of 'novel' software will eventually make it possible for them to sort it out is akin to believing that the 'Elves of Cologne' will one day return.[2] If archives are to function in this new technological environment, they will need to be transparent, accessible and responsive to user needs and expectations.

The umbrella term 'digital curation' encapsulates the many activities involved in caring for digital entities such as selection, documentation, management, storage, conservation, security, preservation and provision of access. Curation focuses not just on preserving digital entities but on keeping them functional, supporting their continuous annotation and maintaining their fitness for purpose. Preservation is a lot narrower in focus. To paraphrase the Report of the Task Force on Archiving of Digital Information, it has the objective of retaining the ability to display, retrieve, manipulate and use digital information in the face of constantly changing technology.[3]

The problem with digital materials is that many factors seem to conspire to make them inaccessible. Technological advances foster obsolescence of access mechanisms and accelerate the loss of material. For example, while it is true that media degrade over time, even before they do, devices to access particular classes of media become scarce and curators can find it impossible to get the contents off the media. Often, even where the digital object is accessible, it remains unintelligible because insufficient descriptive, technical, structural and management information about the object survives. So, while the aim of digital preservation is to preserve digital information or objects that are authentic, understandable and accessible over time, digital curation involves not only the preservation of digital materials but also the updating, correcting and annotating of materials.

Digital curation and preservation are broad fields of enquiry and practice.[4] Here we aim to provide an overview of digital curation and preservation and to provide you with an intellectual framework within which to think about the challenges of curation and preservation.[5] The chapter will approach these discussions against the backdrop of new research in this area.[6]

At the heart of preservation lies planning and the recognition that 'digital curation and preservation is a risk management activity at all stages of the longevity pathway'.[7] In undertaking preservation, individuals and organisations must 'right size' their risk. Many of the approaches to preservation described in the literature are designed to be implemented and used by large organisations, and in particular national archives and libraries. Do the costs and processes perceived to be associated with preservation mean small and medium-sized institutions have no chance of preserving or actively curating digital entities in their care? As we shall see, there are proactive steps and scalable approaches that make the application of preservation strategies accessible to nearly all institutions.

Obstacles to long-term access

The preservation literature makes much play of the fragility of digital materials, although, as we know from the recovery of data held on damaged media such as the tapes recovered from the Atlantic Ocean crash site of the Challenger Space Shuttle, this claim is overstated.[8] As a result, we often identify media degradation as a significant culprit in the loss of digital materials. It can be, but it is not the reason most commonly cited by data recovery companies. Moreover, Ontrack DataRecovery has demonstrated a disjuncture between customers' perception of the causes of data loss and the actual causes of loss (see Table 6.1).

Other causes of loss include deliberate destruction; in late 2004 the Spanish Prime Minister, Señor Zapatero, reported that: 'In the Prime Minister's Office we did not have a single document or any data on computer because the whole Cabinet of the previous Government (Aznar) carried out a massive erasure. That means that we have nothing about what happened, information that might have been received, meetings or decisions that were taken from March 11 until March 14 [2004].'[9]

Technological developments and obsolescence can lead to the loss of digital materials. Digital objects are represented as streams of binary digits, commonly known as bits. These streams must be interpreted (using hardware and software) before they can be manipulated or rendered, whether for display, printing or analysis. Raw bit streams are generally of little value and often meaningless.[10] Sometimes it may be impossible to access and render them because a syntactical interpretation

Table 6.1 Causes of data loss

Cause	As perceived by the customer	As noted by Ontrack engineers (2005)	As noted by Ontrack for the period 1995–6
Human error	11%	26%	36%
Computer viruses	2%	4%	8%
Natural disaster	1%	2%	3%
Hardware or system problem	78%	56%	49%
Software corruption or program problem	7%	9%	4%

of the bit stream cannot be performed. In other instances semantic opaqueness arising from loss of context or process and their dynamic nature may leave the objects unintelligible.

Archivists and records managers will be aware that the organisational structure of institutions and the way information creation and management tools are deployed by them have in themselves become a preservation obstacle. The lack of collaboration between records managers, creators and IT staff contributes its share of problems as well. The failure of many records management approaches to link records management strategies with organisational objectives leaves records management without a strong corporate base. The role that records management plays in the area of compliance and risk management could be exploited to move preservation into a core business focus. Preservation is perceived as expensive and often the scale of this investment is under-appreciated and certainly almost never balanced against recognisable benefits.

The likelihood that digital materials will be properly curated over time is closely tied to their recurring value or to their continued active usage. Recurring value arises from the use of digital objects for their evidentiary value, say to limit corporate liability, to demonstrate primary rights to an idea, invention or property, to meet compliance or regulatory requirements or to achieve competitive advantage. Recurring value can arise when a resource can be re-exploited whether through repackaging or release in some new and unexpected way. Certain data sets that are regularly exploited for commercial or research purposes, such as metrological or scientific data sets (e.g. protein databases) are likely to benefit from a level of care that will ensure their longer-term accessibility.

Ensuring evidential value – authenticity and trust

Digital preservation aims to ensure the value of digital entities. 'When we work with digital objects we want to know they are what they purport to be and that they are complete and have not been altered or corrupted.'[11] These twin concepts are encapsulated in the terms authenticity and integrity. As digital objects are more easily altered and corrupted than, say, paper documents and records, creators and preservers often find it challenging to demonstrate their authenticity. As digital objects that lack authenticity and integrity have limited value as evidence or usefulness as an information resource, the ability to establish authenticity of and trust in a digital object is crucial.[12] A well-documented chain of custody helps with establishing authenticity, and we shall return to this later.

Each rendition of a digital object must carry the same force as the initial instantiation, sometimes labelled as the original. Reflecting on the conclusions from research conducted by ERPANET,[13] the DELOS Digital Preservation Cluster[14] and InterPARES, the very concept of 'original' seems an inappropriate label for digital objects. If there ever is an original of a digital document it exists only for a fleeting moment in the memory of the computer on which the digital object was created at the time it was created. Perhaps first renderings of digital objects might best be referred to as an initial 'representation or instantiation' (II). The problem is: how can we record the functionality and behaviour as well as the content of that initial instantiation so that we can validate subsequent instantiations? Where subsequent instantiations (SI) share precision of resemblance in content, functionality and behaviour with the initial instantiations, the 'SIs' can be said to have the same authenticity and integrity as the 'IIs'. So there is no copy in the digital age; every validated re-representation is in a sense 'the original'.

Could general characteristics of authenticity be identified that would apply to all digital objects? Or do different types of digital objects, record-keeping procedures and digital object creation practices, alongside the diversity of institutional requirements, mean that digital object preservation would require a variety of mechanisms to enable users and preservers to ascertain the authenticity of material? InterPARES argued that reliability and authenticity were two areas of independent responsibility – the creator was responsible for reliability and the preserver took responsibility for authenticity.[15]

While authenticity could be the subject of much new research at both practical and theoretical levels, here we can only draw attention to the issue. Confronted with digital representations, users appear to assume that, unless there is obvious evidence to the contrary, if the creator or holder of a digital object says that it is authentic then it is. As authenticity depends upon 'establishing identity and demonstrating integrity',[16] users require background services to allow them to verify the inferences they have drawn about the status of materials and the documentation.[17] Archivists and records managers need mechanisms to assist in the maintenance of authenticity. For example, users need to know where the digital materials came from, how they came to be deposited, how they were ingested (e.g. under what conditions, using what technology, how the success of the ingest was validated), why they were created, where they were created and how they were created, and they need information as to how the digital object was maintained after its creation (e.g. was it maintained in a secure environment, was the software used to store and represent it changed?). This 'data about data' or metadata provides, as we shall see in an examination of a few legal cases, a crucial source of information to support assessments of the authenticity of digital entities. Where metadata is severable from the content, users will require evidence to demonstrate that the link has been maintained and that no new unvalidated links have been created.

While some professions such as archival, legal and accountancy emphasise the significance of authenticity it does not appear to be the primary focus of current digital repositories. A small-scale survey conducted by Rachel Bradley in mid-2003 received responses from 22 out of 40 digital repositories contacted in the USA and Canada. 'The majority felt that ensuring authenticity and integrity represented a low priority compared with increasing access and preserving content.'[18] She noted that many of these institutions were aware that they needed to address the authenticity and integrity issue, and planned to do so. Of course, if we adopt the InterPARES point of view, preservation of content without ensuring authenticity and integrity is pointless. Her conclusions are at odds with the work of Park (McGill University) who examined how practitioners viewed authenticity.[19]

At the heart of establishing authenticity lies trust and this is an area where, as Lynch has noted, we are just beginning to understand the issues.[20] The maintenance of authenticity and integrity requires control of ingest and its verification and depends on immutability of the data store. But it is not just technological; it also depends upon the organisation that is managing the digital store and how it is perceived. This is one reason why the most commonly employed archival reference model, the Open Archival Information System (OAIS), puts such emphasis on designated communities and also why there is a resurgent interest in the processes of auditing and certifying of repositories.

How do European institutions view digital preservation?

ERPANET, in an effort to understand better how record keepers, information technology staff and business managers viewed electronic records and their longer-term retention, conducted nearly 100 case studies between 2002 and 2004.[21] Our studies provide insights into current preservation practices in different institutional, juridical and business contexts as well as across both the public and private sectors. These insights we hoped would help us to understand contemporary approaches to digital longevity, enable cross-sectoral comparisons, provide an indication of the kinds of tools and education needed, and identify issues requiring further research.

The research was conducted by a combination of structured questionnaire and interview. Interviewees received the questionnaire in advance of the interview, which was normally conducted by telephone. In the course of developing the questionnaire and interview protocol we examined how other projects, including the Pittsburgh Project and InterPARES I, conducted surveys. We aimed to avoid the pitfalls that these projects encountered, but of course created our own. The template is available on the ERPANET website; perhaps those conducting similar studies will adopt it. To obtain a holistic picture of organisational attitudes towards digital preservation, we aimed to interview three different classes of individual within an organisation: a business manager, an IT manager and an archivist/records manager. Where many other studies aim to provide reports of this kind in as anonymous a way as possible, we took the decision that we wanted to identify the organisations that participated in the case studies. With a few exceptions the participating organisations allowed us to do just this.

Our sample was drawn from across Europe, although countries in which ERPANET had a presence (Italy, the Netherlands, Switzerland and the United Kingdom) are over-represented. We contacted just over 500 organisations and by the close of ERPANET we had achieved a participation rate of around 15.6 per cent. Convincing organisations to take part was a challenge. More than 60 per cent of the organisations did not respond to the initial enquiry or subsequent follow-up attempts. Others initially expressed willingness to take part but subsequently withdrew. A good example of the latter case was the Banca di Roma where archival and ICT staff indicated they wished to participate, but superiors in the Bank could not be encouraged to sign off on participation.

The case studies investigated five themes. First, we aimed to understand how aware organisations were of the risks posed by storing material in digital form and how they perceived the potential impact of those risks on their organisation. Second, the survey was intended to provide us with information about how digital preservation impacted on the organisation. Third, we wanted to gather an impression of the actions that organisations took to prevent the loss of digital materials. Fourth, the study was intended to provide us with an appreciation of how organisations with preservation activities monitored them. Finally, the studies were designed to give us an indication as to how organisations would be planning to address their future preservation requirements. Drawing on the case studies we hoped to be able to establish evidence of best practice and to identify preservation approaches and justifications that other institutions could use to build business cases for preservation.

In this chapter, I cannot discuss the findings in detail; preliminary findings are available in print elsewhere,[22] and others will appear shortly. Awareness of the issues surrounding digital preservation varied across organisations more than across sectors. When we assessed the drivers for preservation action we found that cultural and historical value (as noted above) was given the lowest priority; this may reflect in part the nature of our target cohort, which included few cultural heritage institutions. Four core drivers stood out: core business focus, reuse, legal and regulatory compliance, and experience of information loss. Broadcasters recognised preservation as essential if they were to maximise the reuse potential of their resources, whereas pharmaceuticals were motivated to address preservation issues to ensure regulatory compliance. Others noting reuse were public sector bodies (European Patent Office), news agencies (Deutsche Presse-Agentur, Swiss News Agency) and oil companies.

Discussions by participants and presenters at the ERPANET Workshop on policies for digital preservation indicated that preservation policies and procedures 'represent an issue that still needs a lot of attention. Little practical experience yet exists and most of the ideas are still rather theoretical, although there are organisations that have a relatively longstanding experience with digital preservation.'[23] This conclusion was borne out in the results of the case studies. When developing or purchasing new systems, respondents noted that preservation strategies were not usually articulated in the specifications.

Retention policies were not often noted and where they were they were not necessarily implemented across the organisation.[24] There was a general recognition that preservation and storage problems were aggravated by the complexity, diversity of types or formats and size of the digital entities. Few organisations took a long-term perspective and those that did were either national information curating institutions (e.g. libraries) or institutions that felt regulatory risk exposure. In general, a sense emerged from the case studies that preservation required a pragmatic approach.

The organisations participating in the research acknowledged that they have little information about the costs of digital preservation and, where they had tried to predict the costs, they had done so poorly – this is a conclusion borne out by other studies.[25] Respondents noted that when they could quantify the costs they would be difficult to justify in the corporate environment. While the Deutsche Presse-Agentur (dpa) 'was not in a position to reveal detailed figures' it did acknowledge that 'long-term preservation costs are roughly in the dimension of one per cent of the company's turnover'.[26]

The Centraal Bureau voor de Statistiek (CBS)[27] in the Netherlands reported that it had:

> ... identified the cost benefits of digital records management and archiving as threefold: first, the records management can become an integral part of the automated working processes of the organisation; secondly, a decrease in the use of paper and increase in the management of digital records enable better sharing of documents and fewer localised collections of records; and thirdly, digital records management and archiving allows for organised maintenance of the organisational historical memory. There is no separate funding available for digital preservation activities, and the budget of the IT department is expected to cater for ongoing maintenance of the records.[28]

Benefits to commercial businesses to be derived from long-term digital preservation have proved elusive and ERPANET's seminar on Business

Models did not actually succeed in identifying them.[29] In general, the value of digital preservation is only apparent long after the initial investment has had to be made.

One of the primary justifications given in the literature for digital preservation is access. Within the cohort interviewed by ERPANET access was seen as primarily for internal use. Where external access was provided it was done with different approaches: intermediaries, information provided on CDs and more rarely through online portals. The obstacles to access were security, privacy and technical challenges (e.g. lack of standard file format).

What was surprising among the 78 case studies analysed here was just how great the variation of awareness of risk was – some were not aware that there was any risk and a very small number had a highly attuned sense of risk. The value placed on the digital materials by organisations depended in part on how dependent the organisation was on the material for business activity, with the highest value placed on information by organisations who either saw or exploited the potential reuse of information or identified the risks associated with its not being available. Responsibility for digital preservation was rarely taken at corporate level. Organisations did not have a single point of contact for preservation and within organisations there was not always a clearly identified individual who had responsibility for the activity.

Preservation strategies were rare. The secretive nature of many organisations does not support collaborative action to address the preservation problem. What really stood out was the preponderance of the point of view that organisations should not invest internally in defining solutions but should wait for them to be provided externally.

The findings of the ERPANET studies are complemented by those conducted elsewhere.[30] For instance, a working group jointly sponsored by the Online Computer Library Center (OCLC) and the Research Libraries Group (RLG) on Preservation Metadata: Implementation Strategies (PREMIS) reported that 'there is very little experience with digital preservation.'[31] More recently a survey that ICABS conducted for the Koninklijke Bibliotheek, Building Networks in Digital Preservation: Recent Developments in Digital Preservation in 15 National Libraries (draft July 2005), found that libraries have not adopted a single strategy to achieve long-term preservation and access to the diversity of digital objects entering their collections. In fact, some have still not adopted any strategy, despite being cognisant of the risks posed by the poor curation of digital materials. In many cases this appears to reflect a lack of access to appropriate information resources, training and repository support, the need for audit and certification services, and a need for access to research results. Surveys of national and local archives tell the same story; as Hans Hofman noted in the report on Enabling Persistent and Sustainable Digital Cultural Heritage in Europe (September 2004):

> [d]espite the resolutions and charters decided upon by the European Council of Ministers, the General Assembly of UNESCO and the NRG [National Representatives Group], and despite the fact that they have raised a lot of awareness, the consequences have not yet been integrated or formulated into concrete action plans nor have they taken it beyond the level of a stand-alone topic. As long as the practical integration of persistence into our daily economic, social, cultural and policy issues is not achieved, it will be difficult to raise it and to make it politically appealing and interesting for funding.[32]

What was intriguingly absent from the discussions with the ERPANET case study interviewees was a focus on technology and this is despite IT staff having been interviewed.

A case study – e-mail

Preservation of e-mail is a challenge, even without the attachments. We are producing them by the billions each day, some 9.6 billion a day in 2001. For thirty years we have recognised the evidential significance of e-mails, although in an unpublished survey of National European Archives conducted in 1994 Edward Higgs and I found only three of the twenty responding archives had acquired any e-mails and even these were from their own administration systems. We see e-mails exploited in contemporary litigation (e.g. *Zubulake* v. *UBS Warburg*[33] or the use of the Presidential e-mails in *US* v. *Philip Morris USA, Inc., et al.*[34]) or in the case of long-term accountability of government (e.g. *Armstrong* v. *Executive Office of the President*). In *Armstrong* v. *Executive Office of the President*, commonly referred as the PROFS case, the courts found that in creating printed versions of electronic communications government agencies had not met their obligations under the Federal Records Act. The appellate court affirmed, stating '[w]ithout the missing information, the paper print-outs – akin to traditional memoranda with the "to" and "from" cut off and even the "received" stamp pruned away – are dismembered documents indeed.'[35] In the original decision, Judge

Charles R. Richey had noted that the loss of searchability and linkages between messages made the printouts inadequate substitutes.[36] Few organisations actually succeed in managing their e-mails effectively. Indeed few employees consider e-mail to be records or, as Jean Samuel put it, 'User perception of e-mail status is in direct contradiction to the legal perception and the matter of unguarded remarks in e-mail (made because the writer deems the message to be unofficial) ...' exposes organisations to unanticipated risks that may result in financial loss or litigation (or both).[37] Perhaps this claim is old but it is still relevant, as an AIIM survey in early 2005 demonstrated.[38]

Predicting the kinds of research that might be possible in digital archives of the future is difficult. As Perer, Shneiderman and Oard have noted:

> Historians and social scientists believe that archives are important artefacts for understanding the individuals and communities they represent. However, there are currently few methods or tools to effectively explore these archives ... By presenting new ways to approach the exploration of email archives, not only do we provide a new step for exploration, but also raise awareness for the difficult task of understanding email archives.[39]

In the instance of e-mail, we might consider for a moment how we could use contextual information in e-mail (e.g. 'to' and 'from') data to identify both formal and informal communities within organisations and even to identify those individuals who play leadership roles within these communities. Josh Tyler and his colleagues at Hewlett-Packard developed a tool for doing this and then applied it. They '... found that it does an effective job of uncovering communities of practice with nothing more than email ("to:" and "from:") data.'[40] In other instances, we might wish to apply visualisation tools to reveal 'the data and patterns that are hidden within the email archive.'[41] What is evident is that users of digital archives will expect to be able to access, manipulate and analyse material in ways that were never possible in the past and the relationship between the user and the archive will shift. This really changes the way we need to think about digital curation and preservation.

Here I have used e-mail as an example. Databases, especially scientific ones, might as easily have been selected. 'Databases have been, and continue to be, a key technology for the storage, organisation and interrogation of information. They are a core module in most of today's information systems.'[42] In 'Archiving scientific data', Buneman et al. explore many of the challenges of database preservation from performance to ensuring semantic continuity.[43] The National Library of Australia has developed a tool, Xinq, to support the automated creation of interfaces to archived databases.[44] The Swiss Federal Archives identified ingest of databases into the Archives as a fundamental challenge.[45] The crucial point is that archives will be confronted with a broad range of digital materials from databases to documents to e-mail to websites, and the current models all require a tremendous amount of human intervention on the part of the ingesting organisation to prepare material appraised for ingest to be ingested, documented and made accessible. Current approaches do not facilitate the effective initial ingest and longer-term management within the archival environment of digital materials. There is a growing demand for tools to support ingest and management of digital entities ranging from databases to documents to e-mails to software.

Some archives, to reduce costs and minimise the diversity of skills required and the variety of file formats, convert all incoming files to a single format type for each type class, chosen because the type maximises the likelihood of longevity. This can lead to problems. First, what are the appropriate mechanisms to use to evaluate the ability of a file format to support long-term preservation? Second, what impact might 'standardisation' have on information embedded in the proprietary functionality of particular software packages? For instance, the functionality inherent in some documentary editing software to track changes in documents will provide invaluable documentary evidence for future scholars. Contemporary evidence for this comes, for example, from the release in October 2005 by the United Nations of the Microsoft Word version of the UN report into the murder of the former Lebanese Prime Minister Rafik Hariri. It emerged that key names had been dropped from the official report when 'an electronic version distributed by UN officials on Thursday night allowed recipients to track editing changes'.[46] The fact that hidden information in digital documents often provides a window on intentions and original ideas and can enable subsequent users to track how arguments and ideas developed will make the ability to delve into these digital footprints as crucial to future scholars as the editing and interlinear and marginal notes of authors (or even users) are to those working with analogue documents.[47]

Technical preservation approaches

Some archivists and records managers say that the only good approach to the preservation of electronic records is to print them to paper or to microfilm. During the ERPANET case study on preservation practices at the Council of Europe, conducted in mid-2003, representatives of the organisation reported that '[f]or certain categories of records, print-to-paper is the only means of preservation available. This holds especially true for email, where no possibility of digital archiving exists ... [within the organisation]'.[48] As a solution, this is a non-starter. As we saw in the PROFS case above, paper representations lose the richness associated with digital media including searching capabilities, linkages between digital entities and relationships between information elements.[49] There is an increasing expectation that digital materials will be produced electronically in litigation. As early as 1972, courts in the USA had recognised that digital representations of records had benefits in terms of accuracy and place in the chain of evidence that printouts lacked.[50] They also benefited in terms of functionality and essentially the expectation is that, if evidence is created and used in digital form, then it should be made available in that way to litigants.[51]

Computer forensics and digital archaeology lie at the other extreme.[52] This approach suggests that we do nothing now. Conversion or recovery only happens after the original mechanisms, such as a hardware device or software application, for accessing the digital entity ceases to work effectively. This approach has the advantage that it reduces near-term costs. It does not necessarily make the costs higher in the future either, as it is possible that, as approaches to software design become more sophisticated, reverse engineering will become a much more cost-effective and viable process. Of course, you will recognise this as a high-risk strategy as it assumes capability, financial resource, media durability, motivation and continued development of computer forensic technologies.

Other approaches more commonly cited in the literature include conversion and migration. The Library of Medicine (USA) has developed tools to enable users to convert from fifty types of electronic files into five output types (i.e. Portable Document Format (PDF), Multi-page Tagged Image File Format (TIFF), Single-page TIFF, Text, and Synthesized Speech).[53] The CAMiLEON project devised the concept of 'migration on request'.[54] Migration essentially involves moving a file of one type to a new environment before the pathway from the older format to the newer one disappears. Migrations will be time and labour dependent and will be influenced by processes, systems and best practices. Rarely will a migration be clean. Migration options can range from format change to re-representation of data. There is certainly going to be loss of information, functionality, meaning or renderability as a result of migrations. Even six years on, it is still the case that:

[b]efore we can see migration as a viable aid to preservation, more work is needed in the development of metrics for benchmarking and supporting the evaluation of the risks to the functionality of the data set, or losses resulting from particular changes. The question of 'how much loss is acceptable', whether this is in functionality, integrity, authenticity, or meaning has not been adequately addressed by any commercial or research initiatives.[55]

Part of the problem is that we do not have a clear indication as to the properties that a digital object must retain if that object is to have been migrated successfully. If we defined the preservation action and documented the process, could this be a way to compensate for the intrinsic loss of character as a result of migration? The National Archives of Australia introduced the concept of performance to explain the interaction between the source and the process. Some approaches migrate the source, while others migrate the process. Rarely are both migrated accurately.

Emulation is another promising approach to preservation. In one guise it involves running a piece of software on machine 2 which makes it possible to execute code on machine 2 that was designed for machine 1. An early example was Trimble's emulation of an IBM S/360 on a microcomputer. His reason for conducting the work was to investigate the price–performance ratio, which was shown to be better in the emulated environment than in the native S/360.[56] Emulation is designed not merely to maintain the ability to represent and manipulate the digital resources but to do it in the native environment.

In order to approach preservation effectively you need to characterise what you have, define the options that can enable you to handle it most effectively and work out the way in which you carry out these processes. As we have seen, there are a number of different approaches to ensuring that digital materials remain accessible. Work being conducted under the digital preservation cluster of the DELOS Network of Excellence in Digital Libraries examines the use of utility analysis to select the most appropriate preservation option.[57] This research is delivering tools to support preservation choices that can be applied within a test-bed environment, whether the DELOS DPC test-bed or some other, which will enable those doing preservation planning to select the optimum preservation approach.[58]

Preservation of digital information requires active intervention; left unsecured it is susceptible to loss through the physical breakdown of the media, rendered inaccessible by technological advances or left meaningless through lack of or insufficient contextual evidence.[59]

Metadata

Courts have come to recognise, where digital documents are concerned, that different types of digital representations have different values to the end user. For instance, in a class action securities case in the USA, the court noted that production of documents in the tiff format was insufficient and it ordered that the defendant produce 'responsive electronic documents in their native .pst format if that is how they were stored in Defendants' usual course of business'.[60] Furthermore, in this case the court noted that the searchable electronic format should include all available metadata. The contemporary value of metadata is increasingly recognised within the legal profession, although it is still poorly understood and little studied. One of its crucial roles is to support processes of validating the authenticity of the record; as printouts rarely include such system metadata they are not adequate substitutes.[61] In the case of *Zenith Electronics Corporation* v. *WH-TV Broadcasting Corporation*, the court ruled that the defendant should supply the documents to the plaintiff electronically because the printed copies already provided lacked metadata and could not be easily searched.[62]

Contemporary legal cases, particularly in the USA, indicate that metadata are valuable in understanding and verifying the reliability and authenticity of digital materials from documents to databases. But the metadata discussed so far is intrinsic to the digital object itself and not something that was specially structured and mapped on top of the object to support its management and reuse. From the point of view of preservation there is general theoretical agreement that 'the right metadata is key to preserving digital objects'.[63] As Ballegooie and Duff recently commented in an essay that explores 'Archival metadata', '[a]rchivists and records managers have always been metadata experts'.[64]

Predicting the value of metadata to future users of digital materials is difficult, but we can be fairly certain that future users will include both people and machines. They can play a role in rendering, understanding and validating digital materials. Metadata, 'data about data', serves the primary function of making other data useful. As NISO noted, metadata is 'structured information that describes, explains, locates, or otherwise makes it easier to retrieve, use, or manage' digital materials.[65] It is common now to classify metadata by function: descriptive, structural, administrative and contextual. Although we tend to consider metadata as an esoteric and specialised topic, we are all familiar with it in one way or another, although we may not refer to it as metadata.[66] There are a huge number of metadata initiatives and a broad range of metadata standards. In 2004 James Turner of the Université de Montréal developed the MetaMap 'as a study aid and reference tool for understanding metadata standards, sets and initiatives (MSSIs) in the area of information management'.[67]

Based on our contemporary evidence we suppose that metadata are important, but in reality '[w]e do not have enough experience to indicate whether the metadata these systems record, or plan to record, are adequate for the purpose'.[68] To manage digital objects it will be essential to adopt good descriptive, structural and administrative metadata standards and there is much good guidance that can be given in this area. The crucial metadata that need concern us is preservation metadata. PREMIS defined preservation metadata 'as the information a repository uses to support the digital preservation process'.[69] This includes, for example, evidence of provenance and relationships, as well as technical, administrative and structural metadata.

PREMIS has proposed a Data Dictionary that provides a core set of preservation metadata elements along with a detailed description. The PREMIS team adopted the point of view that the critical metadata were those that function in 'maintaining viability, renderability, understandability, authenticity, and identity in a preservation context'.[70] In deciding which metadata to use PREMIS puts stress on core metadata, which are 'things that most working repositories are likely to need to know in order to support digital preservation'.[71] The PREMIS data model rests on a conceptualisation of metadata that is clear and implementable. From a records management vantage point, other emerging models such as ISO 23801-1:2005 will probably be of even greater pertinence, but at the beginning of 2006 ISO 23801 is still a work in progress.[72]

We might now wonder where metadata come from. Some metadata are inherent in the digital object itself (as we have seen from the discussions of legal cases above). A small amount can be extracted automatically (e.g. the National Library of New Zealand (NLNZ) tool to extract technical metadata from a narrow class of digital object types) or is captured at creation, modification or ingest (e.g. event metadata). However, most metadata must be generated by human intervention and this is especially true for contextual metadata. It is this need for human intervention that makes metadata so costly and the relationship between cost and benefit so difficult to justify. How much metadata is enough and what is too much? Crucial in all this is establishing a cost–benefit relationship between the effort necessary to create the metadata and the usefulness of the metadata in ensuring access, management and preservation. Currently metadata is labour-intensive to create and one of our objectives should be to change this. Recovering digital objects and recreating the interrelationships between them without adequate metadata is complex, as the data recovery industry shows.[73]

Metadata interoperability will become increasingly important. The Clever Recordkeeping Metadata Project (CRKM) (at Monash University) is leading the effort to support the exchange of metadata between different business, archival and records management systems. This ability to translate metadata between systems will allow us to go beyond the use of metadata to support the reuse over time of digital entities and their exchange between repositories to:

> enable archivists in the 21st century to go beyond Scott's original vision of sequential multiple provenance to build archival systems that encompass Chris Hurley's 'parallel provenance' and Jeannette Bastian's communities of records and negotiate the complex matrices of mutual rights and obligations that Eric Ketelaar's vision of shared ownership and joint heritage invokes.[74]

Curiously, we have few practical examples of the implementation of preservation metadata and, to the best of my knowledge, can point to no cases as of the end of 2005 where they have been used in practice to support preservation processes.

Automation and preservation

What is evident is that automation is a critical step in the development of preservation solutions.[75] For example, the quantities, quality and level of metadata consistency required for managing digital objects within repositories require that its extraction be in some way automated.[76] To aid the process of ingest, selection and appraisal, for the preservation of digital material, the goal of a Glasgow-led team is to look at ways of automating the semantic metadata extraction process and create a prototype tool, and to integrate this tool with other metadata extraction tools and ingest processes used to underpin the automatic population of document repositories.[77] While our research focuses on metadata extraction in the area of textual documents, some very good work has been done with audiovisual content elsewhere.[78] We are using linguistic and layout analysis techniques to automate this process of metadata extraction. The research within this task can be divided into six domains: (a) selecting metadata to be extracted and that can be extracted; (b) integrating previous and current related research; (c) designing a prototype metadata extraction tool; (d) implementing a prototype metadata extraction tool; (e) establishing a well-designed corpus of documents to validate the effectiveness of the prototype; and (f) testing and refining the prototype. Progress has been made with (a) to (c) above. As this research focuses mainly on automation of the acquisition of descriptive metadata, it will be of most immediate value to the digital library community and will only provide a part of the metadata required in the archival environment.

Even where the exchange of a limited range of metadata can be instituted it results in reduced costs and improved accessibility of digital information by end users. There are numerous projects that aim to improve access to information through maximising the availability and use of metadata. For instance, the Commonwealth Metadata Pilot Project aims to improve access to Australian government information published online by automating the contribution of metadata to the national bibliographic database, and by automating the archiving of content associated with the metadata in PANDORA, Australia's web archive.[79]

In general, however, if preservation is to become mainstream then automation of as wide a range of processes as is possible is essential. Automation combined with workflow modelling and streamlining will reduce costs and help to focus preservation processes. Stephan Heuscher, formerly of the Swiss Federal Archives, has argued that, if we are to manage the process of ingest effectively, we need both methods and tools for modelling these processes.[80] Essentially the objective has to be to shift as much of the preservation activity from a manual process to an automatic (or at least a semi-automatic) one. By automating the work flows we can integrate services (e.g. checking of file format or representation information registries to determine whether the form in which a particular piece of data is represented is appropriate), logging and record creation can be standardised, and costs can be reduced, errors eliminated, and security and reliability enhanced.

Ingest

One of the challenges for digital preservation professionals is to decide at what level to ingest materials. Imagine for a moment that your archives or library was offered an unplanned bequest of the computer files of a local Member of Parliament who had unexpectedly died. The executors of his will offer to make copies of the files onto portable media themselves or to deposit copies along with the laptop and desktop computers the parliamentarian had been using for the past three and six years respectively. What do you do? Obviously the copy onto some portable medium has advantages; it is easy to handle and can probably be put on a shelf until you have time to deal with it (say, for a year or so), but a copy, as any computer forensic professional will assure you, is not necessarily complete – metadata may be missing and certainly deleted files will not appear in the copy although they might be present on the existing hardware.[81] If you do not accept the computers, you should at least seek a clone of the discs.

In most situations this kind of scenario will not arise as most ingests will be planned and the archive will have some influence over the process of preparation of material for submission. Indeed it may even have had a hand in the specification of the system that was used to generate the digital materials.

The ingest process is not just about ensuring that the digital materials that you have acquired are effectively placed in the repository; it is also about controlling the ingest process so that you can verify that the items ingested have not compromised the reliability, usability or authenticity of the digital entities themselves. This ensures that no extra baggage (e.g. viruses) is inadvertently brought into the repository, which might put the contents of the repository at risk.

Archives will be ingesting digital objects from one of four main classes. Each of these classes has its own unique properties which have an impact on an archive's ability to select, acquire, manage, preserve and provide access to them. The ease with which the archive can control the process by which materials are prepared for appraisal and acquisition and the amount of effort that will be involved in ingesting the material into its repository will depend not only on the types of objects. It will also reflect such factors as the number of instances of the object type, the complexity of any individual instance, the file formats and to a lesser extent the volume of the object. For example, it may prove less labour-intensive and technically challenging to ingest large digital objects of low complexity in comparison with large numbers of smaller composite digital objects created using specialised software and having a high degree of interconnectedness between elements. The ease of handling composite objects will also be influenced by the degree of stickiness of the bindings between the composite elements.

Digital entities are likely to be presented to collecting or institutional archives in one of four ways. The handling of each class of digital material will require different policies and procedures. In each case it is likely that collecting archives will encounter a greater diversity of content than, say, corporate or institutional archives.

- *Portable objects.* This includes CD-ROMs, tapes, solid-state devices and other portable media that house content ranging from databases, documents, audio, images or even software. The collecting archive is likely to have little control over how this material is submitted, although some archives will be in a position to collaborate with the content creators to improve the process by which digital objects are created and presented for archiving. In many instances organisations will put in place systems that add metadata and functionality to ease ingest. The diversity of organisations producing digital objects on portable media and the variety of types of objects mean that the archives will be confronted with an expanding, rather than narrowing, range of digital objects. Some will require specialised analysis and attention if they are to be ingested into the digital repository and even then it may only prove feasible to preserve the bit stream and not the capability to render the content of the object or to recreate its functionality. The archive will need to decide whether ingesting the bit stream is sufficient or whether the original medium (and any packaging) needs to be retained as well, even though it is unlikely that suitable peripheral devices (e.g. tape drives) will be available in the future to access the material subsequently.[82]

- *Transfers.* These will usually arrive as electronic transfers (frequently online) from within the organisation itself, although in the case of national or local archives the depositing bodies may be different institutional units. In general, these will be planned deposits and the institutional archive will have some control over how the content was created and submitted (e.g. formats, documentation).

- *Unpublished personal digital materials.* These digital objects will be mainly documents (e.g. drafts of publications, e-mails) of authors and politicians and are most likely to be encountered in a collecting archive. For the most part these will in the near term be produced with fairly standard application packages and be primarily stand-alone documents, suites of images, small-scale personal databases or e-mail records. Discussions with potential depositors would provide information about how the material should be configured and presented for deposit and enable the depositor to provide contextual metadata which otherwise might be unobtainable. For instance, where depositors can be encouraged to produce crucial metadata or where they can note the interrelationship between particular materials, the processes of ingest and cataloguing can be enhanced and the labour required reduced.

- *Outputs of digitisation programmes.* Archives increasingly aim to represent their analogue holdings in digital form and, as Anderson's chapter in this volume makes evident, users expect access in digital form even to materials that were created in analogue. By controlling how digital objects are created, the metadata that is created along with them, and the processes by which they are delivered to the digital repository, the effort required to ingest can then be contained.

The nature of the objects has an impact on the effort that is involved in bringing the objects into the archive holdings. Standards in handling digital objects have an impact on their preservation, authenticity and integrity, and how they can be delivered to users. It is widely recognised that, where preservation functionality can be built into systems that are employed to create the digital objects, the costs of selection, ingest, preservation and access can be reduced.[83] The application of the continuum model (see Chapter 1 in this volume) should mean that those institutions and individuals using a records management system would not encounter situations of this kind. In general, collectors of digital objects rarely have control over the construction of any of the digital objects that they will be ingesting. Cunningham and Phillips, commenting on the situation in Australia in relation to government publications, noted that '[t]here is no standard approach by government agencies for creating, describing and organising their publications, and each is different.'[84] They recognise the need to impose standards if the costs of ingesting these materials are to be contained.[85] ERPANET investigated issues surrounding the ingest of some classes of digital materials and released guidance on the process.[86]

Perhaps a model will help

Adopting a shared model to approach digital preservation may improve communication between curators and users. One preservation model in common use is the Reference Model for an Open Archival Information System (OAIS) (ISO 14721:2003),[87] which specifies a conceptual framework for a generic archival system. OAIS was developed by key players in the space community under the aegis of the Consultative Committee for Space Data Systems and is now an ISO Standard. In creating OAIS, space researchers noted that observations made in space science were both irreplaceable and were not reproducible.[88] If the data were to be made accessible in the future, they and their associated metadata would need to be moved across different technologies. The model reflects a recognition that information will be represented in different formats and that these representations will change over time. OAIS details all the functions of a preservation environment. It charts the preparation, submission, storage, maintenance, retrieval and delivery of digital objects. The model is implementation independent and could be delivered using a range of technologies and at a variety of scales.

The OAIS reference model establishes a common framework of terms and concepts and maps the basic functions of an archival system: ingest, data management, archival storage, administration, preservation planning and access. Representation information (RI) details how the intellectual content is represented and how to extract meaningful information from a stream of bytes. Content information (CI) is the combination of the original bit stream along with the representation information. Preservation description information (PDI) contains the additional information required to identify the object, describe the processes applied to it and support the understanding of the content over time. A designated community identifies the users of the preserved data and itself will change over time. The knowledge base for a designated community indicates that the group has some prior level of knowledge and familiarity with the content, allowing the representation information required to be limited. The model classifies information into object information classes – content, preservation description, packaging and description. A content data package is then represented using a series of information packages; a container encapsulates the content information and the preservation description information. There are also information packages for submission, archival storage/management and dissemination, which identify the changes that are made to the information package as it passes through the system.

Key to OAIS is the concept of the designated community and the relationship between the producer and the consumer of information. The key step is to use OAIS to develop repositories. It is the repositories that will 'carry the load'. Where these repositories instantiate concepts expressed in the OAIS model, they go a long way towards ensuring that the architectures will be robust enough to ensure the ability to ingest, manage and make accessible the materials the designated communities expect them to handle. Do bear in mind, however, that the OAIS model is just one model preservation environment. The OAIS model is not without its critics,[89] and there are other approaches emerging such as a bottom-up approach proposed by David Rosenthal and his colleagues[90] or the one that underpins ISO 15489.

Get a digital repository

Underpinning all digital preservation activities is repository design. Repositories are not unlike the buildings that house traditional archives and libraries – they need to be renewed and the contents they hold shifted to upgraded shelving or newer environments.[91] As we have seen earlier, one of the characteristics of technology is its fluidity. This means that a repository is only a temporary holding bay, even if we are thinking in five- to ten-year time spans. Although taking a strongly OAIS and library-centric view, OCLC and RLG's report on the attributes of trusted repositories[92] provides a high-level model for the design, delivery and maintenance of a digital repository. It outlines the processes that need to be certified and auditable if an institution is to be said to be running a trusted digital repository. For example, they press for clear statements by repository owners on such matters as policies and assumptions (e.g. practices, environment and security), definition of processes in place to manage fidelity checks for ingest, and metadata creation and management processes. Central to the RLG/OCLC model is the recognition that all processes related to the running of the repository need to be well documented, auditable and validated.

At the simplest level, a repository must be able to accept digital objects regardless of type, format or medium.[93] Once the items have been ingested into the repository they must be held in a secure way and the authenticity and integrity of the digital entities must not be compromised. Materials ingested into the repository must be capable of being output in formats that could be ingested into a 'next-generation repository'. Documentation must be accessible and disaster recovery functionality inherent in the design. Repositories will be used by both people and machines. Repositories will be of value to depositors and to organisations needing to ensure secure access to their digital records and assets.

During the process of ingesting materials, metadata including descriptive, administrative and contextual types will be attached to the objects. Among these metadata will be persistent identifiers. Persistent identifiers provide a method of uniquely identifying a digital object. There are almost as many persistent identifier schemes as there are flavours of ice cream. Examples include DOI (Digital Object Identifier), Persistent Handles, ARK (Archival Resource Key) and Persistent Uniform Resource Locator (PURL). Each one has its strengths.[94] Your repository will need to adopt one scheme and decide at what level of granularity it will be used.

Change will be a feature of all repositories. The underlying storage technologies will be replaced on a regular basis, services will be closed down and new ones started, and workflows will be adapted as technology, policies or processes change. The holdings of the repositories will need to be moved to new storage media (i.e. refreshed), migrated or just emulated. If change is a feature of repositories, then flexibility in technical infrastructure and organisational approach is the necessary response.

In this volume Currall examines the security issues associated with digital information. Here we note only a few of the risks associated with information because, with an effective repository supported by robust policies and procedures, it is possible to manage these risks. Among the risks are accidental loss of records and digital assets, information leakage,[95] record duplication, unauthorised modification, loss of accessibility, severing of the relationship between the data and their metadata and loss of provenance evidence,[96] integrity and authenticity.

The Swiss Federal Archives' Archiving of Electronic Digital Data and Records (ARELDA) project sought a solution to the permanent archiving of digital records to enable it to fulfil its obligations under the Swiss Federal Archives Act. They are investing some 11 million euros in the development of the digital archive during the period 2001 to 2008. They expect their data storage requirements will grow at around 20 TB per year. We could have chosen the UK National Archives (Kew), the Dutch National Archives, the Swedish National Archives, the National Library of New Zealand (NLNZ) or the US National Archives as our examples. All these institutions are making substantial investments in establishing digital repositories to facilitate the storage of and access to digital assets, whether records or published resources. These are all expensive operations with development costs ranging from 24 million NZ$ in the case of the NLNZ to more than 300 million US$ in the case of the National Archives and Records Administration (NARA). These will all be gold-plated solutions. Most institutions cannot afford solutions of this kind. This does not mean that you should do nothing.

The National Archives of Australia (NAA), in defining its digital preservation repository for public records, has interpreted the OAIS model in a way that has made it possible for them to establish a cost-effective preservation environment.[97] The functional requirements at repository level can be made quite simple where the need is to link the digital object, which might be stored as a bit stream in the file system, with an XML or SQL database containing the metadata about the object. The digital repository structure deployed by the NAA is designed to minimise access to the underlying repository layer by users. By isolating users from the raw storage, the repository provides an additional layer of information security. Another key feature is the decision by the designers to enable the objects to be examined at ingest (e.g. checked for such unwanted payloads as viruses), processed and wrapped before being placed into the repository.[98]

The heart of repositories is not the technology. It is the policies and procedures that underlie them: deposit agreements, submission information guidelines, management plans, access policies, disaster recovery plans and preservation strategies (e.g. migration). The greatest challenges to the survival of repositories is not the technology, but the organisational and cultural apparatus that makes the operations work and how the institution establishes the trust of the communities of repository users. How can a repository secure the trust of depositors, users (people and machines) and regulatory bodies that they have the mechanisms in place to secure digital assets for the long term? What steps will they need to take to maintain that trust? And, most importantly, what happens if they lose it?

Repository management can be a highly complex task. One way to reduce the complexity is to identify a set of basic repository management functions such as storing, copying, depositing and maintenance of disparate types of data. For the objects and metadata it holds, a digital repository must provide secure storage, facilitate the maintenance of integrity and authenticity, and permit the authorised destruction of items. Five primary functions that must be enabled at an administrative level are ingest, retrieve, track, verify and destroy, and at a user level retrieval and verification are the key services that are needed.[99] A number of projects have focused on laying down the foundations for the long-term storage of digital objects.[100] There are projects that have developed off-the-shelf architectures and solutions: Flexible Extensible Digital Object and Repository Architecture (Fedora),[101] DSpace[102] and LOCKSS.[103] None these are general information preservation environments or can fulfil the requirements of being a trusted repository application.

More importantly, none of these repository models or applications integrates preservation functionality. The DELOS Preservation Cluster's Cologne Team has led the establishment of a complete design for the persistency modules that need to be included in the design process of any digital repository.[104] The work completed includes a Unified Modelling Language (UML) model for preservation components that could be used in the design of any digital repository.

One way to address the trust problem noted above is through establishing an audit and certification process for repositories. So far mechanisms to support audit and certification of repositories are still in the developmental phase. In the USA, RLG and NARA established the Digital Repository Certification Task Force, which in 2005 published a draft checklist for certifiable elements of a digital archive.[105] There are, however, approaches open to institutions of all sizes from archives to companies that will position your organisation to be prepared to take advantage of audit and certification schemes that may come into place. With the best will in the world, audit processes do not shield organisations against security breaches or disasters that result in leakage or loss of information.

If your organisation wishes to establish itself as a trusted repository, the following nine steps should lay the foundation for a sustainable repository infrastructure:

- Define the objectives and aims of your repository and from those specify the services it will provide. The objectives and services should be documented.

- Determine whether your organisation is best placed to develop a repository on its own or whether it should establish a shared repository or purchase use of repository services.

- Develop policies and procedures for managing all processes: ingest, data management, archival storage, administration, preservation planning and access.

- Put in place mechanisms to monitor the application of these policies and how effective they are.

- Define senior management roles and responsibilities in relationship to repositories.

- Ensure that all services, technologies (hardware and software), exceptions and practices are documented.

- Develop and maintain risk registers that clearly identify risks, indicate their likelihood, specify their probable impact, describe how you would address the risk if it did occur and note what you are doing to avoid its arising.

- Maintain status reports and minutes of meetings.
- Define, implement, monitor and test disaster recovery services.

Future research directions

Digital curation and preservation is a fertile research domain. Research problems include theoretical issues, methodological challenges and practical needs. After more than twenty years of research in digital curation and preservation, the actual theories, methods and technologies that can either foster or ensure digital longevity remain startlingly limited. If you contrast Roberts (1994) with Tibbo (2003) it is obvious that, although our understanding of the problems surrounding digital preservation has advanced, the approaches to preservation remain limited.[106] There are many possible explanations for this situation; for instance, there has been a lack of appreciation of the research challenges posed by digital preservation, a lack of a sense of urgency, the lack of proven business cases that might have encouraged the development of this as a research or technology sector, the fact that in the past the research agenda has been driven by information professionals working in memory institutions or corporate records management teams, the limited funding for this kind of research and, of course, the speed of technological development. Recently, changes in the research and technology landscape have raised research interest in the challenges surrounding digital curation and made it evident that there are substantial commercial opportunities. For instance, in 2001 the National Science Foundation (NSF) in the United States through its Digital Library Program (DLI2) and the European Commission through the Network of Excellence it funds in the area of Digital Libraries (DELOS) supported a workgroup to propose a research agenda in the area of digital preservation.[107] This research agenda has been used by the European Commission and others to plan funding programmes. More recently an international workshop co-sponsored by the Joint Information Systems Committee (JISC), the Digital Curation Centre (DCC), the Council for the Central Laboratory of the Research Councils (CCLRC) and the British Library brought together experts to examine the challenges to digital curation and what our research focus should be during the next decade.[108]

Conclusions

Long-term access to digital materials is a process. Charles Dollar commented that to secure digital materials for 100 years we should think in shorter periods because there is currently no 100-year solution.[109] Preservation is hard and the hype has made it harder. There is a general belief that digital technologies make work easier and securing access cheaper. In many ways this is so. Preservation requires active engagement. Solutions that you will put in place today you will replace tomorrow. You should think of digital preservation as a dynamic process that requires focus, policies, procedures and planning. You should not think of it as primarily a technical activity because it is not.

Digital preservation processes should ensure that we pass usable, authentic and reliable evidence to the future. Current approaches are inadequate. There are seven proactive steps that practising archivists and records managers can take to ensure that they are acting to secure digital records and resources in their care:

- Keep skills appropriately up to date.
- Act as an active advocate for digital preservation activities.
- Ensure that your organisation has effective policies and procedures governing the creation, management (both retention and disposal) and curation of digital materials.
- Be attentive to the maintenance of the digital materials in your care (e.g. note when it is time to refresh media and track formats in which your holdings are represented to make certain that you migrate before 'migration pathways' for the format disappear).
- Avoid proprietary standards for representation, encoding, software, hardware and especially for back-up services.
- Do not assume that there is a single solution to all your preservation challenges or that, if you adopt one approach for a set of digital materials at a given time, you will not in ten years' time use a different approach.
- Whatever preservation approaches you apply (e.g. media refreshing, migration, emulation) they must be controlled, monitored, documented, audited and validated.

The conceptual and methodological developments in the creation and management of trusted repositories, user needs assessment and evaluation, and the appraisal and ingest of digital materials are radically altering how we think about and handle digital materials. By understanding just how these developments enable us to document society in the digital age, we can appreciate the impact that changes in the way we communicate and create documents is having on the record we will be passing to future generations. The commoditisation of information leads to a change in the perception of how and why it should be managed. The archival profession is at the heart of this change.

Acknowledgements

Thanks to my Digital Curation Centre colleagues Andrew McHugh, Maureen Pennock and Adam Rusbridge, and to Hans Hofman of the Dutch National Archives, Professor Andrew Prescott of the University of Sheffield, Professor Helen Tibbo of the University of North Carolina (Chapel Hill) and Alistair Tough of the University of Glasgow, who all made valuable suggestions. I am grateful to Michael Day for discussions of PREMIS. Any errors or omissions are, of course, my own.

Notes

1. Cunningham, A. and Phillips, M., 'Accountability and accessibility: ensuring the evidence of e-governance in Australia', *Aslib Proceedings: New Information Perspectives*, 57 (4), 2005, p. 314.
2. Tharlet, Eve, *The Elves of Cologne* (Zurich, 2005), and Kopisch A., *Die Heizenelmannchen* (Cologne, 1836).
3. Commission on Preservation and Access and the Research Libraries Group, *Preserving Digital Information*, Report of the Task Force on Archiving of Digital Information (Mountain View, CA, 1996).
4. An excellent source for information about work in digital preservation is the PADI subject gateway (*http://www.nla.gov.au/padi/*). Another is the Kennisbank/Knowledge Bank of Digitale Duurzaamheid, *http://www.digitaleduurzaamheid.nl/index.cfm?paginakeuze=65&categorie=2* (accessed February 2006).
5. Discussion about the issues of web archiving figure hugely in the current literature. We have excluded them from discussion here because website preservation is a sub-set from an archival point of view of good records management. See, for instance, Dollar, Charles, *Archival Preservation of Smithsonian Web Resources: Strategies, Principles, and Best Practices* (Washington, DC, 2001), *http://www.si.edu/archives/archives/dollar%20report.html*; McClure, Charles and Sprehe, Timothy, *Guidelines for*

Electronic Records Management on State and Federal Agency Websites (New York and Washington, DC, 1998), *http://slis-two.lis.fsu.edu/~cmcclure/ guidelines.html*; Phillips, John T., 'The challenge of web site records preservation', *Information Management Journal*, 3 (1), 2003, pp. 42–51. There are tools for harvesting websites remotely, such as HTTrack, *http://www.httrack.com/page/1/en/index.html* (accessed February 2006).

6. Ross, S. and Day, M. (eds), *DCC Digital Curation Manual* (Glasgow, 2005 onwards), *http://www.dcc.ac.uk/resource/curation-manual/*, includes some 45 chapters on issues surrounding digital preservation and is managed by the Digital Curation Centre.

7. Ross, S. and McHugh, A., 'Audit and certification: creating a mandate for the Digital Curation Centre', *Diginews*, 9 (5), 2005, *http://www.rlg.org/ en/page.php?Page_ID=20793#article1* (accessed February 2006).

8. An excellent summary of the problem is Cordeiro, M.I., 'From rescue to long-term maintenance: preservation as a core function in the management of digital assets', *VINE*, 34 (1), 2004, pp. 6–16.

9. Sharrock, D., 'Aznar accused of destroying Madrid bomb evidence and deceiving the public', *The Times*, 14 December 2004, *http://www .timesonline.co.uk/article/0,,3-1402824,00.html*.

10. Ross, S. and Gow, A., *Digital Archaeology? Rescuing Neglected or Damaged Data Resources* (London, 1999), *http://www.ukoln.ac.uk/ services/elib/papers/supporting/pdf/p2.pdf* (accessed February 2006).

11. InterPARES Authenticity Task Force, *Authenticity Task Force Report on the Long-term Preservation of Authentic Electronic Records: Findings of the InterPARES Project* (Vancouver, 2002), *http://www.interpares .org/book/index.cfm* (accessed February 2006).

12. Ross, S., 'Position paper on integrity and authenticity of digital cultural heritage objects', *Integrity and Authenticity of Digital Cultural Heritage Objects*, Thematic Issue 1, 2002, pp. 7–8; also available at *http:// www.digicult.info*.

13. ERPANET, with funding from the Swiss Federal Government and the European Commission (IST-2001-32706), led by the Humanities Advanced Technology and Information Institute (HATII) at the University of Glasgow (United Kingdom), and its partners the Schweizerisches Bundesarchiv (Switzerland), ISTBAL at the Università di Urbino (Italy) and Nationaal Archief van Nederland (Netherlands), worked between November 2001 and the end of October 2004 to enhance the preservation of cultural and scientific digital objects.

14. *http://www.dpc.delos.info*. DELOS: A Network of Excellence on Digital Libraries funded under the 6th Framework's IST Programme. The Project falls under thematic Priority: IST-2002-2.3.1.12 (Technology-enhanced Learning and Access to Cultural Heritage). Its project number is: 507618. DELOS focuses on six primary research domains ranging from digital library architectures to evaluation. The DELOS digital preservation cluster (DELOS-DPC) brings together researchers from seven European countries to lead cutting-edge research in digital preservation.

15. Duranti, L. (ed.), *The Long-term Preservation of Authentic Electronic Records: Findings of the InterPARES Project* (San Miniato, 2005).

16. InterPARES Authenticity Task Force report, op. cit.
17. Ross, S., 'Reflections on the impact of the Lund Principles on European approaches to digitisation', in *Strategies for a European Area of Digital Cultural Resources: Towards a Continuum of Digital Heritage*, Conference Report, European Conference, The Hague, The Netherlands, 15–16 September 2004, pp. 88–98.
18. Bradley, R., 'Digital authenticity and integrity: digital cultural heritage documents as research resources', *portal: Libraries and the Academy*, 5 (2), 2005, pp. 165–75.
19. Park, E., 'Understanding authenticity in records and information management: analyzing practitioner constructs', *American Archivist*, 64 (2), 2001, pp. 270–91.
20. MacNeil, H., 'Providing grounds for trust: developing conceptual requirements for the long-term preservation of authentic electronic records', *Archivaria*, 50, 2000, pp. 52–78; MacNeil, H., 'Providing grounds for trust II: the findings of the Authenticity Task Force of InterPARES', *Archivaria*, 54, 2002, pp. 24–58.
21. ERPANET conducted around 100 case studies between 2002 and the end of 2004, of which 78 are published on the ERPANET website and are forthcoming in Ross, S. et al., *ERPANET Case Studies in Digital Preservation* (San Miniato, forthcoming 2006).
22. Ross, S., Greenan, M. and McKinney, P., 'Digital preservation strategies: the initial outcomes of the ERPANET case studies', in *Preservation of Electronic Records: New Knowledge and Decision-making* (Ottawa, 2004), pp. 99–111, or Ross, S., Greenan, M. and McKinney, P., 'Strategie per la conservazione digitale: descrizione e risultati dei primi studi di casi di ERPANET', *Archivi e Computer*, XIV/3.04, 2004, pp. 99–122.
23. ERPANET, 2003, 'Policies for Digital Preservation', ERPANET Training Seminar, Paris, 29–30 January 2003, *http://www.erpanet.org/events/2003/paris/ERPAtraining-Paris_Report.pdf* (accessed February 2006), p. 16.
24. The findings of ERPANET in Europe are also borne out by evidence in the USA. In the recent case of *In re Old Banc One Shareholders Securities Litigation*, 2005 US Dist. LEXIS 32154 (ND Ill., 8 December 2005), 'Bank employees testified they did not know missing documents should have been retained, and the bank did not inform employees of the need to retain documents for this litigation or have employees read and follow the electronic version of the policy that was established.'
25. Sanett, Shelby, 'Toward developing a framework of cost elements for preserving authentic electronic records into perpetuity', *College and Research Libraries*, 63 (5), 2002, pp. 388–404.
26. Ibid.
27. *http://www.cbs.nl* (accessed February 2006).
28. ERPANET Case Studies, *http://www.erpanet.org* (accessed February 2006).
29. ERPANET, Business Models Related to Digital Preservation, 2004, *http://www.erpanet.org/events/2004/amsterdam/Amsterdam_Report.pdf* (accessed February 2006), p. 17.
30. For example, InterPARES I (*http://www.interpares.org*, accessed February 2006).

31. PREMIS Working Group, *Implementing Preservation Repositories for Digital Materials* (Dublin, OH, and Mountain View, CA, 2004) (available at *http://www.oclc.org/research/projects/pmwg/surveyreport.pdf*, accessed February 2006), p. 13.

32. Hofman, H. and Lunghi, M., 'Enabling persistent and sustainable digital cultural heritage in Europe: the Netherlands questionnaire responses summary and Position Paper', 2004, *http://www.minervaeurope.org/publications/globalreport/globalrepdf04/enabling.pdf* (accessed February 2006); XLIV, presented at the *Dutch Presidency on Towards A Continuum of Digital Heritage – Strategies for a European Area of Digital Cultural Resources.*

33. *Zubulake v. UBS Warburg*, 217 FRD 309 (SDNY 2003). This is one of a series of rulings in this case.

34. See Memorandum Opinion in *U.S. v. Philip Morris USA, Inc., et al.*, Civ. Action No. 99-2946 (DDC), dated 7 July 2004, at 2 n.3, available at *http://www.dcd.uscourts.gov/99-2496ak.pdf* (accessed February 2006).

35. *Armstrong v. Executive Office of the President*, 1 F.3d 1274 (DC Cir. 1993). (Note: The decision was reversed on other grounds, 90 F.3d 553 (DC Cir. 1996).)

36. Wallace, D.A., 'Recordkeeping and electronic mail policy: the state of thought and the state of the practice', Society of American Archivists (Orlando, FL, 1998), *http://www.mybestdocs.com/wallace.html* (accessed February 2006).

37. Samuel, J., 'Electronic mail', in Higgs, E. (ed.), *History and Electronic Artefacts* (Oxford, 1998), p. 111.

38. A study in early 2005 conducted by AIIM and Kahn Consulting, 'Electronic Communication Policies and Procedures', which attracted over 1,000 respondents, found among responding organisations that while '86% tell employees how they should use e-mail, ... only 39% tell employees where, how, or by whom email messages should be retained' (Skjekkeland, Atle, 'Email mismanagement: a looming disaster', *M-iD*, 2005, pp. 49–50).

39. Perer, A., Shneiderman, B. and Oard, D.W., 'Using rhythms of relationships to understand email archives' (n.d. but probably 2005), (*http://hcil.cs.umd.edu/trs/2005-08/2005-08.pdf*), p. 18. In this study the team applied a new approach to understanding e-mail archives in a study of 45,000 messages collected over 15 years by a single individual (accessed 7 December 2005).

40. Tyler, J.R., Wilkinson, D.M. and Huberman, B.A., 'Email as spectroscopy: automated discovery of community structure within organizations', *Communities and Technologies*, 2003, pp. 81–96 (alternatively at: *http://www.hpl.hp.com/research/idl/papers/email/email.pdf*). These communities often transcend organisational structures. Currently there are few instances where it is possible to obtain data to carry out more complex studies. One possible source that archivists might use to investigate how researchers in the future might examine archives of e-mail will be to experiment with the Enron Email Dataset. The dataset is available at *http://www.cs.cmu.edu/~enron* and contains over 500,000 messages. B. Klimt and Y. Yang noted that the original dataset contained some 619,446 messages

from 158 users before they produced a 'cleaned Enron corpus' and this includes some 225,000 e-mails of 151 senior executives during the period 1997 to 2004 (see, for example, *http://sonic.ncsa.uiuc.edu/enron/about.htm*). There is a discrepancy between the scale of 'clean' corpus as described on the website and by Klimt and Yang in 'Introducing the Enron Corpus', 2004, *http://www.ceas.cc/papers-2004/168.pdf*. Most of the interest in the dataset has so far been from communications and information retrieval experts. The cleaning of the dataset removed, for example, duplicates, but that reduces the archival value of the dataset as duplicates tell their own story. (Sites accessed February 2006.)

41. Donath, J., 'Visualizing email archives – draft', 2004, *http://smg.media.mit.edu/papers/Donath/EmailArchives.draft.pdf* (accessed February 2006), p. 2.
42. ERPANET, 2003, 'The long-term preservation of databases', *http://www.erpanet.org/events/2003/bern/Bern_Report_final.pdf*.
43. Buneman, P., Khanna, S., Tajima, K. and Tan, W.-C., 'Archiving scientific data', *ACM Transactions on Database Systems*, 29 (1), 2002, pp. 2–42.
44. For Xinq, see *http://www.nla.gov.au/xinq/download.html*.
45. Heuscher, S., Järmann, S., Keller-Marxer, P. and Möhle, F., 'Providing authentic long-term archival access to complex relational data', European Space Agency Symposium on *Ensuring Long-Term Preservation and Adding Value to Scientific and Technical Data* (Frascati, Italy, 2004), *http://arxiv.org/pdf/cs.DL/0408054*.
46. Bone, J. and Blanford, N., 'UN office doctored report on murder of Hariri', 22 October 2005, *Times Online*, *http://www.timesonline.co.uk/article/0,,251-1837848,00.html* (accessed 15 December 2005). In another case the failure of authors to note that Microsoft Word also holds revision history metadata enabled Richard M. Smith to identify the individuals who had been responsible for the last edits of a document and this contributed to our understanding of how the document evolved. 'IRAQ – Its Infrastructure of Concealment, Deception and Intimidation', released by the Prime Minister's Office on 6 February 2003. An analysis of the log can be found at *http://www.computerbytesman.com/privacy/blair.htm*. These tracking facilities within documentary editing software are often referred to as 'hidden dangers', but in litigation and to future scholars they may provide sources of valuable information. As a reaction to this, there is an increasing tendency for official documents to be released as PDFs rather than in their native word-processed formats (e.g. Danish Prime Minister, Anders Fogh Rasmussen, see Norup, T., 'Danish PM's private communications disclosed by MS Word', *The Risks Digest: Forum on Risks to the Public in Computers and Related Systems*, 23 (12), 12 January 2004, *http://catless.ncl.ac.uk/Risks/23.12.html#subj4*). See also the case of the SCO Group suit against DaimlerChrysler (2004) where a document created in Microsoft Word enabled lawyers to see that the SCO Group had spent time trying to aim the suit at Bank of America.
47. For a further discussion of this from a risk point of view, see Byres, S., 'Scalable exploitation of, and responses to information leakage through hidden data in published documents', 2003, *http://www.user-agent*

.org/word_docs.pdf, or Byres, S., 'Information leakage caused by hidden data in published documents', *IEEE Security and Privacy*, 2 (2), 2004, pp. 23–7. Remarkably, Byres found that among 100,000 documents downloaded from the web all had hidden information with 50 per cent having more than 50 words, 33 per cent having up to 500, and 10 per cent more that 500 words. This provides us with a contemporary example of the creation of tracks of document development that may help future scholars to understand how they were shaped.

48. ERPANET Case Studies. We had similar findings at other institutions, such as the International Labour Organisation.

49. In earlier cases the court recognised the plaintiff's need for access in electronic form in *National Union Elec. Corp. v. Matsushita Elec. Ind. Co.*, 494 F. Supp. 1257 (ED Pa. 1980), and *In re Air Crash Disaster at Detroit Metro*, 130 FRD 634 (ED Mich. 1989), flight simulation data was ordered to be provided on computer-readable nine-track magnetic tape. In printouts it lacked the operational capabilities. Even when data was provided on paper in legal cases courts have ordered their production on digital media; see, for instance, *Timken Co. v. United States*, 659 F. Supp 239 (Ct. Int'l Trade, 1987).

50. See, for example, the ruling in the employment discrimination case *Adams v. Dan River Mills, Inc.*, 54 FRD 220 (WD Va. 1972).

51. *Linnen v. A.H. Robins Co.*, 1999, WL 462015 (Mass. Super. 16 June 1999). There are numerous other cases such as *Storch v. IPCO Safety Prods. Co.*, 1997 WL 401589 (ED Pa. 16 July 1997), where the court ruled that in a world '... where much of our information is transmitted by computer and computer discs, it is not unreasonable for the defendant to produce the information on computer disc for the plaintiff.'

52. Ross and Gow, op cit.

53. *http://docmorph.nlm.nih.gov/docmorph/docmorph.htm*; see also Walker, F. and Thoma, G., 'A web-based paradigm for file migration', *Proceedings of IS&T's 2004 Archiving Conference*, San Antonio, TX, April 2004, *http://docmorph.nlm.nih.gov/docmorph/IST2004.pdf*, pp. 93–7.

54. Wheatley, P., 'Migration – CAMiLEON discussion paper', *Ariadne*, 29, 2001, *http://www.ariadne.ac.uk/issue29/camileon/*.

55. Ross, S., *Changing Trains at Wigan: Digital Preservation and the Future of Scholarship* (London, 2000), *http://eprints.erpanet.org/45/01/seamusross_wigan_paper.pdf*, p. 20.

56. Trimble, G.R., 'Emulation of the IBM system/360 on a microprogrammable computer', International Symposium on Microarchitecture, Conference record of the 7th annual workshop on Microprogramming, Palo Alto, CA, 1974, pp. 141–50.

57. Rauch, C. and Rauber, A., 'Preserving digital media: towards a preservation solution evaluation metric', *Proceedings of the International Conference on Asian Digital Libraries* (Shanghai, 2004) (alternatively accessible at *http://www.dpc.delos.info/private/output/rau_icadl04.pdf*). See a case study on the application of the approach to audio and video files: Rauch, C., Pavuza, F., Strodl, S. and Rauber, A., 'Evaluating preservation strategies for audio and video files', *Proceedings of the DELOS Workshop on Digital*

Repositories: Interoperability and Common Service (Crete, 2005), http://www.dpc.delos.info/private/output/rau_digrep05.pdf.

58. Rauber, A. et al., 'DELOS DPC testbed: a framework for documenting the behaviour and functionality of digital objects and preservation strategies', in Thanos, C. (ed.), Delos Research Activities 2005 (Pisa, 2005), pp. 57–9.

59. Ross, op. cit., p. 5.

60. In re Verisign, Inc. Sec. Litig., 2004, WL 2445243 (ND Cal. 10 March 2004).

61. Williams v. Sprint/United Mgmt Co., 2005, WL 2401626 (D. Kan. 29 September 2005), the Memorandum and Order in the case (http://www.ksd.uscourts.gov/opinions/032200JWLDJW-3333.pdf).

62. Zenith Elec. Corp. v. WH-TV Broad. Corp., 2004, WL 1631676 (ND Ill., 19 July 2004).

63. Duff, W., Hofman, H. and Troemel, M., 'Getting what you want, knowing what you have, and keeping what you need', ERPANET Training Seminar Marburg, Briefing Paper (Glasgow, 2003), http://www.erpanet.org/events/2003/marburg/erpaTraining-Marburg_BriefingPaper.pdf, p. 3.

64. Van Ballegooie, M. and Duff, W., 'Archival metadata', in Ross, S. and Day, M. (eds), DCC Digital Curation Manual (Glasgow, 2006), http://www.dcc.ac.uk/resource/curation-manual/chapters/archival-metadata. They provide detailed discussions of the Pittsburgh Project's Business Acceptable Communications (BAC) model, Australian Recordkeeping Metadata Schema (RKMS), ISO Records Management Metadata, and the Public Record Office Victoria (VERS). There are many others.

65. NISO, Understanding Metadata (Bethesda, MD, 2004), http://www.niso.org/standards/resources/UnderstandingMetadata.pdf, p. 3.

66. Day, M., 'Metadata', in Ross, S. (ed.), DCC Digital Curation Manual (Glasgow, 2005) (available at http://www.dcc.ac.uk/resource/curation-manual/chapters/metadata, accessed 7 February 2006).

67. Turner, J.M., 'The MetaMap: a tool for learning about metadata standards, sets, and initiatives', in Bischoff, F.M., Hofman, H. and Ross, S. (eds), Metadata in Preservation: Selected Papers from an ERPANET Seminar at the Archives School Marburg, in Veröffentlichungen der Archivschule Marburg, Institut für Archivwissenschaft, 40, 2003, pp. 219–32. For the map itself, see: http://mapageweb.umontreal.ca/turner/. Other documentation schemata of note are those used in the audiovisual sector; see, for instance, Bauer, C., Rosensprung, F., Lajtos, S., Boch, L., Poncin, P. and Herben-Leffring, C., PrestoSpace Deliverable D15.1MDS1: Analysis of Current Audiovisual Documentation Models (Paris, 2005), http://www.prestospace.org/project/deliverables/D15-1_Analysis_AV_documentation_models.pdf.

68. PREMIS Working Group, 2004, p. 5.

69. PREMIS Working Group, Data Dictionary for Preservation Metadata (Dublin, OH and Mountain View, CA, 2005), OCLC and RLG, http://www.oclc.org/research/projects/pmwg/premis-final.pdf.

70. PREMIS Working Group, 2005, p. 9.

71. Ibid.

72. ISO 23081-1:2005, *Information and Documentation – Records Management Process – Metadata for Records – Part 1 – Principles* (Geneva, 2005), in conjunction with the subsequent two sections, will provide mechanisms to implement and use metadata within the framework of ISO 15489, *Information and Documentation – Records Management* (Geneva, 2001).

73. Ross and Gow, op. cit.

74. Evans, J., McKemmish, S. and Bhoday, K., 'Create once, use many times: the clever use of recordkeeping metadata for multiple archival purposes', *15ᵗʰ Annual International Congress on Archives* (Vienna, 2004), *http://www.wien2004.ica.orgimagesUpload/pres_174_MCKEMMISH_Z-McK%2001E.pdf*, p. 13.

75. Ross, S. and Hedstrom, M., 'Preservation research and sustainable digital libraries', *International Journal of Digital Libraries*, 5 (4), 2005, *http://eprints.erpanet.org/archive/00000095/*, pp. 317–25.

76. Greenberg, J., Spurgin, K. and Crystal, A., 'Final Report for the AMeGA (Automatic Metadata Generation Applications) Project', *International Journal of Metadata, Semantics and Ontologies*, 1 (1), 2006, *http://www.loc.gov/catdir/bibcontrol/lc_amega_final_report.pdf*, pp. 3–20.

77. Ross, S. and Kim, Y., 'Digital preservation automated ingest and appraisal metadata', in Thanos, C. (ed.), *DELOS Research Activities* (Pisa, 2005).

78. PrestoSpace, the FP6-funded project in the area of digital curation of audiovisual materials, has produced two state-of-the-art reports that deal with these issues – one looking at approaches to automated analysis of audiovisual content: Bailer, W., Höller, F., Messina, A., Airola, D., Schallauer, P. and Hausenblas, M., *PrestoSpace Deliverable D15.3 MDS3 State of the Art of Content Analysis Tools for Video, Audio and Speech* (Paris, 2005), *http://www.prestospace.org/project/deliverables/D15-3_Content_Analysis_Tools.pdf*.

79. *http://www.nla.gov.au/ntwkpubs/gw/65/html/p04a01.html*

80. Heuscher, S., 'Workflow modelling language evaluation for an archival environment', *Archivi e Computer*, XIV (3/04), 2004, pp. 123–40.

81. A good summary of this digital persistence can be found in Chapter 7 of Farmer, D. and Venema, W., *Forensic Discovery* (Boston, 2004). See also Ross and Gow, 1999, op. cit.

82. Johan Steenbakkers, in *The NEDLIB Guidelines – Setting up a Deposit System for Electronic Publications* (The Hague, 2000), argued that digital documents should be separated from their original carrier because the carriers were intended for publishing and not for archiving. While in digital management terms he is absolutely correct, there may be some curatorial benefits from retaining the original carriers. D. Swade of the Science Museum (London) has for more than a decade promoted this view ('Collecting software: preserving information in an object-centred culture', in Ross, S. and Higgs, E. (eds), *Electronic Information Resources and Historians: European Perspectives* (St Katharinen, 1993), pp. 93–104). Indeed, in at least one legal case the carrier was considered to be metadata.

83. Ross, 2000, op. cit., p. 15.

84. Cunningham and Phillips, op. cit., p. 310.

85. Ross, S., *Digital Library Development Review, National Library of New Zealand* (Wellington, 2003), *http://www.natlib.govt.nz/files/ross_report .pdf*, pp. 43–52.

86. ERPANET, 2004, *erpaguidance: Ingest Strategy, http://www.erpanet.org/ guidance/docs/ERPANETIngestTool.pdf.*

87. *Reference Model for an Open Archival Information System (OAIS)* – ISO 14721 (2002), *http://www.ccsds.org/documents/650x0b1.pdf* (accessed 10 October 2005).

88. Esanu, J., Davidson, J., Ross, S. and Anderson, W., 'Selection, appraisal, and retention of digital scientific data: highlights of an ERPANET/CODATA Workshop', *Data Science Journal*, 3, 30 December 2004, *http://journals.eecs.qub.ac.uk/codata/journal/Contents/3_04/3_ 04pdfs/DS390.pdf*, p. 230.

89. See, for instance, PREMIS Working Group, 2004, pp. 27–8.

90. Rosenthal, D.S.H., Robertson, T., Lipkis, T., Reich, V. and Morabito, S., 'Requirements for digital preservation systems', *D-Lib Magazine*, 11 (11), 2005.

91. Anderson, S. and Heery, R., *Digital Repositories Review* (London, 2005), *http://www.jisc.ac.uk/uploaded_documents/digital-repositories-review- 2005.pdf.*

92. RLG/OCLC Working Group on Digital Archive Attributes, *Trusted Digital Repositories: Attributes and Responsibilities*, 2002, *http://www.rlg .org/longterm/repositories.pdf.*

93. It might be possible to run a repository that specialised in handling a narrow range of object representation types, for example only handling image formats.

94. ERPANET, Workshop on Persistent Identifiers, 2004, *http://www.erpanet .org/events/2004/cork/Cork%20Report.pdf.*

95. There are many high-profile cases of this, among them the *loss* by United Parcel Service (May 2005) of a back-up tape belonging to the retail division of Citigroup in the USA and containing social security numbers and transaction histories on both open and closed accounts for nearly four million customers.

96. For a helpful discussion of provenance from the vantage of scientific datasets, see pages 179–83 of the Digital Archiving Consultancy (DAC), the Bioinformatics Research Centre (University of Glasgow (BRC)) and the National e-Science Centre (NeSC), 2005, *Large-scale Data Sharing in the Life Sciences: Data Standards, Incentives, Barriers and Funding Models (The 'Joint Data Standards Study')*, prepared for the Biotechnology and Biological Sciences Research Council, the Department of Trade and Industry, the Joint Information Systems Committee for Support for Research, the Medical Research Council, the Natural Environment Research Council, the Wellcome Trust, *http://www.mrc.ac.uk/ pdf-jdss_final_report.pdf.*

97. Stephen Ellis and Andrew Wilson of the NAA described the plans during a March 2003 interview with Seamus Ross.

98. *http://www.naa.gov.au*

99. Ross, 2003, op. cit.

100. Ibid.
101. *http://www.fedora.info*. An excellent discussion of Fedora can be found in Payette, S. and Staples, T., 'The Mellon Fedora Project: digital library architecture meets XML and web services', in Agosti, M. and Thanos, C. (eds), *ECDL 2002, LNCS 2458*, pp. 406–21.
102. *http://dspace.org/index.html*
103. *http://lockss.stanford.edu/*
104. Herrmann, V. and Thaller, M., 'Integrating preservation aspects in the design process of digital libraries', *DELOS Deliverable 6.5.1*, 2005, *http://www.dpc.delos.info/private/output/DELOS_WP6_d651_finalv3_5__cologne.pdf*.
105. RLG/NARA Task Force on Digital Repository Certification: Audit Checklist for Certifying Digital Repositories, *http://www.rlg.org/en/pdfs/rlgnara-repositorieschecklist.pdf* (last accessed 10 October 2005).
106. Roberts, D., 'Defining electronic records, documents and data', *Archives and Manuscripts*, 22 (May 1994), pp. 14–26; Tibbo, H.R., 'On the nature and importance of archiving in the digital age', *Advances in Computers*, 57, 2003, pp. 1–67.
107. Ross and Hedstrom, op. cit; Hedstrom, M. et al., *Invest to Save: Report and Recommendations of the NSF-DELOS Working Group on Digital Archiving and Preservation* (Pisa and Washington DC, 2003), *http://delos-noe.iei.pi.cnr.it/activities/internationalforum/Joint-WGs/digitalarchiving/Digitalarchiving.pdf*, Report of the European Union DELOS and US National Science Foundation Workgroup on Digital Preservation and Archiving (alternatively at *http://eprints.erpanet.org/94/01/NSF_Delos_WG_Pres_final.pdf*).
108. *Digital Curation and Preservation: Defining the Research Agenda for the Next Decade*, report of the Warwick workshop, 7–8 November 2005, *http://www.dcc.ac.uk/training/warwick_2005/Warwick_Workshop_report.pdf*.
109. Charles Dollar, 'Public in Conversation with Director of HATII', HATII University of Glasgow and Digital Curation Centre, 6 December 2004.

7

'Seek and destroy' – an archival appraisal theory and strategy

Rachel Hosker and Lesley Richmond

Introduction

This chapter describes work in progress on functional appraisal that is being undertaken at the University of Glasgow on both the records created by the university and those collected from external business organisations. It discusses the role of archivists and the types of appraisal in general as well as the particular application of appraisal methodology at the University of Glasgow. One major outcome of this work is a toolkit for documenting the appraisal of collections of business archives. The toolkit has been developed out of a strategy that balances archival appraisal theory with archival reality. The authors hope that Glasgow University's experience may prove useful to other archive services and may stimulate further work on testing the toolkit on other types of records.

The role of the archivist

There are two basic types of archivist: the corporate archivist and the collecting archivist. The former is employed by an organisation to preserve, maintain and exploit its records for the good of the organisation. The latter is employed by an organisation to preserve, maintain and exploit the records of other organisations and individuals that the organisation collects as part of its function to provide historical, cultural, scientific, legal or educational materials for the benefit of its constituents, customers or clients. The actual remit of both types of archivist varies greatly, but the mission of both is to acquire, preserve, maintain and ensure the use of the records under their care. The principles and responsibilities of any archivist are to 'remember' for both the institution that employs them and for posterity (if that is in the job description).[1] The main difference between the two is in user base and the access rights of users. A corporate archivist remembers, or ensures that remembrance is possible, for those who have the rights to use or access the information, the owners and management (and employees, customers and others if the legislation is in place).[2] Often archivists of collecting institutions are wholly entrusted with remembrance for posterity, with the right to 'remember' accessible to any citizen of the world. Often the two types of archivists are merged. Many corporate archivists are also collecting institutional archivists and vice versa, the boundaries where the corporate archives become part of the holding of the collecting repository being very blurred.

Richard Cox has called appraisal the archivist's 'first responsibility' from which all else flows; all subsequent archival processes – description, conservation, exhibition, outreach, access – flow from this primary process. He has produced an intimidating list of the appraisal tasks, which he describes as

> daunting, if not impossible, including preserving and protecting any aspect of the documentary heritage that is endangered; acquiring a systematic documentation of particular aspects of society; serving diverse constituencies with very different objectives; meeting the institutional needs of the creators of records; providing a cultural or public memory role; safeguarding records as both artifacts and information systems; endorsing a legitimizing for certain segments of society; ensuring the accountability of public officials, civic, and corporate leaders; managing records of all media; and serving as a repository of last resort for records that have been stranded by their creators.[3]

Ever since the 1940s when archivists first began to acknowledge the appraisal problems caused by burgeoning documentation and record creation, they have had a major role in deciding the nature of the small proportion of records of any organisation or individual that will be preserved in an archive.[4] They have also granted authority to destroy all the rest. Archivists' main role in today's society is one of identifying, selecting, appraising and choosing archives – not one of just keeping archives.[5]

Appraisal is all about making choices.[6] For archival institutions the choice is between being a collecting or selecting organisation, whether to garner or winnow records for permanent preservation. Many other choices subsequently flow, including the decisions that balance the resources of the archival institution with its selection or collection criteria.

The selection versus collection debate does not equate to corporate archive versus collecting archive. Corporate archives must also choose between selecting and collecting. It is also not a debate that equates with the public archive institution versus the manuscript library institution; in both cases a choice between actively selecting or passively collecting is there to be made.

When Terry Cook asked the question whether the administrative and cultural values of archives are compatible, he laid bare the core issue that fuels division and uncertainty about the nature of archives. This has a direct bearing on the role of appraisal. He identified the unresolved tension between the concept of archives as evidence or as memory. Are archives to be primarily administrative and juridical organisations or to be cultural, educational and heritage institutions? Are archives 'passive objective documentary evidence of past actions or active subjective constructions of social memory'?[7] Can these two concepts of archives coexist? Both concepts have implications in theory and practice for appraisal decisions.

Types of appraisal

There are three main types of appraisal used by the archive profession: the older traditional approaches of creator and user appraisal and the more recently developed archivist appraisal.

Creator appraisal

Allowing the creator to determine value was the theory put forward by Jenkinson, the father of passive appraisal. He was very uneasy about archivists deciding what was to become an archive: 'The business of the archivist, put in the simplest terms, is to take over such documents, conserve them, and make them available for study.'[8] Archivists were not to be involved in creating their own selection criteria, as selection, in his opinion, was best left to the records creator, 'who was well placed to identify the records required to document their activities and retain sufficient evidence of their accountable decisions.'[9] However, the assumption that the original actors in the events are best qualified to do this selection because they know the issues has many flaws. These include the fact that the creators have long since declared that this is no longer their function, as they lose the battle to control their records as technology allows ever quicker and ever cheaper means of copying documents and records. Creators may be aware of the 'best records' of the functions and activities in which they are involved but they do not have the broader picture. They are also in a position to select records as evidence that places the institution and its record creators in the best light. At its worst, creator appraisal may also allow the destruction of archivally valuable records (evidence) for any reason that the creator may determine – from fear of corporate or personal scandal, obstructing openness in government or a desire to change history by destroying evidence of past actions. The traditional archival perspective of appraisal for social, cultural, accountability and historical values goes well beyond that of the employing institution's need for the preservation of a small portion of its own records for administrative continuity, legal defence, bottom-line profit and corporate memory.

It was Jenkinson's view that any personal judgement by the archivist would damage the impartiality of archives as evidence, as would any thought of selecting archives to meet the needs of current or future historians or other researchers. Here the archivist was to act in proxy of the original record creator, to ensure the authenticity and trustworthiness of the record. However, allowing the creator to determine 'value' privileges the powerful and the institutional in society, who have the resources and infrastructure to create and manage records in an organised way and have time to allow a natural residue to form which at the end of the life cycle can pass to an archive for preservation.

User appraisal

Allowing user needs (actual or anticipated) to determine the appraisal of records was best argued by Theodore Schellenberg[10] and his American successors, who tried to broaden the institutional bias of Jenkinson by considering the needs of a much wider range of users. It was a pragmatic approach to determining value; if the user uses the record, then it has value. If there is no use of the record, it is self-evident that there is no value. Schellenberg developed the concept of primary uses for records – the original use for which the record was created – and secondary uses, which included evidential, legal, fiscal and informational research values. If researchers, especially historians, found uses for records, then it was to be assumed that the records must fill the needs of society and societal memory.

This approach to determining value left archives subject to the loudest lobbying groups of researchers or the latest trends of historical research that inevitably privileged certain records and records creators and marginalised or silenced others. Archivists themselves have warned of the dangers of being 'too closely tied to the ... academic marketplace', with the ultimate result 'that archival holdings too often reflected narrow research interests rather than the broad spectrum of human experience. If we cannot transcend these obstacles, then the archivist will remain at best nothing more than a weathervane moved by the changing winds of historiography.'[11] It also left the historical user-orientated archivist unable to engage with non-historical uses and users of records such as those in medicine, science, business, sociology and environmental studies. While trying to predict future research trends, the archivist was neglecting to document the wider society in which the record creators and the institutions functioned.

Use-driven archival models also removed records from their natural context within the functions and activities of the creator. Appraisal criteria became external to the record, undermined its provenance and so devalued the role of archives in cultural memory.

Archivist appraisal

Cook called for an archival theory of appraisal, a theory of value created by archivists and not by creators, users or society at large. He argued that only once an archival theory of appraisal had been defined can an appraisal strategy, methodology and practice be implemented.[12] This theory was for archivists to decide on value. Neither the values of Jenkinson's creators or Schellenberg's users are archival values. In both cases, appraisal has been taken from the domain and professional competence of the archivist, who then is left merely to interpret and implement the wishes of others, whether creators or users.

The functional approach to appraising the long-term value of the functions and activities of an organisation provides the basis for an archival theory of determining the value of records. Records are the evidence of transactions and activities carried out in the pursuit of a function. It is not the evidential or contextual nature of the record that is valued but the various and differing contexts of the activities and transactions or, at a higher level, of the functions that caused the record to be created, and this determines whether a record is preserved or destroyed. Some functions can be deemed to have long-term importance while others may not.

Society functions by assigning greater or lesser value to different dimensions of the interplay of social structures, societal functions, and citizens and groups. Archival appraisal theory explores the nature of these functions, agents and acts, and the interconnections or interrelationships between them, and assigns greater importance or value to certain functional–structural factors compared with others.[13] It is known as functional appraisal, as the functional context of creation and contemporary use establishes value and is a provenance-based approach to appraisal.[14]

In the digital age archivists can no longer afford to wait for the end of the life cycle and the arrival of dormant digital records, but must actively intervene to shape the creation and capture of the future archival record. Archivists on the continuum model are usually seen to be working at the outer edge, in the fourth dimension, where collective memory and broad societal purposes operate, while records managers are seen to work within the inner first circle where administrative values and the creation and maintenance of evidence are the drivers. For archivists who are institutional record keepers or those with active relationships with the record creators of non-institutionally created records of the collecting repository, using archival functional appraisal opens up a gateway through which to work and make appraisal decisions within the inner circle of the continuum.

Archivists will inevitably inject their own values into all decision-making, appraisal and other practices. In a postmodern world archivists should rejoice in this self-knowledge but at the same time document all that they do in order to aid the reconstruction of their actions by those who will examine the work of the archivist in the future. Archivists are no longer neutral, if they ever were, but are actors on the postmodern world stage. Documenting decisions and assumptions will help meet the issues raised by the postmodern discussion about the function of archivists.[15]

Documentation

Archivists cannot help but be influenced by the environments in which they live and work but they must ensure that record descriptions are created to a standard that will allow appraisal and selection decisions to be understood. While archivists have become more sophisticated in how they consider appraisal, the public perception of what archives are about, especially in their selective identification and preservation of material, is still very limited. The mediation and intervention of the archivist in the construction of memory based on documentary evidence must be acknowledged and archivists must modify their claims that archives as evidence are impartial and objective.

During the mid-1980s Tom Nesmith and Terry Cook developed the concept of 'the history of the record'[16] to describe a major focus of archival work and of archivists' research, namely that each record has its own history, that it evolves and constantly changes over time, both before and after it comes to an archive. Cook at that time wrote of records moving from a status of information to knowledge and that, as they do so, they develop or acquire complex, changing relationships, connections and interconnections. The archival record question should be viewed as content linked to an extended and continually evolving contextual metadata, thus continually changing the record object as it acquires new or additional contextual metadata.[17] This supports the notion of the fond as being the whole of the records, extant and not extant, created by an entity and allows appraisal to cross an institution's functional and structural boundaries and cross archival jurisdictions.[18] The work of archivists must be accountable, transparent and well documented. The finding aids that archivists create must show clearly why the records being described have been selected for preservation and what related records have been destroyed and why.

Like many other commentators, Richard Cox[19] is concerned about the lack of communication about the role of the archivist in society, and he is particularly concerned about archivists explaining themselves to the public and winning their support especially when it comes to appraisal. Glasgow University Archive Services (GUAS) is undertaking to communicate its role as a selector of university records by documenting its appraisal within surveys of current records as well as in archival finding aids.[20] GUAS has also begun to appraise the functions and activities of the university that it is attempting to document over time and to document that process.

Glasgow University Archive Services case studies

Corporate records appraisal strategy

Glasgow University Archive Services (GUAS) acts both as a corporate archive for the records of the University of Glasgow since its foundation in 1451 and as a collecting archive preserving the history of Scottish business and industry.[21] This has been an ideal laboratory to explore, test and develop a function-based approach to appraisal for both collecting and corporate archivists. In particular as a corporate archive for the University of Glasgow, GUAS is attempting to provide by its appraisal approach the means to answer both corporate evidential and accountability and posterity questions over time. The JISC HEI (The Joint Information Systems Committee Higher Education Institution) Function and Activity Model[22] has been used for the generic functional analysis of the records of the University.

The themes that Glasgow University Archive Services attempt to document are:

- origin, growth and organisation
- policies, planning and decisions
- teaching
- research
- students and staff
- finance and physical resources
- Glasgow University and the wider community

in attempting to provide answers to questions such as:

- what did the institution do?
- why did it do it in a particular way?
- when and how did it do it and where?

To give an example, in conjunction with the *substantive* elements of the *facilitative* function of Strategy Development and Implementation, the record series being documented are those that answer the following:

What:

- were the goals of the institution?
- did the institution do to achieve those goals?
- policies did it put in place and why?
- did it decide to teach and why?
- were the results of what it did?

- were the internal management and organisational structures and how did they evolve?
- part did academic staff and students play in the development of strategy?

Why:

- was the institution established?
- did it evolve in a particular way?
- was it located where it is?

How:

- was the organisation structured and why?
- did that structure change over time and why?
- was policy decided (the process) and why?
- was policy communicated and implemented?
- were academic staff selected?
- were investment decisions made?

Who:

- were the main players in the life and development of the institution?
- was responsible for the governance of the institution?

When:

- was the institution established?
- were individual units within it established, merged, changed or abolished?

All business functions, activities and transactions are in the process of being appraised, so that an appropriate record is captured to enable such questions to be answered. Value will be applied to these functions, activities and transactions, and then strategies will be developed to capture the small percentage of all the records created that have enduring, long-term value, not just to the creator, not just to contemporary society for accountability purposes, but to a larger society, across time and space. Such an approach may also have important governance issues as, if it is discovered that a function is important but the records available are of low quality and so badly organised as to be unusable, then the record creation of the organisation in that particular instance will be investigated and reviewed. Important policies and processes are possibly not being captured in a record. It may also be the case that some functions and activities are not being captured within formal institutional record-keeping systems and the archivist needs to look to non-corporate systems. This is often the case within universities with research records created and curated by individual researchers.

Once the link between creator or primary business curator and record has been broken, the appraisal of the value of records becomes much more difficult by a non-creator or curator. This is often the position in which collecting repository archivists find themselves. The organisation, function and activities have to be understood to value the record. It was this realisation that led partly to the development of an archival appraisal strategy for business archives at Glasgow University Archive Services.

Business archives appraisal strategy

Background

The business collections managed by Glasgow University Archive Services are known as the Scottish Business Archive. Appraisal in the past had (on the whole) been carried out by individual archival professionals, often working in very difficult conditions. Frequently businesses had ceased to trade before an archivist was involved. Liquidators imposed severe time limits; the work was carried out in unheated and unlit premises and the threats of vandalism and arson added to the urgency of the situation. These time constraints often still apply today. Professional training had provided archivists with some skills towards making appraisal decisions through the knowledge of theory and practical exercise. With major businesses going bankrupt every month for a period of years in the 1960s and 1970s, there were scant opportunities for carrying out thorough appraisal. It is known from comments by historians, interest groups and employers that appraisal decisions had not always provided the survival of the records they would have wished to have preserved. Appraisal decisions had been influenced by a number of factors: trends in academic research; trends in popular leisure pursuits; trends in archival thought; and available resources for storage and processing.

Archivists are limited by their knowledge and training and they cannot retrain as an accountant, lawyer, engineer or some other professional every time a new specialised collection is due to be appraised. An individual professional archivist facing the dilemma of appraisal needs support. They need a process and understandable criteria to measure their decisions against and to create clear informative documentation. This is not to suggest a rigid approach to appraisal but that appraisal should be a fluid, clear, documented process.

> Our appraisal and descriptive tools must be linked, so that destroyed records and kept records, and the reasons for both decisions, are well researched, documented, transparent, and available to our many publics, now and over time. When people read an archival series description, they should also see what related records were destroyed and why. This is a minimum level of accountability to which the appraisal process, and appraising archivists, should be held.[23]

The dilemma created by trying to satisfy both professional obligations and pressure from stakeholders has often led to cautious decisions resulting in too much material being kept taking up scarce repository space. Professionals in all repositories are aware of collections that should be reappraised but limited resources often do not allow reappraisal to take place while new unprocessed collections await appraisal for the first time. Appraisal is often carried out within a very constrained environment with tight deadlines and a dearth of information. Often very little is known about how a company operated, how and why its records were created or the environment within which it functioned. How under all this pressure and lack of information can an archivist make the best decisions?

Developing a process and documentation strategy is essential. Balanced with professional judgement it can provide documented decisions that clearly state what influenced decision-making. Such documentation will explain to subsequent users why records were retained or destroyed. Although it is impossible to retain everything, it may be possible to record its existence and the reasons why it no longer exists. Satisfying the needs of all stakeholders of the Scottish Business Archive is an unobtainable goal but a practical and sensible approach to appraisal is obtainable. Possessing the knowledge of appraisal theory, however, is not enough for hard-pressed archivists; there is a requirement also to provide step-by-step guidance that will capture appraisal decisions.

Apart from Greene and Howells's[24] 'Minnesota Method', no comprehensive approach has been attempted to deal with the diverse and complex nature of business records. Business records are not standard sets of records. Although there are often set core governance and accounting records such as minute books, ledgers and journals for nineteenth-century business, the records that are created by a company are very much dependent on its business sector as well as the way in which it operates. The records of a bank are very different compared with those of a cotton mill. The Scottish Business Archive at the University of Glasgow comprises hundreds of collections of business records from different sectors that had different processes and created different records.

The lack of practical guidance has exacerbated many of the problems faced by archivists managing business archives, whether 'in-house' or within a collecting repository. A collecting repository often has a wider set of stakeholders to satisfy when making appraisal decisions, as it serves both the business (if it is still live) as a provider of a corporate archive service and users as a provider of a research service and a research resource. However, the need for documenting and justifying actions of disposal has greatly increased for both the 'in-house' and collecting repository. Business archivists are under pressure, with the increase in legislation and regulation on corporate governance, to document in order to be accountable. Some appraisal theorists warn against addressing accountability in appraisal. In practical terms, however, it has to be addressed, as it is a major influencing factor on appraisal decision-making. It also requires to be addressed as there is a danger that litigation and risk management considerations will encourage business managers, liquidators and receivers to destroy records at the end of their minimum retention period or at the completion of a legal process, rather than consider whether they have any long-term value. The promotion of a clear practical framework, which can support business needs such as knowledge and records management and still ensure compliance, may go some way to discouraging the disposal of records and provide corporate memory and research material for the future.

The focus of the GUAS appraisal strategy and method

Howell and Greene put forward the following observations about appraisal, which the GUAS strategy has adopted:

- All appraisal has been local and subjective; documenting decision-making ensures that the wider picture is examined.

- The potential universe of the documentation will always exceed the resources of any repository.
- There is a working archival reality; business records should not be appraised with 'Roman Heroics'.
- It is possible to make selection more rational, efficient and relative to a specific repository's goals and resources.[25]

It was concluded that the focus of GUAS had to be practical and realistic, not idealistic. Issues raised by the 'influencing factors' – accountability, stakeholders, statutory and regulatory requirements, time and resources, scenario of disposal, provenance and context, the impact of appraisal on arrangement – had to be acknowledged and tackled head on. These issues are often the most complex to deal with when making appraisal decisions and the ones that cause hesitancy in many professionals.

Appraisal is an activity that is accountable to a number of stakeholders. Legislation and regulation make archivists accountable when retaining or disposing of records. Archivists are also accountable to their employers (and clients in the case of the collecting archive). Appraisal decisions require to fit with company policy and business need and sometimes even company image. The corporate archivist is ultimately an employee who must put the company needs first. However, when appraising, this responsibility to an employer can be balanced with accountability to memory and researchers. These stakeholders are part of a larger group whose activities and opinions also influence appraisal. Researchers of all kinds, including the historical and legal, have a need for information for different purposes.

Resources, including time, are an influencing factor faced by all archive services as under-funded information services. Funding, the ability to acquire experienced professional staff, lack of equipment and storage are all realities that impact on what can be preserved and managed by a service. The appraisal process should ensure that disposal can mean distribution.

Interlinked with this is the scenario of disposal. GUAS has had experience of acquiring records both through positive proactive approaches to and from companies and also in dealing with receivers and liquidators of companies. The latter scenario often requires rescue work where instantaneous appraisal decisions have to be made *in situ* while uplifting a collection of records often days or hours before offices or factories are completely cleared. Secondary appraisal is then carried out once the records have been transferred to the repository. The scenario of disposal is often the strongest influence on appraisal, as the decision as to what survives to be appraised may have already been made by the business before an archivist has had a chance to see the collection as a whole. Working with a clear process with clear documentation will capture information about how a collection was acquired, which is invaluable to researchers as it puts surviving records in context. It also provides information on provenance and can inform arrangement.

Documentation

The only way to ensure that all of these influencing factors are taken into account in a practical methodical way is by documentation. This is the key to appraisal. Documenting as much information at the time of the acquisition and appraisal has two major advantages. It removes any reliance on the memory of individuals and negates the need to scrabble around gathering information months or years after the collection has been acquired. One of the descriptive elements of the General International Standard Archival Description (ISAD(G)) is 'custodial history'. This information helps the user interpret the information held within the records and can provide greater intellectual access to a collection. It is at the point of acquisition and appraisal that this information can be found in its most abundant, reliable state. Less is available as time goes on, as memory fades and companies cease to exist and employees are not available to assist.

Documentation provides consistency in the appraisal process, offering guidance on what to think about during the process, and also provides a means of recording the process. It provides the user with confirmation of what existed and the reasons for subsequent disposals. Even if a researcher is disappointed that particular records have not survived, they will know reliably that the records no longer exist and will not continue to search fruitlessly for them. The archivist is therefore accountable, open and can provide justification for disposal through this process. In an ever increasingly litigious society, documentation will also provide protection for the professional. To this end Glasgow University Archive Services is developing a toolkit to aid documentation.

The appraisal toolkit

The development of this strategy and methodology is still in its initial stages. Further testing, especially of the consolidation of fields and whether an assessment element would prove useful in the decision-making process, requires to be undertaken. The aim of this method is to provide documentation of appraisal decisions and to guide the appraiser through the appraisal process. The sections and fields provide prompts for decision-making at the macro and record type level. This strategy and methodology informs the collecting policy of GUAS.

The appraisal form has been heavily influenced by elements from the Minnesota Method,[26] ISAD(G) 2nd edition,[27] DIRKS[28] and the Functional Retention Model for HEIs.[29] These standards were used to enable the appraisal form to be consistent with professional best practice and recognisable in style and language to record-keeping professionals.

Sections on the appraisal form

An example of the appraisal form is given in Appendix 7.1 at the end of the chapter.

- *Section 1 – Cover information.* This provides information about what is being appraised and who is appraising it.

- *Section 2 – Scenario of appraisal/disposal.* This identifies and clarifies the situation that has prompted the acquisition of the material and provides information for timetabling of resources to appraise, select, document and move the material to the repository.

- *Section 3 – Essential information.* This section has ISAD(G) type fields to gather context and provenance needed for the appraisal decisions. If the material is not kept, this section can act as a record that provides evidence and information of the existence of records of a business or part of a business or collection.

- *Section 4 – Influencing questions.* This section documents the influences on appraising the business records. This information can again provide context to interpret and properly appraise the records as a whole or by record type.

- *Section 5 – Business and record type questions.* This section documents the processes and functions of the business and highlights where and why the record types were created. It also deals with archival administration questions required to make appraisal decisions.

- *Section 6 – Interaction questions or overview questions.* This section provides the focus on the importance of the business in the wider world, both as a corporate body and within society. These fields are designed to clarify the importance of the collection of records within a collecting policy and point to the best place of deposit.

- *Section 7 – Record of decision made.* This section can include further notes on individual items of importance or influences not accounted for.

Assessment

This is an area that requires further investigation as to whether an element of scoring is needed to guide decision-making. On its own it does not provide any kind of reason for keeping or disposing of any material. It is intended that an assessment element would be optional, an add-on to help decision-making and to clarify where the important issues lie with an individual collection throughout the process. It is an indication, not a finite decision. Currently, this does not fit well with the fields and may be construed as oversimplifying or over-mechanising the intellectual process of appraisal. It will be tried and tested further to see if a practical benefit can be gained.

Appendix 7.1 Appraisal toolkit

Appraisal form structure

Section 1: Basic title information for form

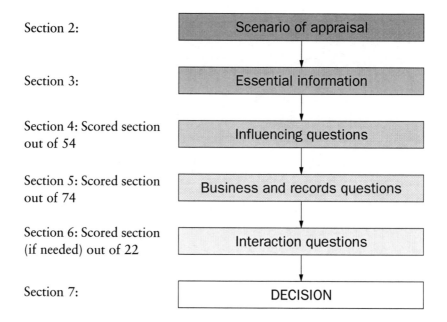

Section 2:	Scenario of appraisal
Section 3:	Essential information
Section 4: Scored section out of 54	Influencing questions
Section 5: Scored section out of 74	Business and records questions
Section 6: Scored section (if needed) out of 22	Interaction questions
Section 7:	DECISION

Appraisal and selection form

Section 1: Basic title information for form

Organisational name:
Organisation or archive department appraising:
Archivist appraising:

Section 2: Scenario of appraisal

This section clarifies the situation that has prompted the acquisition of material and provides information for timetabling of resources to appraise, select, document and move the material. The information gathered in this section should document any pressures that could influence decisions to keep material or not.

Tick the most appropriate scenario:

1. Records need to be moved immediately   ☐
2. Records need to be moved within a few weeks   ☐
3. Provision by the company/organisation for time
   to appraise records *in situ*   ☐
4. Reappraisal of a collection   ☐

Section 3: Essential information

Non-scoring

This section gathers information that provides a background for appraisal. Some of this information has a bearing on appraisal decisions and the aim of this section is to clearly document such background information. If a decision is taken not to keep material then this section can act as a record that provides evidence and information for the existence of a business.

Field area questions	Further questions	Comments
Unique identifier		
Name of corporate body		
Name of subordinate bodies		
Date of establishment		
Location of main offices and productive operations		
	Is there a comprehensive creation of records for all functions? Y/N Is there obvious physical bulk of records? Y/N	
	What factors may negatively affect appraisal decisions?	
Non-preferred terms		
Alternative names		
Administrative structure		
Legal influences	Are there any limitations on records – legislative, regulatory, access, confidentiality? Y/N Describe	
Other significant information		
ISAD reference (final reference or reappraisal)		
Name of creator		
Administrative history		
Physical characteristics	Format of records? Are there other limitations to keeping anything in another media, e.g. conservation, cost, etc.?	
Scope and content/abstract	Is there a comprehensive set of records? Y/N Describe Can you identify record types? Y/N List	

Field area questions	Further questions	Comments
	Are core records types identifiable? Y/N If N why? *Item level*: Is this record type of high informational content/value? Y/N Why?	
Appraisal and retention scheduling		
Semi-current storage		
Destruction methods		
Scenario of appraisal		
Rules or conventions		
Record created by and on		
Altered by and on		

Section 4: Influencing questions

This section documents any influencing factors that should be taken into consideration when appraising business records. Unless documented these influencing factors can be missed. It provides us with an assessment for portential researchers of that which documents the success or unique qualities of a business.

Field area questions	Further questions		Answers	Assessment Score	Possible total
Corpus (complete set of records) *Choose 1 from record type list and 1 from function list*	Record type (list):	Complete ☐ Moderate survival ☐ Incomplete ☐			4
	Function (list):	Complete ☐ Moderate survival ☐ Incomplete ☐			

Field area questions	Further questions	Answers	Assessment	
			Score	Possible total
Social/ gender/ethnic minority business *Social inclusion*	Business owned by a particular social/gender/ethnic minority ☐ Business employees from a particular social/gender/ethnic minority ☐ Business reflective (products and customers) of a particular social/gender/ ethnic back-ground ☐			6
National or local identification	Significance at an international level UK ☐ Significance at national level UK ☐ Significance at national level Scotland ☐ Significance at regional level ☐ Significance at local level ☐			10
Illustrative example for sector	Records created ☐ Business functions ☐ Products or services ☐			6
Technological innovation	Products ☐ Research ☐ Processes ☐			6
Organisational innovation	Management ☐ Customer care/client care ☐ Staff development ☐			6
Cultural significance	Geographical ☐ Industry sector ☐ Cultural sector/discipline ☐			6
Product/ market	Unusual or unique product ☐ Particular market leaders ☐ Illustrative of dealing with markets in sector ☐			6
Industry leader	Financial (investment in/funds available) ☐ Products/services ☐ Processes/operations ☐			6

Total score out of 55 =

Section 5: Business and records questions

This section deals with documenting business process and function-specific questions that provide further information on the records created. It also deals with archival administration questions that can influence decisions on appraisal such as any apparent records keeping systems or legal restraints.

Field area questions	Further questions	Comments	Assessment Score	Possible total
Main functions of business	What access is there to information on business functions? Company organisation charts? Y/N Contained within records identified? Y/N Is it comprehensive? Y/N			6
	What are the major functions and activities of this business?			10
	Can the functions be attached to a section, department or a team (a creating body)? Y/N If no describe why not.			6
	Is there a comprehensive creation of records for all functions? Y/N Is there obvious physical bulk of records? Y/N			
	How are these functions of historical/research value?Y/N If Y describe. Do they fall into current research trends? Y/N If Y describe.			4
	Did these functions or activities make money for the company? Y/N List			2
	Do the surviving records clearly indicate the functions of the company? Y/N			2

Field area questions	Further questions		Comments	Assessment	
				Score	Possible total
Geographical scope *Choose 1*	World-wide and Scotland UK wide and Scotland Scotland Scottish region Local area	☐ ☐ ☐ ☐ ☐			2
No other repository *Choose 1*	No other part of the collection elsewhere Part of collection elsewhere Related material elsewhere	☐ ☐ ☐			2
Sector records in Scotland (or of significance to Scotland) *Choose 1*	Best or unique example for sector Good example Standard example of sector Not illustrative of sector	☐ ☐ ☐ ☐			2
First offer to an archival repository/ institution *Choose 1*	First offer Second offer (give reason) Offered to more than two repositories (give reason)	☐ ☐ ☐			2
Corporate responsibility initiative *Choose 1*	Department exists Dealt with by existing department Adheres to principles. Not part of corporate structure	☐ ☐ ☐			2
Paper record systems					6
Computer record systems					6
Corporate record systems use					2
General systems notes	Devolved systems? Y/N Describe				2
	Legislative, audit and regulatory framework? Y/N Describe				2

Field area questions	Further questions	Comments	Assessment	
			Score	Possible total
Archival history	Are there any record types unique to a particular industry or to the business itself? Y/N Describe			2
Scope and content/ abstract	Is there a comprehensive set of records? Y/N Describe Can you identify record types? Y/N List Are core records types identifiable? Y/N If N why? *Item level*: Is this record type of high informational content/value? Y/N Why?			
Accruals	Is this or will it have been part of a series of records? Y/N Describe if Y.			2
System of arrangement				2
Location of originals				2
Existence of copies	Do some record types duplicate information (e.g. can it be found elsewhere?) Y/N If Y describe where else. *Item level*. Is this the only surviving or unique type of evidence for the existence or functions and activities of the company? Y/N Is this the only survivng or unique type of evidence for the existence of this industry or business sector? Y/N *Item level*: Is this the only surviving example of this type of record for this comany? Y/N			

Total score out of 74 =

Section 6: Interaction questions

This section provides questions that focus on the importance of a business and its collection of records that can influence an appraisal decision. These questions provide a section to clarify any issues on the potential importance of business to a society that can be used to consolidate a decision.

Field area questions	Further questions		Comments	Score	Possible total for field
				Assessment	
Politically important/ stakeholders	Top level ☐ Mid-level stakeholder ☐ Low-level stakeholder ☐				6
Top sector employer/ citizenship	World-wide ☐ Europe ☐ UK ☐ Scotland ☐				8
Top 25 national employer	Top 25 employer UK ☐ Top 25 employer Scotland ☐				4
Top 5 regional employer	Geographical ☐ sector ☐				4

Total score out of 22 =

Section 7: Decision

Score out of 152 =

Influencing factors:

Comments:

Notes

1. Richmond, Lesley, 'The memory of society: businesses', *COMMA, International Journal on Archives*, 1–2, 2002, p. 113.
2. Since 2005, for instance, within the United Kingdom public bodies are subject to freedom of information legislation that allows worldwide scrutiny of public bodies within the United Kingdom – see *http://www.opsi.gov.uk/acts/acts2000/20000036.htm*.
3. Cox, Richard J., *Archival Appraisal Alchemy*, paper delivered at Choices and Challenges: Collecting by Museums and Archives, 1–3 November 2002, Benson Ford Research Center at the Henry Ford, 2002 (available at *http://www.thehenryford.org/research/publications/symposium2002/papers/cox.asp*, accessed 30 June 2005).
4. For a review of the development of the role of the archivist in appraisal, see 'Muddied waters and conflicting currents: an overview of appraisal thought', in Boles, Frank, *Selecting and Appraising Archives and Manuscripts* (Chicago, 2005), Chapter 2.
5. Cook, Terry, *Overview of Appraisal*, presentation to Appraisal Seminar, Monash University, Melbourne, 15 March 1999 (available at *http://www.recordkeeping.com.au/march99/terrycookadmincultural.html*, accessed 15 September 2005).
6. McKemmish, S. et al. (eds), *Archives. Recordkeeping in Society* (Wagga Wagga, 2005), p. 174.
7. Cook, T., 'Are the administrative and cultural values of archives compatible?', Presentation to Appraisal Seminar, Monash University, Melbourne, 16 March 1999 (available at *http://www.recordkeeping.com.au/march99/terrycookadmincultural.html*, accessed 6 December 2005).
8. Jenkinson, H., 'Reflections of an archivist', in Daniels, Maygene F. and Walch, Timothy, *A Modern Archives Reader: Basic Readings on Archival Theory and Practice* (Washington, DC, 1984), p. 15.
9. McKemmish et al., op. cit., p. 174.
10. 'Those records of any private or public institution which are adjudged worthy of permanent preservation or reference and research purposes and which have been deposited or have been selected for deposit in an archival institution': see Schellenberg, T., *Modern Archives: Principles and Techniques* (Melbourne, 1956), p. 16.
11. Ham, F. Gerald, 'The archival edge', *American Archivist*, 38, January 1975, pp. 5–13.
12. Cook, *Overview*, op. cit.
13. For an example of such interaction in the world of business and business records, see Baer, Christopher T., 'Strategy, structure, detail, function: four parameters for the appraisal of business records', in O'Toole, James M. (ed.), *The Records of American Business* (Chicago, 1997), pp. 75–135.
14. Booms, Hans, 'Society and the formation of a documentary heritage', *Archivaria*, 24, Summer 1987.

15. Terry Cook discusses many of the issues in his article, 'Fashionable nonsense or professional rebirth: postmodernism and the practice of archives', *Archivaria*, 51, 2001, pp. 14–35.
16. *Appraisal and the Continuum*, Presentation to Appraisal Seminar, Monash University, Melbourne, 15 March 1999.
17. This is the reality of the approach adopted with the Glasgow University records held within the GASHE Project: see *http://www.gashe.ac.uk*. The creation and use of function and activity descriptions across the record-keeping continuum are discussed in Chapter 8 in this volume.
18. Although it may often be impossible for either the collecting or corporate archivist to know the true scope of non-extant records, corporate archivists, operating as record professionals across the record-keeping continuum, are in a position to know, or to discover, and document the records created by their organisation.
19. *http://www.thehenryford.org/research/publications/symposium2002/papers/cox.asp*
20. See Chapter 8 in this volume, and Table 8.3 – Example of ISAD(G) compliant description of series created during survey work at Glasgow University – in this volume.
21. See *http://www.archives.gla.ac.uk* for further details.
22. The current model for the functions of higher education in the United Kingdom can be found at *http://www.jisc.ac.uk/srl_structure.html* (accessed 1 August 2005). It was compiled by Elizabeth Parker in 2003 and is a revised version of the model commissioned by JISC and published by Parker in 1999.
23. *Appraisal and the Continuum*, Final Commentary Session of the Appraisal Seminar, Monash University, Melbourne, 16 March 1999 (available at *http://www.recordkeeping.com.au/march99/terrycookfinal.html*, accessed 15 December 2005).
24. Greene, Mark A. and Daniels-Howell, Todd J., 'Documentation with an attitude: a pragmatist's guide to the selection and acquisition of modern business records', in O'Toole, James M. (ed.), *The Records of American Business* (Chicago, 1997), pp. 161–229.
25. Ibid., pp. 161–3.
26. Ibid.
27. See *http://www.icacds.org.uk/eng/standards.htm* (accessed 1 August 2005).
28. *http://www.naa.gov.au/recordkeeping/dirks/dirksman/dirks.html*
29. See *http://www.jisc.ac.uk/srl_structure.html* (accessed 1 August 2005).

8

Divided no more: a descriptive approach to the record-keeping continuum

Victoria Peters and Lesley Richmond

Introduction

This chapter describes the results of an applied research project testing a function-based approach to archival representation. The project, entitled 'Developing Archival Context Standards for Functions in the Higher Education Sector', was funded by the Arts and Humanities Research Council and carried out by Glasgow University Archive Services between August 2003 and February 2006. The major outcomes of the project, in which there was perpetual feeding of theory on practice and practice on theory, were not only a more flexible and dynamic system of archival representation but also the creation of a practical application of the concept of the records continuum, namely a continuum of care between records management and archives management. The chapter describes both the immediate outcomes and the wider implications of the project and proposes that archivists can be record-keeping professionals whose roles move seamlessly between the present, future and past. It is the authors' hope that Glasgow University's experience may prove informative and stimulating to other records professionals as well as demonstrating the value of carrying out research within a working environment.

Background to project

The Developing Archival Context Standards for Functions in the Higher Education Sector project arose out of the realisation that archivists were failing in one of their primary goals: the preservation of the context of archives in order to safeguard their evidential value and historical authenticity. The importance of context has long been recognised. In 1990, the Society of American Archivists published *Arranging and Describing Archives and Manuscripts*, a manual prepared by Fredric Miller, part of a new series on basic archival functions. The following definition of archival description distilled current thought:

> Archival description is the process of capturing, collating, analysing, controlling, exchanging, and providing access to information about (1) the origin, context, and provenance of different sets of records, (2) their filing structure, (3) their form and content, (4) their relationships with other records, and (5) the ways in which they can be found and used.[1]

Indeed, the principle of provenance has been described by Horsman as 'the only principle' of archival theory.[2] Records are not created in a vacuum and their interpretation and significance are dependent on the context of their creation and use. Barbara Reed places context at the very heart of what differentiates records from mere documents.[3] She argues that records are 'a construct, always virtual, consisting of the physical object and its relationships, links and contextual information, defined as much by the processes applied to their management as by the physical object itself'.[4] She argues that 'a record has to be linked to doing something – it is inherently transactional in its nature'.[5] Of course, records, and record series in particular, can be linked to more than one transaction and they can have more than one relationship. They can be created by one organisation or individual for one purpose and then later reused by the same or a different organisation or individual for another purpose. For example, at Glasgow University, student records were created by the University Registry to record biographical and educational information about students. The records were later reused by the Development and Alumni Office in connection with organising reunions and fundraising campaigns. Which is the most important activity? Postmodernists argue rightly that these subsequent uses are of no less importance for our interpretation of the records than their original and very first use. Terry Cook argues that records have multiple and changing contexts, and that records are dynamic, not static.[6] As Sue McKemmish (quoted by Barbara Reed) puts it, 'the record is always in a process of becoming'.[7] Records 'are not fixed; they are fluid, ever-forming'[8] – in other words organic. They are created by living organisms, whether institutions or individuals, and are therefore liable to change and grow with the living organism. These changing contexts open records quite legitimately to different interpretations at different points in their existence. It is precisely these different contexts that archivists must strive to record. If they choose to favour any one context at the expense of others, then they leave themselves open to justifiable criticism.

Archivists in Australia are meeting the challenge of representing multiple contexts very well. Archival descriptive systems are based upon the Series System first developed by the National Archives of Australia in the 1960s as the Commonwealth Record Series (CRS) System.[9] Under this system, the record series is taken as the basic unit of accumulation rather than the fond, and context is entirely separated from content. Series are not fixed in a rigid hierarchical structure. Instead, each series can be linked to any number of contexts, whether creator or activity or related records. The system is therefore flexible enough to capture different and changing contexts.[10]

It is still the norm in the UK, however, to describe or represent records in a single, static arrangement, usually based on administrative or organisational structure. The advent of ICT has done little so far to change this. In most examples of online finding aids in the UK, the computer has simply been used to provide an online, albeit searchable, version of a traditional paper-based list. A static arrangement cannot easily (if at all) accommodate multiple contexts. These have been sacrificed for the convenience and neatness of a single view, which can only provide a snapshot of the records at a specific point in time. Vital contextual information is being lost, if not actually being destroyed, by archivists.

Authority records for the creators of records have gone some way towards addressing this problem and enabling the capture of some contextual information. They enable the recording of valuable background information on the creators of the records, whether organisations, office bearers, individuals or families. Even more importantly, by recording this information separately from but linked to descriptions of the actual records, they open up possibilities for more dynamic descriptive systems. Rather than the traditional static, mono-hierarchical representation based on administrative structure, records can be linked to more than one office bearer or department, removing the need to connect a record series artificially to a single creator. Authority records, however, do not provide all the contextual information that is required. It is not enough simply to equate context with the individual or organisation that created the record. Usual practice in the UK today, however, is to describe the records according to ISAD(G) and the creators according to ISAAR(CPF). This provides the user with the knowledge of what the records are and who created them, but this is surely not enough. Users are being short-changed. They are not being provided with all the information they need to interpret the records. Archivists must attempt, as the guarantors of the authenticity and trustworthiness of archives, standing in, by proxy, for the creators of the records, to explain to potential users: the reasons why the records were created and subsequently used, i.e. what transactions they were recording; the purpose or function of the records within the organisation, i.e. what functions and activities they were fulfilling; and the interrelationship of records within and between creating organisations. The capture and representation of this contextual information must result in what Megan Winget refers to as a description of the 'continuum of relationships and interrelationships over time and place'.[11] Referring to Horsman,[12] she continues: 'To comprehend context, Horsman argues that the archivist not only has to describe and define the structure of the fonds in its series and sub-series, but also to define and describe the relationships between the agency's characteristics or functions, and the records it has created throughout the range of its existence.'[13] Archival representations that include such information will be of far greater value than those that simply provide background information on creators.

In addition to the realisation that archivists are failing to preserve context, it was also evident that they are not providing an adequate retrieval mechanism for potential users of any archive collection. Researchers interested in one particular area or activity of an organisation often have to undertake a great deal of work to guarantee the retrieval of all the records relating to that activity. Usually they are required to find out which office bearers or departments within the organisation were responsible for that activity. Then they must consult a number of different finding aids to ensure that they have tracked down all relevant records. The process can be very time-consuming. An example from the University of Glasgow will highlight the issues.

Student registration at the University of Glasgow

Student registration records are a popular source for both academic and non-academic researchers. The history of registration at the university, however, is a complex one. It has not always been compulsory, different officers of the university have been responsible for it at different times, the format of the records has changed, the level of informational detail in the records has changed and even the name of the activity has changed.

Using the traditional 'original order' based approach to cataloguing, archivists have arranged such records by each creator or custodian of the records – in this case, the Faculty, Clerk's Press, Library and Registry. A potential user must first work all this out, discovering which creator or custodian was responsible either for the activity or for looking after the records of the activity for the time period in which they are interested, and then look in the finding aids of all these bodies to retrieve all the records relating to student registration. The controlled indexing and free-text searching of online systems help to a certain extent in the retrieval of these records, but they do not guarantee complete records retrieval and they do not help the user to understand the context or relationship of the records retrieved. To be able to fully understand and interpret the records, the user must know why the records were created and understand their original purpose and function.

Functional description: a complementary approach

In order to remedy these failings, Glasgow University Archive Services turned to functional analysis and records management practice. Functional analysis has long underpinned records management practice and is used as the basis for classification or arrangement rather than administrative structure. Records managers understand that the fundamental relationship of records is with the functions and activities that brought them into being rather than the office bearers who created them. New departments, offices and committees are created within an organisation all the time, and responsibilities constantly pass from one to another. However, the basic functions of the organisation, i.e. what an organisation does to achieve its goals and strategies, remain the same. In higher education, the main functions that universities undertake to achieve their goals are student administration, teaching, research and governance.

A number of identifiable activities are carried out in the course of each of these functions. Handling student discipline, the administration of student records and student recruitment are all examples of activities carried out under the function of student administration. It is these functions and activities that records managers use for analysing and classifying the records in their care rather than organisational or administrative structure. The thesis of the Developing Archival Context Standards for Functions in the Higher Education Sector project was that, if a functional provenance approach could be applied equally well to older, historical records and, if that was then used as one strand of an archival descriptive system, it could both provide vital contextual information on the purposes and functions of records and determine a practical outcome of the records continuum model.

The thesis did not advocate an arrangement based solely on function instead of one based solely on administrative structure; function-based descriptions were only to be one strand of a descriptive system. They were to constitute a separate but complementary strand in order to record the multiple and changing contexts of records so that researchers would have as much contextual information as possible to interpret a record at any point in time. The test-bed for this approach was the records of Scottish higher education institutions held on the electronic Gateway to the Archives of Scottish Higher Education (GASHE).[14] The records of these institutions date back to 1215 and they themselves are large, very complex and constantly evolving organisations. Therefore they make an ideal basis for a test. The Joint Information Systems Committee (JISC) Higher Education Institutions Business Function and Activity Model[15] was used for the generic functional analysis of the records of the organisations.

Activity descriptions

The project selected certain activities from the JISC model and compiled an activity description for each of those activities in a number of different higher education institutions. Time constraints meant that it was impossible to describe every activity carried out by every higher education institution in Scotland. Selection of activities, therefore, was determined in the first instance by their usefulness in explaining the context of surviving records. Student records, for example, are a heavily used source and so activities that led to the production of these records were selected as a priority for description. In addition, the selection was driven by the need to test the functional approach in as many different scenarios as possible. Accordingly, activities of different longevity were selected. Activities were chosen to include some that went right back to the foundation of the institution, such as student admission or financial accounting, whereas others were chosen that only emerged in relatively recent times, such as childcare services management. Also, institutions of different ages were chosen to include both ancient, such as Glasgow University, founded 1451, and more modern, such as Glasgow School of Art, founded 1845.

The activity descriptions comprise a number of elements. The structure mirrors and complements the structures of the General International Standard Archival Description (ISAD(G)) and the International Standard Archival Authority Record for Corporate Bodies, Persons and Families (ISAAR(CPF)).[16] A draft activity standard has been created as one of the outcomes of the project.[17] This standard is currently being used by the International Council on Archives Provisional Section on Standards and Best Practices for the development of an international archival standard for functions.[18]

The description contains an identity statement area, which comprises the names of the institution, function and activity and the covering dates of the activity; a context area, which includes a history of the activity from its first appearance within the institution and a list of all the office bearers and departments that were involved in the performance of the activity; an allied materials area, which comprises a list of all the records created in the course of the activity and a list of related activities; and a note area where information on the compilation of the description and the rules and conventions used are recorded (see Table 8.1).

Table 8.1   Example of description of activity of student discipline at Glasgow University

Activity description	
Institution	University of Glasgow
Function	Student administration
Activity	Student discipline

Table 8.1	Example of description of activity of student discipline at Glasgow University (*cont'd*)

Activity description	
Date(s) of activity	1451 to date
Activity performed by	Rector Principal Regents and Professors Jurisdictio Ordinaria Faculty Senate Court
Activity history	In the earliest years of the University, student discipline was primarily the responsibility of the Principal and regents. The ultimate responsibility, however, rested with the Rector, who, as the active head of the University, exercised jurisdiction over all its members. On his election to office, the Rector had to swear an oath to defend discipline and to expel from the University all rebels and any who refused to obey the instructions of the University officers. Serious cases of student misdemeanour that could not be kept within the bounds of the University were dealt with by the Bishop's courts or the City Magistrates. By the early eighteenth century, a University court called the Jurisdictio Ordinaria was in existence. This met occasionally for the exercise of discipline over junior students. After the evolution of the Senate and Faculty in the 1600s, these too became involved in disciplinary matters. Although there is evidence of both bodies dealing with such matters, it appears that gradually this responsibility fell mainly to the Faculty. In 1771, a meeting of the Faculty enacted regulations concerning the exercise of discipline over students. The regulations state that all acts of discipline over the students belonged in the last resort to the Faculty, which had the right to review all cases of discipline exercised by individual professors or the Jurisdictio Ordinaria. This power of discipline of the Faculty was held neither to interfere with nor encroach upon the civil or criminal jurisdiction belonging to the Rector. The regulations further state that every sentence of expulsion had to be recorded but that there was no need to record admonitions, rebukes or fines. With the passing of the Universities (Scotland) Act 1858, the Faculty was abolished and responsibility for

Table 8.1	Example of description of activity of student discipline at Glasgow University (cont'd)

Activity description	
	superintending and regulating the discipline of the university passed to the Senate, subject to the control and review of the University Court. The Universities (Scotland) Act 1889 added that the Court could only review decisions of the Senate in matters of discipline upon appeal by the Senate or by a member of the University directly affected. The powers of discipline vested in the Senate by these acts were regularly delegated to the Senate's Principal and Deans Committee. In 1966, however, discipline procedure was reviewed with the result that, in 1967, a code of discipline was drawn up and a Senate Disciplinary Committee, comprising the Principal, Vice-Principal, nine members of Senate and two students nominated by the Students Representative Council, was appointed. Three Assessors for Discipline were also appointed. Allegations were initially reported to these Assessors who could administer punishment or report the matter to the disciplinary committee as appropriate. Students could appeal to the University Court against any decision taken by the Disciplinary Committee. Any disciplinary action taken against a student was recorded by the Registry in the student's record.
Scope and content	Annales Collegii Facultatis Artium in Universitate Glasguensi 1451–c.1580 Ref: GB 0248 GUA 26614 (Clerk's Press 2) Includes statutes concerning student discipline 1580/1581

Bonds and obligations from students as surety for good behaviour 1633–1700 Ref: GB 0248 GUA 46770–46801

Liber decani facultatis 1640–1654 Ref: GD 0248 GUA 26621 (Clerk's Press 9) Includes statutes concerning College discipline 1645 and minutes of Faculty meetings

Minutes of meetings of moderators and other miscellaneous records c.1644–1727 Ref: GB 0248 GUA 26622 (Clerk's Press 10) Includes Leges de Pietate et Moribus Discipulorum (four versions)

Faculty meeting minutes 1663–1669, 1701–1859 Ref: GB 0248 GUA 26626, 26631–26632, 26634–26635, 26647–26650, 26690–26703 |

Table 8.1	Example of description of activity of student discipline at Glasgow University (*cont'd*)

Activity description	
	Minutes of trial of student for murder 1670 Ref: GB 0248 GUA 43232
	Act of Privy Council empowering College to impose fines on disorderly students and requiring magistrates of Glasgow to uphold its sentences 1693 Ref: GB 0248 GUA 2011
	Letter from John Maxwell of Pollock, Rector, to Gerschom Carmichael, Philosophy Regent, concerning conduct of English student 1716 Ref: GB 0248 GUA 30178
	Records of Senate 1730 to date Ref: GB 0248 GUA SEN The Senate minutes, papers and letter books all record cases of student discipline
	Papers relating to proceedings against student for body-snatching 1749 Ref: GB 0248 GUA 43172–43173, 43323
	Bond of caution by students to University as result of assault on dancing master 1756 Ref: GB 0248 GUA 351
	Papers relating to Edward Kennedy, student, v James Stewart, dancing master 1764–1765 Ref: GB 0248 GUA 30181–30189
	Papers relating to proceedings against David Woodburn, student 1765–1770 Ref: GB 0248 GUA 26682, 29200–29202, 29204–29242
	Papers relating to conduct of Russian student, Simon Desnitzkoy 1767 Ref: GB 0248 GUA 30190–30191
	Papers relating to complaint by Duncan Ruthven, sedan chair man, against William Grant, student, and others 1767 Ref: GB 0248 GUA 30192–30194
	Minute of meeting with Lord Provost of Glasgow concerning riot said to be committed in street by Mr Blackwood, student 1769 Ref: GB 0248 GUA 30202
	Papers relating to meetings of Faculty regarding conduct of students 1782–1783 Ref: GB 0248 GUA 34638–34639, 30212
	Schedule of registration and protest of Professor John Anderson to Principal and Faculty relating to expulsion of James Wilson, student 1783 Ref: GB 0248 GUA 27333
	Calendars 1826 to date Ref: GB 0248 GUA SEN 10 The calendars contain the full text of the code of discipline

| Table 8.1 | Example of description of activity of student discipline at Glasgow University (*cont'd*) |

Activity description

	Summons by order of Faculty by John Calder, Bedellus, for students to attend meeting of Faculty following disorderly proceedings in College and its neighbourhood 1846 Ref: GB 0248 GUA 3907
	Printed notice to students warning of severe punishment in case of disregard of decency and propriety at public meetings of University 1849 Ref: GB 0248 GUA 34558
	Records of Court 1860 to date Ref: GB 0248 GUA C
	The Court minutes, papers and letters all record cases of student discipline
	Papers relating to power of review of decision of Senate in matters of discipline possessed by Court 1906 Ref: GB 0248 GUA 31595
	Discipline Committee minutes and correspondence relating to various discipline cases 1940–1943 Ref: GB 0248 GUA 66048
	Papers on amendments to code of discipline drawn up by Court 1967–1972 ref: GB 0248 GUA 62109
	Notes concerning jurisdiction of city magistrates over students n.d. Ref: GB 0248 GUA 15793
	Papers and correspondence concerning code of discipline n.d. Ref: GB 0248 DC 157/6/30
	Memorandum of overtures to be proposed at visitation of College concerning students' conduct n.d. Ref: GB 0248 GUA 440
	Records relating to disciplinary cases may also be found among the papers of individual principals, masters and rectors
Related activities	For individual student records, see: Student administration/Student records administration, University of Glasgow
Rules and conventions	Titles of function and activity taken from JISC HEI Business Function & Activity Model, compiled by Elizabeth Parker in 2003. Activity description compiled according to GASHE Standard for Creating Activity Descriptions
Creation date	Activity description compiled by Victoria Peters, research archivist, 1 April 2004

The description provides information on the office bearers and administrative divisions that performed the activity and how and why this changed over time, and brings together in one place all the records created in the course of that activity. This enables users to locate all relevant information much more quickly than by using traditional finding aids and, more importantly, allows improved interpretation of the records. As has already been stated, the activity descriptions are designed to complement both authority records and descriptions of the records themselves. They are an additional feature to the ISAD(G)-compliant finding aids and ISAAR(CPF)-compliant authority records already available on GASHE.

Users of GASHE can enter the system via a record description or an activity description and can then navigate through these descriptions to other record descriptions and activity descriptions as well as to related authority records. The user can also search across all three types of information at once using either controlled index terms or free-text searching. The intention was to create a flexible system that accommodates the needs of users without abandoning the requirements of the records themselves. The records are still arranged and described according to archival principles but users are thereafter offered an alternative way into the records, by activity, as well as a great deal of extra contextual information.

Data delivery

The original GASHE software was designed in collaboration with the Navigational Aids for the History of Science, Technology and the Environment (NAHSTE) project[19] by EDINA, the JISC-funded national data centre based at Edinburgh University Data Library.[20] For the Developing Archival Context Standards for Functions in the Higher Education Sector project, EDINA improved and adapted the GASHE software[21] to incorporate the new activity descriptions and to provide extra functionality. All descriptions in GASHE were created in eXtensible Mark-up Language (XML). The traditional record descriptions were created in Encoded Archival Description (EAD)[22] and, as the GASHE and NAHSTE projects pre-dated the introduction of Encoded Archival Context (EAC),[23] the authority records were created with a specifically designed document type definition (DTD). The activity descriptions have also been created in XML. Project staff designed an XML DTD both to reflect the elements set out in the project's activity standard and to complement EAD and EAC. Glasgow University Archive Services intends to offer this DTD to the international archive community for further testing.

Initial results of the project

Activity descriptions have been created for activities performed at a number of different institutions, both ancient and modern, in connection with a broad spread of functions, including governance, financial management, student administration and student support services management. Initial results have been very positive. The advantages of the approach are clear. First, activity descriptions provide the vehicle for the extra contextual information that slips through the net with standard cataloguing. Record descriptions can be linked to as many activities as necessary, thereby allowing records to be described in multiple contexts. Furthermore, activity descriptions are fluid and can be easily updated when the responsibility for an activity or the creation and maintenance of a record series changes, appropriately reflecting the fluid and dynamic nature of the records themselves. They also provide very useful, additional retrieval points for the user. Very good results have been produced for the longest-lived and most complex universities, allowing the seamless description of records from their origin right up to the present.

A continuum of record keeping

In addition to providing a more flexible and dynamic and therefore less subjective means of representing archives, the project has had another, perhaps even more fundamental, outcome. Traditionally, records managers at the University of Glasgow have handled current records but have not necessarily understood the historical origin and evolution of these records. Conversely, archivists have cared for historical records but have not necessarily had an awareness of how they linked to current records. Similarly, records managers have used one set of standards for the classification and identification of records and, on the metamorphosis of these records into archives, archivists have used another set to produce archival descriptions or representations. The two approaches failed to join up. Activity descriptions, however, enabling the seamless description of records from their origin to the present, have proved the perfect means of joining them up. This project provided a 'eureka moment' when it became clear that the concept of a records continuum is not just a model but can be applied to produce tangible results. This realisation is transforming record-keeping practice within Glasgow University Archive Services. In saying this, we are not claiming that our approach reflects Upward's version of records continuum thinking. Our variant of the continuum more closely matches that of Ian Maclean.[24]

Activity descriptions are becoming the heart of a system embracing information about both past and current records. There are many potential developments that are beginning to be explored further, such as linking activity descriptions to retention schedules in order to eradicate unnecessary duplication or using activity descriptions as a tool to facilitate access under freedom of information legislation, acting like the UK government's information asset registers. The project has already, however, led to radical developments. The concept of a continuum of care has been developed with one set of documentation to cover past and present information.

Archivally trained records professionals are being utilised to carry out basic record survey work using archival documentation. Tables 8.2 and 8.3 are examples of documents created during survey work at the university. This use of archival documentation enables records of long-term evidential value and potential value as corporate and/or societal memory to be documented to archival standards of representation from the time of creation or as early as possible after creation. The use of archival standards to describe the records of an organisation as they are created ensures documentation of records that may help meet the issues raised by the postmodern discussion about the function of archivists.[25] Archivists cannot help being influenced by the environments in which they live and work, but at least records could be documented by records professionals to a standard that would allow subsequent archival activities such as appraisal and selection also to be adequately documented.

Table 8.2	Example of ISAAR(CPF)-compliant authority record created during survey work at Glasgow University
Name of corporate body	University of Glasgow | Archive Services
Other forms of name	Formerly known as: University of Glasgow | Archives 1955–1998

Table 8.2	Example of ISAAR(CPF)-compliant authority record created during survey work at Glasgow University (*cont'd*)

	University of Glasgow | Business Records Centre 1975–1998 University of Glasgow | Archives and Business Records Centre 1998–2000
Dates of existence	2000 to date
History	Archive Services was created in 2000 following the renaming of the Archives and Business Records Centre. Archive Services is the central place of deposit for the records of the University created and accumulated since its foundation in 1451. The oldest records are charters dating from 1304 conveying land and privileges which eventually came into University hands. The department acts as the guardian of the University's collective memory as revealed in the records of management, administration, staff and students and thus protects the rights of all members of the University community. The department is also the guardian of Scotland's business and industrial history. The central aims of the department are to assist and promote the study of the past through the use of the archives it holds, in order to inform the present and the future and to advise the University on record-keeping issues and related information policy matters.
Places	Archive Services is located at three sites. The University Records Centre is at 12 Dunaskin Street, an office is at 77–87 Dumbarton Road and the searchroom is at 13 Thurso Street.
Administrative structure	In 1991, the service became part of the Academic Services Planning Unit. It subsequently became part of the Information Services Planning Unit. In 2004, following a reorganisation of the University's administration, it became part of the Information Services Division of Administrative, Information and Management Services.

Table 8.2 Example of ISAAR(CPF)-compliant authority record created during survey work at Glasgow University (*cont'd*)

Main function of business	Information Resources Management
Reference of records	GB 0248 GUA AS
Rules or conventions	NCA Rules, ISAAR(CPF), 2nd edition, 2004
Authority record created by	Moira Rankin, Senior Archivist, 4 February 2004
Authority record altered by	Victoria Peters, Research Archivist, 9 December 2004

Table 8.3 Example of ISAD(G)-compliant description of series created during survey work at Glasgow University

IDENTITY STATEMENT AREA

Reference code:

GB 0248 AS/5

Title:

Project management files

Dates of creation of material:

c.1990–

Creator:

University of Glasgow | Archive Services

Level of description:

Series

Extent of the unit of description:

0.5 metres

CONTEXT AREA

Administrative history:

A new paper file and computer folder is opened during the planning stages of each project and kept as part of the department's central filing system

Table 8.3	Example of ISAD(G)-compliant description of series created during survey work at Glasgow University (cont'd)

throughout the life of the project. The life of projects varies greatly and can be particularly short if a funding bid is not successful. The files may be subject to audit or inspection by external bodies which have funded the projects. Whilst projects are live the computer files are vital to the successful completion of the project. The routine back-up procedures are enough to protect this series.

CONTENT AND STRUCTURE AREA

Scope and content:

All significant papers relating to the management of an individual named project. This includes final bid documents; correspondence with project funding bodies, project partners and stakeholders; project plans; project reports.

It does not normally include monthly financial breakdowns or details of the recruitment and performance management of individual staff unless at bid stage the names of individuals are allocated. These are held in the related series noted below.

Appraisal, destruction and scheduling information:

Draft documents and irrelevant routine circulars from funding bodies are not normally retained on file. On completion of the project and submission of any final report, files are closed and sent to the University Records Centre. They are retained there for five years and the contents reviewed for permanent preservation purposes. Files will be retained permanently if seen after five years to have been particularly influential on the development of the department or on the archive profession more widely. Individual project management files may be required for different retention periods if the funding body so requires for audit purposes. Exceptions will be noted at individual file level. Files appraised as unworthy of permanent retention are confidentially destroyed.

Accruals:

Constant during the life of an individual project. Number of project files opened per year varies but rarely more than four.

System of arrangement:

There is normally one file per project, the contents are entered chronologically and indexed by a sheet inside the cover. For larger projects, there may be more than one file cover and different part numbers allocated. The current files are kept alphabetically by project title.

Table 8.3	Example of ISAD(G)-compliant description of series created during survey work at Glasgow University (cont'd)

CONDITIONS OF ACCESS AND USE AREA

Access:

The files are on open access to all current members of Archive Services staff. They are open for inspection by University and funding body officials or their authorised agents. More generally they are open one year after the completion of each project because, depending on the exact nature of the enquiry, disclosure of information during the project may affect intellectual property rights.

Physical characteristics:

The paper files are the central authoritative versions and are kept in the standard departmental labelled folders.

Digital documents relating to projects are filed on the drive shared by all members of Archive Services staff. Significant e-mails about projects are most likely to go to the Head of Department's staff e-mail account with the key documents being printed out and retained in paper form.

Finding aids:

File list available within the department including a list of files transferred to the custody of the University Records Centre and those kept permanently in the University Archive.

ALLIED MATERIALS AREA

Location of originals:

The contents of the project management files are mainly original documents created by Archive Services staff. However, files may also contain copies of documents gathered from elsewhere.

Existence of copies:

No known copies of the entire files although some documents from the files may be held elsewhere in the University or by funding bodies.

Related units of description:

Archive Services monthly financial reports
Finance Office Agresso finance system
Archive Services staff files
Human Resources staff files
Archive Services staff e-mail accounts
Archive Services project websites

Table 8.3	Example of ISAD(G)-compliant description of series created during survey work at Glasgow University (*cont'd*)

Research & Enterprise project approval forms
Information Services files

Publication note:

Regular project progress reports are normally published online in *Dunaskin News* or, if relevant, on the project's website. Summary project reports are also given in the Archive Services Annual Report.

NOTE AREA

Series level description compilation details:

Compiled by Moira Rankin, Senior Archivist, 04 February 2004.

Archivist's notes:

Description compiled in line with the following international standards: International Council on Archives Ad Hoc Commission on Descriptive Standards, *ISAD(G) General International Standard Archival Description* and National Council on Archives, *Rules for the construction of personal, place and corporate names.*

Archivist's notes (private):

Future action notes:

1. Some thought should be given to separating this file series depending on the different retention periods for different types of document or different stages of the bid.
2. The duplication of this documentation across University departments is likely to be minor.
3. Consideration should be given to appraising and weeding Records Centre project management files.

SUBJECT ENTRIES

Project management

ACTIVITY ENTRIES

Research Project Management

This sudden realisation of what now appears blindingly obvious, namely that the records continuum provides the constant between records management and archives management, has led to a rethink and redesign of the approach to records management support within the University of Glasgow. Archivists and records managers have merged into record-keeping professionals whose roles can move seamlessly between the present, future and past.

Faculty support teams

The concept of a continuum of care led to the creation within Glasgow University Archive Services of Faculty Support Teams, to work with and support academic faculties and departments and central administrative offices to improve their record keeping – for both current and archival records. In the long term, the teams will ensure that the Faculties use Glasgow University Archive Services to the fullest possible degree for public relations, academic research and administrative support. Individual members of staff will be able to specialise in promoting and using their own areas of expertise, for example in teaching archive skills classes and using archives for public relations and general outreach. However, the initial priority was in promoting good record-keeping practice across all departments to ensure a successful implementation of Freedom of Information in January 2005.

A great deal of good practice dissemination was carried out by the Faculty Support Teams, highlighting the guidance already available and encouraging departments to adopt best practice in record keeping. A needs analysis was carried out for training in areas such as vital records protection, filing schemes, record creation, filing system design and use, record-keeping legislative compliance, retention scheduling, record storage and disposal. Work on the production of an information asset register based on archival descriptive standards for record series produced by each department is scheduled to start in 2006. Descriptions of the records created by organisational units have been prepared for several units of organisation, although work was halted as preparations for the introduction of Freedom of Information legislation to Scottish universities diverted resources from this work.

Conclusion

The creation and use of activity descriptions to document over time the record-creating activities of Scottish higher education institutions has led to two major outcomes. First, it has resulted in a much more flexible and more objective system of representation. Instead of providing a highly subjective snapshot of records at a single point in time, we can now provide a whole series of images of records showing their changing uses and functions within the organisation. Users can see how the organisation evolved and how the purpose and use of records evolved with it.

It has also – and equally importantly – led to a practical outcome of the concept of the records continuum – a continuum of care between records management and archives management. The record-keeping context is a constant that should encourage the archives profession to reconsider its approach to records management. Archivists can be record-keeping professionals whose roles move seamlessly between the present, future and past. It is hoped that, when the final report on the Developing Archival Context Standards for Functions in the Higher Education Sector project is published, it will spark considerable debate on both archival descriptive practice and general record-keeping practice.

Notes

1. Miller, F.M., *Arranging and Describing Archives and Manuscripts* (Chicago, 1990), p. 7.
2. Horsman, P., 'Taming the elephant: an orthodox approach to the principle of provenance', in Abukhanfusa, K. and Sydbeck, J. (eds), *The Principle of Provenance. Report from the First Stockholm Conference on Archival Theory 1993* (Stockholm, 1994).
3. Reed, B., 'Records', in McKemmish, S. et al. (eds), *Archives. Recordkeeping in Society* (Wagga Wagga, 2005).
4. Ibid., p. 106.
5. Ibid., p. 102.
6. Cook, T., 'Fashionable nonsense or professional rebirth: postmodernism and the practice of archives', *Archivaria*, 50, 2000, pp. 93–116.
7. Reed, op. cit., p. 128.
8. Ibid.
9. For a discussion of the series approach to cataloguing, see McKemmish et al., op. cit., pp. 168–74.
10. For a practical application of this approach, see the online catalogue of the National Archives of Australia at *http://www.naa.gov.au/the_collection/recordsearch.html* (accessed 9 November 2005).
11. Winget, M., *The Archival Principle of Provenance and Its Application to Image Representation Systems* (available at *http://www.unc.edu/~winget/research/provenance.pdf*, accessed 9 November 2005).

12. Horsman, P., 'Dirty hands: a new perspective on the original order', *Archives and Manuscripts*, 27 (1), 1999, pp. 42–53.

13. Winget, op. cit.

14. GASHE was a project funded by the Research Support Libraries Programme (RSLP) which ran from 1999 to 2002 and was based at the University of Glasgow. It was designed to open up the outstanding collections of records produced by higher education institutions in Scotland and to make them fully accessible on the web via an integrated gateway. The ten partners in the project were representative of Scottish higher education from medieval to modern post-polytechnic universities. The aim was to provide an online resource, describing a variety of educational, intellectual and cultural resources to recognised international standards, which allowed seamless searching of archive and manuscript collections across all the educational institutions and their predecessors. The online resource enabled subject and limited functional guided navigation as well as providing value-added biographical and institutional access points. GASHE is available at *http://www.gashe.ac.uk* (accessed 9 November 2005).

15. The current model for the functions of higher education in the United Kingdom can be found at *http://www.jisc.ac.uk/srl_structure.html* (accessed 9 November 2005). It was compiled by Elizabeth Parker in 2003 and is a revised version of the model commissioned by JISC and published by Parker in 1999.

16. Both standards are available on the website of the International Council on Archives at *http://www.icacds.org.uk/eng/standards.htm* (accessed 9 November 2005).

17. The GASHE standard for creating activity descriptions is available at *http://www.gashe.ac.uk/about/standard.html* (accessed 9 November 2005).

18. Victoria Peters is the Glasgow University Archive Services' representative on the ICA Provisional Section on Standards and Best Practices. Details of the section are available at *http://www.ica.org/body.php?pbodycode=SPS& plangue=eng* (accessed 9 November 2005).

19. Available from *http://www.nahste.ac.uk* (accessed 9 November 2005).

20. EDINA's website is at *http://www.edina.ac.uk* (accessed 9 November 2005).

21. The technology behind the original GASHE and NAHSTE sites is described in Higgins, S. and Inglis, G., 'Implementing EAD: the experience of the NAHSTE project', *Journal of the Society of Archivists*, 24, 2003, pp. 199–214.

22. The official Encoded Archival Description website is available at *http://www.loc.gov/ead/* (accessed 9 November 2005).

23. For EAC resources, see *http://www.iath.virginia.edu/eac/* (accessed 9 November 2005).

24. McKemmish et al., op. cit., pp. 172–3.

25. Cook, op. cit., discusses many of the issues.

9

Archival digitisation: breaking out of the strong box

Ian Anderson

Introduction

There is a nineteenth-century folk tale of a Hebridean minister being dispatched to Glasgow to investigate the new-fangled electric telegraph. Upon his return he reported:

> Weel, it's hard tae explain something you'll nae understand, but imagine yon dog stretched from Stornoway tae Glasgow, if ye tickled his chin in Stornoway, he'd wag his tail in Glasgow.

As analogies go, it is not a bad one and it is tempting to seek similar ones to aid our understanding of digitisation. However, focusing on how the technology works is a limiting perspective. Certainly, our Hebridean forebears would have had to think beyond stretched dogs to imagine the pivotal role the telegraph played in administering Britain's disparate empire, let alone the era of global mass communication that it initiated.

This chapter will not dwell on the myriad technical details of digitisation.[1] As the stage of experimental digitisation projects is well behind us, the technology itself holds fewer mysteries. Although all cultural heritage collections are unique in some way, in terms of actually digitising them the key criteria are collections' size, shape and media. It doesn't matter if a book, manuscript or photograph is in an archive, library, museum or gallery, how it is actually digitised is the same, even if the way in which the digital surrogates are described and presented may well vary.

More important are the decisions that precede digitisation: the why, what and for whom. Although various generic approaches for this decision-making process have been developed, the implications for archival digitisation are not necessarily obvious. This chapter suggests a strategic and reflective approach to digitisation that emphasises the implications for archival practice in a digital age.

Why digitise?

The first question any institution embarking on digitisation needs to ask is not what to digitise, but why digitise at all? Although digitisation may seem de rigueur, it should not be started simply because of cultural heritage 'peer pressure'. As other chapters in this book have indicated, the transition to the digital raises many fundamental issues and the creation of digital surrogates has no fewer implications than that of born digital material or digital preservation for archival practice.

Broadly speaking, we can categorise the reasons to digitise cultural heritage collections into two: access and preservation. The practice of digital preservation is fraught with difficulty. While the need to preserve digital material is a real and present one, we should not be under any illusion that the creation of digital surrogates is in any way a preservation medium. At best, the digital surrogates can be considered an aid to analogue conservation, if access to the original resources is restricted and wear and tear are minimised.[2] Indeed, it is rare to find a digitisation project that claims its primary aim is preservation, if it makes this claim at all.

There are other reasons why an archive might consider digitisation. It can highlight particularly valuable or important collections, raise the profile of the institution and act as a beacon for future funding, donations or collection development. However, none of these reasons should detract from the fact that improving access is, and should be, the overriding aim of digitisation.[3] Typically, this is through the free distribution of digital surrogates over the World Wide Web. Certainly, the inherent ability of networked digital resources to transcend time and space frees cultural heritage collections from those who can only visit the physical collections. However, broadening access is predicated upon people having access to a computer, Internet connection and the freedom to use it. In the developed world this is an assumption we tend to make, but one that still excludes significant proportions of the population, let alone those in the developing world. Equal opportunity, social inclusion and lifelong learning are all laudable aims but one can also argue that money spent on digitisation benefits the white, middle classes more than it does minorities or the deprived. This does not mean we should not strive to achieve these objectives or that digitisation cannot play its part, but we need to be realistic and pragmatic about what we can do and why we are doing it.

However, digitisation for access immediately raises two important questions: access to what and access for whom? The answers to both of these questions are problematic because access has not traditionally been archives' primary concern. Their *raison d'être* has been collection development and preservation. As a result, archival theories, practices and standards have been predominantly orientated towards preservation, not access. Before archivists everywhere swell with righteous indignation, this comment is as much observation as criticism. In opportunity cost terms, preservation should come before access for archives. The problem arises because, whereas this decision is entirely justifiable in the analogue world, it is not so in the digital environment. Here, access must be privileged, but at the same time due consideration must also be given to managing and preserving these digital assets.

While we are offending cultural heritage professionals, we can also generalise that, although libraries have traditionally been accessible institutions, apart from special collections, they have tended to preserve material through accident rather than design. On the whole, material is meant to be borrowed, it is available on open shelves and directly accessible to the public, there are few if any regulations on how material can be used and handled, environmental conditions are not as stringent as in archives and users are not under the same level of supervision. This all aids access, but does little to minimise wear and tear on material. If material has not been rebound, replaced or thrown out it may, by good fortune, last long enough to acquire historical significance. Even then, it may not reach the embrace of special collections but languish in the preservation purgatory of the stack or remote store.

As for museums and galleries, they fall somewhere between archives and libraries. In general, they are more accessible than archives, but compared with libraries they have only ever been able to display a fraction of their collections and have had to strike a different balance between preservation and access. The cultural heritage sector as a whole is faced with the same digital opportunities, costs and problems, but each profession begins at a different starting point and brings different strengths and weaknesses to the digital table. The key is to better understand what archives' strengths and weaknesses are through a structured and strategic approach to planning digitisation.

The question of what to digitise poses problems for archives because many collections remain uncatalogued or have minimal descriptions, particularly to item level. It is only comparatively recently that serious attention has been paid to standards that facilitate online access, such as ISAD(G) and EAD. As we shall see, having existing descriptive metadata is a key factor in selection criteria for digitisation. The 'for whom' question poses a problem because archives have paid relatively little attention to user needs. Although great strides have been made in recent years, particularly through the efforts of the Public Service Quality Group (PSQG), where user evaluation has been undertaken it has focused on satisfaction with service and facilities, not on user segmentation, user needs analysis or establishing appropriate metrics.[4] Given the access rationale for digitisation, user needs is another key factor in shaping effective digitisation plans.

The challenge facing archives embarking on digitising is to transform themselves from organisations that 'store objects' to ones that manage the life cycle of digitised objects while providing access on a hitherto unprecedented scale.[5] As a result, when one considers models for the development of institutional digitisation plans, particular consideration needs to be given to the unique starting position in which archives find themselves. Such a model must help define the intellectual, historic and cultural value of collections, work across all media types, account for institutional objectives and enable strategic thinking, but also respond to archive access and user needs.

During the late 1990s various models or procedures for the selection of content for digitisation were produced.[6] All of these outline similar proposals, posing a series of questions regarding copyright, intellectual value, use, format, delivery, costs, benefits, etc. However, there is little evidence of widespread application of these procedures. In reviews of digitisation projects it is clear that institutions know why they have selected the material for digitisation, but there is little evidence of these decisions being documented arising from a clear institutional policy, or of digitisation being considered in a wider strategic context.[7] Of the selection models put forward, that of Ross provides the most strategic approach while embracing all of the planning issues required for a successful digitisation strategy.[8] Although this model suffers from a profusion of acronyms in its first iteration, it has proved itself as both a planning and an analytical tool.[9] Therefore, we can take the key principles and organisation of this model as a starting point for assessing the issues facing archival digitisation. As its name suggests, the Source-Orientated User-Driven Asset-Aware Model (SOUDAAM) emphasises detailed source surveys, recognises users as key to success and forces consideration of digital surrogates as intellectual assets.

Strategic thinking

No digitisation activity should be started without careful consideration as to how this activity supports an archive's aims, users and collections. Consideration also needs to be taken of an archive's size, organisation, resources and capabilities. This may seem a common-sense approach, but many digitisation projects are just that – small, individual, isolated, opportunistic activities that have little relation to their organisation's aims and objectives or that of their local, national or international counterparts. Indeed, it is not uncommon for projects within an organisation to have little or no relationship to one another. Today, many early adopters are still struggling to integrate their disparate digitisation projects into coherent digitisation programmes.

The adoption of a strategic approach is not limited to the project level. At a national and international level there is recognition that strategy, coordination and cooperation are key to releasing the potential of our cultural heritage. In April 2001 the European Union member states adopted the Lund Principles.[10] The main conclusions were that the member states could make progress on the eEurope objective if they:

- established an ongoing forum for coordination;
- supported the developing of a European view on policies and programmes;
- developed mechanisms to promote good practice and consistency of practice and skills development;
- worked in a collaborative manner to make visible and accessible the digitised cultural and scientific heritage of Europe.

The European Commission could help achieve the eEurope objectives by:

- supporting coordination activities;
- enabling the creation of centres of competence;
- fostering the development of benchmarking standards for digitisation practices;
- encouraging a framework that would enable a shared vision of European content;

- assisting member states to improve access and awareness for citizens through enhancing the quality and usability of content and the development of models to enable eCulture enterprises.

Early digitisation projects also demonstrated selection criteria that reflected curatorial, archivist or librarians' preferences in terms of what the 'best' or most appropriate items for digitisation were. While these characteristics were to be expected in the early, experimental days of digitisation, selection criteria generally have not evolved. The one new characteristic is the extent to which criteria have become funding driven. The consequence of these trends is that collaborative, large-scale and interrelated digitisation programmes are still the exception within the cultural heritage sector. It was these trends that Ross's model sought to address.

The outcome of SOUDAAM is the creation of a Digital Collection Development Plan and the process to achieving this is though strategic thinking and collection surveys. The first step in this process is to involve as many constituencies as possible. This includes managers, archivists and records managers but also users, curators, teachers, publicity and education officers and whoever else may make a useful contribution to, or be affected by, digitisation. Some of these people may not seem immediately relevant to developing a strategic view, but the point is to start from as broad an outlook as possible. An archive may never have considered developing specialist digital content to support secondary school teaching but, unless it allows for the possibility, it never will. Furthermore, irrespective of the direction in which a digital collection develops, it is crucial that it does not encounter internal resistance because key staff were not involved at the inception of the plan. Of particular importance in this respect is ensuring staff who are responsible for the curation of collections are involved in a risk assessment. Although it is easy to exaggerate the risks posed by digitisation, it is best to ensure these fears are allayed at the outset. Secondly, financially sustainable digitisation (that is, not reliant on further external grants) is something of a holy grail; having wider institutional and management support during lean times is crucial to continuity.

One of the other key means by which programmes can ensure broad institutional support is by relating digitisation to the mission of the archive or parent institution. This should include relating to existing policies for managing digital assets where these exist. Archives that exist as part of a larger organisation may not find this process so straightforward. For example, the access-driven aims of digitisation do not necessarily sit comfortably with a business that sees its archive's mission as supporting its compliance and marketing functions. Indeed, where any archive also fulfils records management, freedom of information or data protection roles, articulating an access-driven digitisation policy that does not conflict with these functions requires careful thought and involvement of senior management. At the very least, the scope and nature of digitisation may need to be more tightly defined from the outset.

For most archives, relating digitisation to its mission will involve fewer ethical considerations. Taking Glasgow University Archive Services as an example, it states its aims and objectives as given below.

Aims

The aims of Glasgow University Archive Services are:
- To assist and promote the study of the past through the use of archives in order to inform the present and the future
- To advise the University on record-keeping issues and related information policy matters
- To enhance the competitive position of the University through applied history/memory

Objectives

The objectives of Glasgow University Archive Services in pursuit of these aims are:
- *Selection* – guiding the records management processes for the University and selecting records to provide an information resource for present and future generations
- *Preservation* – preserving the records for current and future use
- *Access* – providing access to the records and promoting their value and use as an information and educational resource

---

An appropriate digitisation policy statement might then read:

Glasgow University Archive Services' digitisation programme supports its core aims and objectives by providing greater access to the records of the University and adding value to their use as information and educational resources. This enhances the study of the past and increases the competitiveness of the University by providing new opportunities for applied history/memory.

This is an innocuous enough statement but it is the process of relating any proposed digitisation activity to an organisation's aims that is important. It is an opportunity to reconsider what an archive is for, for whom and how digitisation may, or may not, support these aims and objectives.

Collaboration

The next aspect of strategic thinking is to relate archival digitisation to other local, national or international initiatives. The purpose of this is to seek and plan for collaboration at the outset. It is only by collaboration that archives can build a critical mass of content, share resources and expertise, and avoid duplication and reinventing the wheel. Unfortunately, there is no single convenient source by which to identify complementary digitisation projects. However, projects should look beyond traditional archival networks and seek out cross-domain cooperation with those in libraries, museums and galleries. It is important to bear in mind that the majority of users will not know, or necessarily care, that the material they seek is in a library, archive or museum. As related collections do not always conveniently reside in a single repository, establishing collaborative partnerships can greatly assist in leveraging the value of individual collections.[11] This is also sometimes the only way in which smaller or poorly resourced archives can gain access to specialised equipment, expertise or services.

Collaboration is also important in one other regard. Despite the utopian vision of its founders, the World Wide Web is not a world of equals. The online information world is a competitive one, and one increasingly dominated by global players such as Microsoft, Yahoo, Google, Springer, Emerald et al. The notion of a global digital library might have seemed entirely fanciful until Google took it upon themselves to shatter a few illusions.[12] If the New York Public Library and the libraries of Harvard University, Stanford University, the University of Oxford and the University of Michigan see the benefits of collaboration, then this suggests that it is imperative for other, less well-endowed institutions to do likewise. Of course, Google's digital library project has not been without its controversies, not least authors' and publishers' legal challenge over copyright.[13] Nor should it be forgotten that full texts will only be made available for public domain works. Nevertheless, the writing is on the wall: even for large institutions, collaboration is key to securing a place in the digital world.

Nor is competition limited to global corporations. In its recent review of digital image provision for UK higher and further education, the Joint Information Systems Committee (JISC) Images Working Group proposes digitising institutional slide collections as a more cost-effective means of providing a critical mass of digital art and culture collections than ongoing subscription fees to multiple commercial image libraries.[14] Even relatively small publishers have access to resources, technical skills and publishing alliances that outweigh even national repositories. Furthermore, there are literally millions of local history societies, professional researchers, academics and genealogists who are providing archival content online, even if the quality of this content is sometimes questionable. Nor can we assume that these small contributions, however imperfect they may be, will remain hidden.[15] There is further evidence from the UK that a more coordinated approach is being taken to such issues. The recent Community Led Images Collection (CLIC) report by the Learning Technologies Group at Oxford University Computing Services has suggested a three-tier network that shares catalogue information from the local to national level to harness community image collections for learning and teaching.[16]

This scenario should not be read as one of archives hopelessly besieged from all sides. It does, however, raise important questions about the role of the archivist in the online information world. As we shall see, the process of developing a digitisation plan also reveals where archives' competitive advantage lies. However, we should be under no illusion that this advantage can be best exploited by going it alone. Collaboration across the cultural heritage sector and potentially with online information providers, commercial publishers, universities and community groups represents opportunities, not threats. After all, how best to provide access to digital cultural heritage content is not an issue unique to archives, or one that can be addressed alone.

User evaluation

If cross-sector collaboration is a highly desirable component of effective digitisation, then an essential feature is consideration of user needs. As digitisation's primary benefit is improved access, we immediately need to ask: what type of access and for whom? Improved access can mean different things to different people, as access can be improved in terms of both increased numbers and more diverse users. These two approaches are not mutually exclusive, and the latter has been the driving force behind much of the government's investment in digitisation in the guise of social inclusion and lifelong learning. However, both approaches require archivists to engage with users and user communities in ways that hitherto they have not shown much evidence of doing.

Becoming user focused may not require as great a shift in professional practice as a decade ago, but archivists are still finding it hard to love their users as much as they love their collections. In a 2003/2004 survey of 70 UK archives, only half had conducted any form of user survey and just eight of these considered user needs.[17] Furthermore, where user consultation did take place this tended to be infrequent, ad hoc and often associated with a particular project or development. In other words, user evaluation was an external, functional activity. One can consider user evaluation in the digitisation process in a similar vein, but to do so would be to miss an opportunity to integrate user evaluation into the archival process. But why should archives do this?

When collections and finding aids only existed in print form and all users visited the repository in person, archivists were able to inform, guide and respond to users' needs on the ground. This type of support simply does not translate into the online digital environment. Users still need as much, if not more, support, but their needs have to be anticipated unless archives are prepared to provide online support 24 hours a day, seven days a week. This issue has not gone unrecognised, but if and how users should be incorporated into the development of archival practices remains unresolved. As Cox points out, 'We also know that many of our traditional views about books and records, libraries and archives, rest on complex assumptions about society, technology, information, and information use that are, in fact, quite prone to change, and these are prone to be challenged.'[18] Digitisation poses one such challenge but also an opportunity to test these assumptions, make archives more efficient, and enhance understanding of their collections and the public's opinion of archives by integrating user evaluation into archival processes.

User evaluation is critical in one other respect, that of trust. Over the last fifty years Britain has become a far less deferential society and we are much less likely to accept the opinion and authority of professionals at face value. Constant media reporting of the fallibility of politicians, police, doctors, teachers and social services has further eroded our faith in the professional classes. This has been accompanied by moves to make professional and public bodies more accountable and transparent and involve patients, parents or users directly. There is no evidence that archives or archivists are suffering any loss in reputation. Indeed, archives, libraries and museums have an enviable reputation as trustworthy sources of information, even if they are not regarded as the most accessible institutions.[19] Digitisation can help solve the access part of the problem, but trust cannot be taken for granted. While it is tempting to dismiss many instances of public-sector consultation as window dressing, involving users in the decision-making process is one activity that will help maintain trust in archives through the vagaries of the digital environment.

To fully exploit the benefits of user evaluation requires a view of archival practice that allows for systematic user input. However, whatever view we take of archive practice or archival science, there appears little room for user input. We can certainly find a systematic approach, based on an internal rationality, that has given archives a functional form and structure. Subsequently, this has been combined with elements of philosophical enquiry and scientific theory to produce a distinctive professional discipline that combines both doctrine and theory. Even if we look in more detail within the discipline we can identify three, broad and sometimes competing approaches, but none that has explicit user involvement. The narrative approach has seen the development of institutional activities such as appraisal, preservation, storage and access. The empirical approach has sought to understand the contents and activities of archival collections in terms of record creators and use. Lastly, the postmodern approach has concentrated on the history of ideas and values, structures and lost information. What is less clear is how these theories can be reconciled with a methodological approach that embodies user input for archives in the digital age.

Berndt Fredriksson has proposed one such model.[20] This starts from the premise that only through establishing differentiated value categories and scales for those values can we obtain the optimum amount of information for archival collections. Fredriksson suggests these value categories might cover issues such as accountability, social justice, research potential and cultural heritage. In order to obtain relevant information for these categories a structural overview of the available, or potentially available, information is required. This information could be produced and recorded by the creator, already exist in archival documentation or be otherwise controlled by archivists (including extending control back to information creators to ensure today's 'black holes' are filled). This in turn requires appropriate methods of information analysis informed by evaluation and it is this evaluation stage that distinguishes this model.

Fredriksson breaks evaluation down into four components – the evaluation of administrative needs, source value, user value and informational value. Indeed, it is only through user evaluation that precise value categories can be determined and appropriate value scales applied. Users will also have an input to source and informational value, and we can also think of archivists themselves as users, certainly in terms of administrative needs of material. As we shall see, a similar evaluation approach is required for digitisation collection surveys. This allows us to marry established procedures for digitisation with those of an archival approach that also incorporates evaluation. Moreover, there is a small but growing body of research that is providing new insights into archive users' behaviour and demonstrating the value of user needs evaluation.[21]

Evaluation in general can be classified into three stages – front-end, formative and summative (before, during and after a project). In the initial phases of planning for digitisation it is front-end evaluation that is of prime concern.[22] This type of evaluation can assist in the selection of content areas and themes, provide feedback about the type of service and functionality required and enable the archive to make a general assessment of users' attitudes towards digitisation. Involving users early on helps ensure that digitisation is more likely to meet their expectations and needs. Front-end evaluation should also provide an opportunity to assess, from a user's perspective, whether digitisation is the best way to meet their needs or whether simpler and more affordable solutions might be more appropriate.[23]

At this stage in the process it is important to consider how we conceive of our users, particularly as existing users may not be those we seek to attract through digitisation. It is tempting to think of users according to their role, and user surveys often ask the question: 'Are you a historian/genealogist/researcher/student?' etc. However, what we are often seeking when asking this question is not what people do for a living but why they are visiting or using the archive. Therefore, a more appropriate question might be: 'Why are you using the resource: academic research, teaching, school project, family history research or general browsing?' We must also bear in mind that users will have a variety of age groups, educational attainment and interests, and other appropriate classifications might include their area, period or subject of interest, age group, educational level, gender or ethnicity.

The exact questions one would ask at this stage will depend upon the particular aims of the digitisation programme. However, there are several questions that any digitisation programme needs to be able to answer before undertaking further planning:

- Who are your anticipated users?
- How large are these groups?
- Are these users different from users of the analogue collection?
- How geographically dispersed are they?
- Do they want remote access to digital surrogates?
- If so, for what type of material?
- Is their priority download speed or image quality?
- Do they want to be able to purchase high-resolution images or a printed version?
- How do users find and work with the analogue material?
- Is there a demand for added functionality, such as zooming, transcriptions, translation and encoded electronic texts?
- How much and what type of information should accompany the digital surrogates?
- Do different user groups require different features?

However well an archive knows its existing users and their methods with analogue material, it is certain that the digital environment will encourage new ways of working, new users and new demands. It might not be possible to meet all of these demands for all users, but the sooner these needs are recognised the sooner that priorities can be established, articulated and incorporated into a digitisation strategy.

Collection survey

Having covered strategic thinking, collaboration and user needs, attention must turn to the collections themselves. For archives this will be more familiar territory, and it is here that archivists have clear transferable skills, even if these skills may need to be applied in different ways.

The first and most crucial aspect of this stage of digitisation planning is intellectual property rights (IPR). Of these, copyright is the most obvious but there are other legal issues to be considered. Before any consideration of what to digitise it is vital to know the copyright status of collections, whether you have the rights to the material and if these rights extend to creating digital surrogates. This may well pose less of a problem for archive collections than for library holdings, but the terms of deposit, if they exist at all, may well not have envisaged the ease with which material can be distributed and copied in the digital age. The majority of depositors or their descendants may well have no objection to creating digital surrogates, but identifying, contacting and gaining permissions is a time-consuming and expensive task. For material that is in copyright and the rights do not reside with the archive, it is probably best left on the shelf. Even if material is out of copyright, or the rights reside with the archive, care must still be taken not to infringe any moral rights or the sensibilities of those associated with the collection. This is particularly the case with correspondence and ethnographic collections. Of course, one can be overly cautious and common sense will dictate where the value of digitisation outweighs the risk of uncertain copyright status.

Although there may be no copyright issues in the original material, there are remaining IPR issues to be considered. Any digital surrogates will become the intellectual assets of the archive that creates them (unless rights revert to the original depositor). The vast majority of these digital assets will have no commercial benefit. Where this does arise, the archive concerned will need to manage their licensing. At a simple level, readily downloadable images will be of insufficient resolution for others to exploit commercially. However, if high-resolution images are to be provided on request, immediate questions arise as to how the use of these images is managed. Various technical solutions to protecting IPR can be adopted, from simple watermarks through to encryption, but the key to success is having the procedures and resources to monitor and enforce these rights and this does not come cheaply.

Alongside IPR, metadata is the second necessary prerequisite that has to be considered as part of any collection's survey. In this respect, archives are somewhat at a disadvantage compared with libraries, museums and galleries. Apart from the backlog of uncatalogued or minimally listed collections, the extent of item-level descriptions is generally limited and/or not available in electronic format. Given that item-level descriptive metadata is essential for digital content discovery, this can put archival collections at an inherent disadvantage. Although it is possible to include descriptive cataloguing in digitisation projects, this will inevitably prove to be more time-consuming, and at least as expensive, as the digitisation itself. If digitisation is going to be the impetus for cataloguing, it is important to remember that it is difficult to disguise overt cataloguing projects as digitisation in funding applications. One can certainly question the merits of millions of pounds being made available for digitisation when such a backlog of archival cataloguing exists. This situation is even more lamentable, given how critical accurate, detailed and accessible descriptive information is to successful digitisation. After all, it makes no difference if archival material is available in digital form if users cannot find it.

The comparative paucity of item level descriptions provides other challenges for archives contemplating digitisation. Archival descriptive practices and standards have been built around the importance of original order and understanding items within the context of the collection as a whole. As a result, recent developments such as ISAD(G) have provided valuable international standards, but ones that work best at higher levels of description. The lack of item level descriptive standards is not unique to archives, but the position here is most acute. It is fanciful to imagine that we will ever have standards agreed that enable archivists to describe every item in every collection. Nevertheless, the absence of such standards inevitably means there is much duplication of effort and inconsistency of description. This in turn provides a real handicap for the development and searching of union catalogues and even more so for cross-domain searching.

As the section on selection below indicates, digitised material may well come from several collections, and not all collections may be represented in their entirety. Therefore, archives need to consider if they are going to include collection level descriptions and, if so, to what extent. Part of this deliberation must also include whether such information is useful to all users in all circumstances. It is easy to envisage, for example, that these descriptions may be of limited use to academics or experienced users. It must also be remembered that many users will not access digitised archive material through the root page of the finding aid. They are far more likely to follow a direct link from a web search engine. In these circumstances, context may become even more important to some users, so how the user is made aware of this information in these circumstances becomes crucial. Even if users locate material through searching or browsing the finding aid directly, there are real issues as to how users can maintain their view of the collection as a whole, while at the same time viewing individual digital surrogates. Within a few paragraphs we have rapidly moved from the existence of metadata as a consideration in collection surveys to the online representation of finding aids. However, it is just such consequences that need to be borne in mind if the maximum benefit is to be obtained through digitisation.

Unfortunately, metadata issues do not end here. All digitisation projects require the creation of administrative and structural metadata. Administrative metadata is created to aid the reuse and management of the digital surrogates. Typically this includes information on IPR issues and technical details of the digitisation process. Given the significance of the collection context for archives, of more concern is structural metadata. This is used to describe both the internal and external relationships of individual digitised items. In this regard archives do at least have the advantage of ready-made structural metadata in the shape of EAD. Creating EAD finding aids is not without its own time and resource demands, but under the circumstances archives do at least have a well-understood starting point.

With these barriers out of the way, the collection survey can proceed to the thorny issue of selecting and prioritising material. Given that we will not be able to digitise everything, at least not in the short term, unambiguous and consistent selection criteria are required. In the early days of digitisation, selection was often based on the preferences of an individual archivist, curator or librarian. This was understandable when an entrepreneurial individual drove digitisation projects and these selection decisions may not have been inappropriate. However, there are good reasons why selection should be put on a more formal basis. First, as previous sections have indicated, digitisation is best carried out in a consultative and collaborative fashion. As digitisation inevitably involves a degree of selectivity, involving archive staff, collaborators and users in this decision-making process can be particularly valuable. Secondly, being able to justify selection decisions on transparent and consistent criteria is a protection against the accusation that archives are privileging one type of material, collection or user group above another. Lastly, this is an area where archivists bring something unique to the digitisation table. While all cultural heritage professionals will assess their collections in one way or another, none do so to the same extent or in the same manner as archivists. Appraisal is bread and butter to any archivist. Weeding, sorting, grouping and assessing material for its cultural, historic and societal value and information significance is routine. Furthermore, this is conducted in the context of the repository's collection policy and related material within the repository and elsewhere. Appraisal may be archivists' least publicised skill, but it is one that is particularly relevant to digitisation.

In many respects the selection parameters applied in digitisation are analogous to those used in standard appraisal; however, the criteria may need to be applied differently. Obviously, archival collections already have historical, cultural, research or informational value. However, the extent of these values will vary within and between collections. Moreover, selection criteria should include consideration by material categories, subjects or themes, geographic areas or other interrelations. This may well result in only parts of collections being selected as candidates for digitisation.

Recognition also needs to be made of the fact that there are often sound reasons for not digitising material. Aside from a low, or lower, informational value, material can be inappropriate for a number of other reasons. Although it is legitimate to hold material that may be offensive in some shape or form, common sense dictates that it is an entirely different matter to make such material freely available in digital format. A less obvious area of concern includes ethnographic, anthropological and medical collections. Many of our forebears did not possess our cultural sensitivity and it is easy to overlook the fact that what had been acceptable a century ago would not be so today. Therefore, while such collections have legitimate historical value, reproducing the sins of the past through digitisation is best avoided. Material in poor condition or where suitable equipment and technology are not available would also constitute legitimate reasons for postponing digitisation. Material that has a low demand may also appear to be justifiably relegated from the selection list. However, this criterion needs to be applied cautiously. Archives need to be sure that the low demand is not due to lack of awareness of the material's existence, difficulty in handling or problems in using and understanding the content. It is entirely possible that in these cases digitisation would release a previously untapped demand.

Implementation plan

Having applied such selection criteria, archives are still likely to be faced with a vast range of potential material for digitisation. With a view to implementation, it is then possible to reapply the selection criteria as prioritisation questions. Exactly which criteria to apply will depend on the specific circumstances of the project, users and archive, and may vary between selection and prioritisation.

In Table 9.1, prioritisation questions have been provided in a weighted matrix. By giving each question a weight, projects are able to produce a consistent, comparative and transparent process for prioritising content for digitisation.

While the intellectual values of materials are essential selection criteria, their physical characteristics also influence selection for digitisation. The first principle of all digital capture is to start from the source material, as it is the relationship between physical properties, document categories and digitisation categories that determines the digitisation process. Where time and resources allow, it is most efficient to conduct an analysis of physical properties during the collection survey. If this is not possible, it is essential that this be done prior to digitisation, as failure to do so has a detrimental effect on workflow, costs and quality. This is because material that shares common physical properties is best digitised together in batches. Ultimately, any survey of physical properties needs to divide the material first into transparent (slides and film) or reflective (everything else, except audio/video sources). The transparency category then needs to be divided into positive or negative and then the various formats, such as 35 mm, 120, 6 × 4, glass plates, then black and white or colour. It may even be worthwhile categorising material according to film stock, as different film has different colour casts that can be time-consuming to optimise.

For reflective material the categories are far greater. The first consideration is the structure of the material – bound, mounted or loose. Loose material is by far the easiest to handle and digitise; mounted, and particularly bound, material often requires specialist cradles or book scanners. If the bindings are tight, and the volume cannot be disbound, it might not even be possible to digitise it effectively at all. Then size and dimensions need to be recorded. Again it is far more effective to digitise material in batches that have uniform dimensions. Standard flatbed scanners will only handle loose material up to A4 size. Anything larger will require a large-format flatbed scanner, digital camera and copystand or wide-format scanner.

Medium type (paper, velum, leather, etc.), content structure (particularly mixed media of image and text) and production process (handwritten, typescript, half-tone print, engraving, gold leaf, etc.) do not affect which technology is used to digitise but they do have a significant effect on capture settings. Different media types provide different levels of background contrast. Where text and images are juxtaposed, it is highly unlikely that capture settings could be optimised for both. In these

Table 9.1   Prioritisation questions

Questions	Score	Weight	Total
Would making the material available diminish or enhance the value of the underlying collection?			
Would conversion of the material leverage the opening up of material in other collections?			
Have other projects digitised complementary material?			
Is the material unique?			
Is there an existing demand for the material?			
Will digitisation create a demand for the material?			
Will the digital content be capable of being reused for multiple purposes?			
Will it be necessary or possible to monitor how the material is used?			
Would digital representation assist in the conservation of the material?			
Is there potential for commercial exploitation where such exploitation would not diminish the value of the item or collection?			
Does the material have untapped research potential?			
Would the improved functionality digitisation would bring enhance the research potential of the item or collection?			
Could the material play a role as a teaching resource?			
Would digitisation lead to financial savings through reducing infrastructure and labour costs associated with supporting collection management and access?			
Would digitisation have publicity benefits?			
Is the current generation of technology suitable or would it be better to wait?			

circumstances a project will need to decide if it is going to optimise capture for one or the other or capture both separately. If the latter, this raises the issue of how the relationship between the two is indicated.

The production process can affect digitisation in more subtle ways. Handwritten and typescript material are resolution-dependent for legibility. Anything printed using the halftone process will probably display the moiré effect. These are digital artefacts that appear as a 'herringbone' pattern and are caused by a conflict between the sampling used in digitisation and the dots and lines used in the halftone printing process. This can be corrected at the capture stage using a 'descreen' tool.

Digitisation can be broadly defined into three categories – bitonal, greyscale and colour. It is useful to categorise material in this way as well as according to its colour information. Material that is pure black and white equates to bitonal scanning. Where the material has tonal range but no colour, this should be captured as greyscale (usually 8 bit) and, whenever colour is present, the material should be captured in colour (usually 24 bit). For greyscale and colour material, noting whether or not it has a wide dynamic range (or tonal range) can be useful. Transparencies and photographic prints tend to have the widest dynamic range that can test the limits of even the best capture equipment. In particular, it can be difficult to capture details in shadow areas and this type of material may need more prolonged experimentation to reproduce faithfully in digital format. Lastly, the condition of the material, its sensitivity to light exposure and any conservation work required are best identified as soon as possible.

Such detailed consideration of the physical properties of collections may seem excessively time-consuming. Certainly, it is not an activity to be taken on lightly, but hopefully at least some information, such as size and condition, may already exist. However, projects should not be tempted to skip this stage in implementation planning. Any estimates of cost, workflow or time and motion that have not been based on this information will be hopelessly optimistic and will inevitably jeopardise success.

With content selection issues out of the way, attention can turn to the last set of factors in any implementation plan, that of institutional capacity. Working in an organisation that already undertakes digitisation is a major benefit. It is far more likely that suitable equipment, for capture, processing, storage and delivery, as well as experienced staff, is already available. Projects that take place in large institutions also benefit from a significant amount of non-project-related investment. Such 'benefits-in-kind' can include local area networks, high bandwidth

Internet connections, networked storage, web servers and backup devices as well as related technical expertise. This infrastructure capacity provides a very valuable framework that helps projects in well-resourced institutions start up quickly even if the real costs of their digitisation activities are often opaque. However, such capacity is not always the advantage it may seem. Archives may find themselves tied into restrictive service level agreements of their parent organisation or unable to access the expertise and infrastructure in a way that matches their project goals and user needs. In these circumstances, developing in-house capacity may be the only realistic alternative, even if it entails some duplication of resources and skills. Whether existing resources are available or not, a thorough identification of resource requirements will enable any archive to better plan its digitisation development.

One significant area that has not been directly addressed is that of costs. In part this is because no estimate of costs can be undertaken until all of the factors mentioned above have been analysed. Furthermore, it is extremely difficult to provide any sort of universal cost model because so many variables are project specific and cost information from comparable projects is rare.[24]

Conclusion

As this chapter has attempted to indicate, successful archival digitisation requires strategic thinking and planning and relating these activities to archival practice. It needs to recognise the primacy of enhanced access and depends upon collaboration, evaluation of user needs, detailed collection surveys and implementation planning. Given that this work requires time and effort, commodities that are in short supply at the best of times, it may seem that this is one can of digital worms that is best left unopened. However, the opportunity cost of archives not taking their place at the digitisation table, and bringing with them their unique skills, is likely to be far greater. There is a great deal of hyperbole surrounding the 'digital age' but archives have too much to offer, and the public too much to lose, if archives fail to fully engage in this process. Taking the approach outlined above will help archives do this from a position of strength and ensure that they can provide high-quality digital surrogates that maximise the value of their collections not just in terms of immediate access but also for long-term use and re-purposing.

Notes

1. TASI is an excellent online resource: *http://www.tasi.ac.uk* for technical information. Kenney, Anne R. and Rieger, Oya Y., *Moving Theory into Practice: Digital Imaging for Libraries and Archives* (Mountain View, CA, 2000); Besser, Howard, Hibbard, Sally and Lenert, Deborah (eds), *Introduction to Imaging,* revised edn (Los Angeles, CA, 2003); and Koelling, Jill Marie, *Digital Imaging: A Practical Approach* (Walnut Creek, CA, 2004) are recent additions to the print cannon.

2. Anecdotal evidence suggests that in the short term at least the availability of digital surrogates can increase the demand for the originals, particularly where awareness of, or access to, the originals has been limited.

3. Smith, Abby, *Why Digitize?* (Washington, DC, 1999), *http://www.clir.org/pubs/abstract/pub80.html*.

4. See *http://www.nationalarchives.gov.uk/archives/psqg/* for the work of the PSQG and *http://www.si.umich.edu/ArchivalMetrics/Index.html* for attempts to address the lack of appropriate metrics for user needs.

5. *The DigiCULT Report, Technological Landscapes for Tomorrow's Cultural Economy*, European Commission, Directorate-General for the Information Society, 2002, pp. 89–90.

6. Research Libraries Group (ed.), *Selecting Library and Archive Collections for Digital Reformatting*, Proceedings from an RLG Symposium, 5–6 November 1995, Washington, DC (Mountain View, CA: Research Libraries Group, 1996); Hazen, Dan, Horrell, Jeffrey and Merrill-Oldham, Jan, *Selecting Research Collections for Digitization* (Washington, DC, 1998), *http://www.clir.org/pubs/reports/hazen/pub74.html*; Ayris, P., *Guidance for Selecting Materials for Digitisation*, Joint RLG and NPO Preservation Conference: Guidelines for Digital Imaging, 28–30 September 1998, *http://www.rlg.org/preserv/joint/ayris.html*.

7. See Chapter 3 of *The NINCH Guide to Good Practice in the Digital Representation and Management of Cultural Heritage Materials*, The Humanities Advanced Technology and Information Institute (HATII), University of Glasgow, and the National Initiative for a Networked Cultural Heritage (NINCH), Washington, DC, 2002, *http://www.nyu.edu/its/humanities/ninchguide/III/*.

8. Ross, S., 'Strategies for selecting resources for digitization: Source-Orientated, User-Driven, Asset-Aware Model (SOUDAAM)', in Coppock, Terry (ed.), *Making Information Available in Digital Format: Perspectives from Practitioners* (Edinburgh, 1999), pp. 5–27.

9. The SOUDAAM model underpinned HATII's feasibility and pilot study for the Wiltshire Wills Project, Wiltshire and Swindon Record Office (for images from the pilot study, see: *http://www.hatii.arts.gla.ac.uk/research/wiltwill.html*) and part of the interview instrument and report for *The NINCH Guide to Good Practice in the Digital Representation and Management of Cultural Heritage Materials*.

10. The Lund Principles can be found in full here: *http://www.cordis.lu/ist/digicult/lund_p_browse.htm*. A review of progress to date can be found in Ross, S., 'Reflections on the impact of the Lund Principles on European

approaches to digitisation', in *Strategies for a European Area of Digital Cultural Resources: Towards a Continuum of Digital Heritage* (The Hague, 2004), pp. 88–98.

11. All too rare examples of such collaboration can be found in many of the NOF Digitise projects at *http://www.enrichuk.net/*. See, for example, *http://www.theglasgowstory.co.uk/index.php*.

12. *http://print.google.com/googlebooks/library.html*. For an alternative approach, see 'European libraries fight Google-ization', *Deutsche Welle*, 27 April 2005, *http://www.dw-world.de/dw/article/0,1564,1566717,00.html*.

13. See, for example, 'Copyright lawsuit challenges Google's vision of digital library', *Christian Science Monitor*, 26 September 2005.

14. JISC Images Working Group, *Steps Towards a National Vision for Images*, JISC, May 2005, p. 8.

15. Yahoo's Content Acquisition Program includes methods for tapping into documents from what is called the 'invisible web', that is content rarely reached by web crawlers or residing in proprietary databases.

16. CLIC, *Investigating Community-Led Image Collections*, CLIC Project, January 2006. See *http://clic.oucs.ox.ac.uk/index.html*.

17. Research conducted as part of the Primarily History project. The survey will form part of a forthcoming paper by Ian Anderson and Professor Helen Tibbo.

18. Cox, Richard J., 'Access in the digital information age and the archival mission: the United States', *Journal of the Society of Archivists*, 19 (1), 1998, p. 26.

19. Usherwood, B., *Perception of Archives, Libraries and Museums in Modern Britain* (Sheffield, 2005).

20. I am grateful to Berndt Fredriksson of the Swedish Ministry of Foreign Affairs and Professor of Archival Science at the University of Stockholm for sharing his views at the Workshop on Archival Information Seeking, Use and Access, Mid Sweden University, June 2005.

21. Mortimer, Ian, 'Discriminating between readers: the case for a policy of flexibility', *Journal of the Society of Archivists*, 23 (1), 2002; Duff, Wendy and Johnson, Catherine A., 'Accidentally found on purpose: information seeking behavior of historians in archives', *Library Quarterly*, 72 (4), 2002; Garmendia, Jone, 'User input in the development of online services: the PRO catalogue', *Journal of the Society of Archivists*, 23 (1), 2002; Tibbo, Helen R., 'Primarily history: how US historians search for primary sources at the dawn of the digital age', *American Archivist*, 66 (1), Spring/Summer 2003; Hallam Smith, E., 'Customer focus and marketing in archive service delivery: theory and practice', *Journal of the Society of Archivists*, 24 (1), 2003.

22. A note on terminology: while formative and summative evaluation are accepted terms, front-end evaluation is less so. In this context it is used to mean pre-project evaluation and should not be confused with user interface evaluation.

23. For a guide to evaluation methods, see *http://www.icbl.hw.ac.uk/ltdi/cookbook/contents.html*.

24. For a good exception, see Puglia, Steven, 'The costs of digital imaging projects', *RLG DigiNews*, 3 (5), 15 October 1999.

10

The function of the archive

Michael Moss

Much contemporary writing about archives and records management
is introspective and defensive. It is dominated by the critique of poststructuralists and postmodernists, who are perceived as problematising
not just content but the archive itself.[1]

A response has been to fetish the document itself and appraisal
(the selection of objects to populate the archive) by emphasising its
supposed objectivity, which has been reinforced by adopting the function
analysis techniques of social scientists.[2] Such an approach has convinced
archivists and records managers that there is an intimate relationship
between their two responsibilities, which transcends the objects
(documents or records) themselves. Another reaction has been to extol
access as a paradigm shift to counter arguments that the way archivists
construct their catalogues and finding aids is a barrier to entry.[3] Such
reasoning has been facilitated by the rise of the Internet, which has made
it possible for users to access catalogues and finding aids globally in ways
that could only be done before with great difficulty and at considerable
expense. This opportunity has been exploited by developing standards
for archival description (EAD, ISAD(G) and so on) and seeking agreement
for naming conventions to enable cross-walking.[4] The difficulty with both
these strands in archival/records management thinking is that they ignore
the profound changes in the realm of information, which are indeed
problematising the archive and the record. Even where archival theory
addresses the identity and morphology of the objects by drawing on the
long tradition of 'diplomatic', there is often a failure to recognise that
there might be something to contribute to ontological understanding in
the digital age.[5] Such introspection excludes archival sciences from the
literature of the disciplines that make direct use of archives, such as
history and literary studies, and those where the recording of information

is either observed or required, such as accountancy, anthropology, ethnography, philosophy and political science.[6]

The management of records is concerned with the control of flows of information within an organisation and is increasingly considered to be a vital component of good corporate governance, as more and more information is exposed to external scrutiny with the relentless advance of the audit society in both the private and, of more concern, the public sector.[7] This now stretches far beyond purely financial audit and has in many countries become an instrument of public policy with serious penalties for non-compliance.[8] The growth of the culture of audit can be traced to the neo-liberals, who combined the highest moral principles with managerial efficiency to foreshadow Francis Fukuyama's end of history.[9] Marilyn Strathern and other anthropologists have argued compellingly that such a constructed audit culture simply seeks to record what is to be audited, often against a normative abstraction.[10] Not only is there a dangerous circularity about the record keeping that is likely to underpin the audit society, the aberrant or anomalous is likely to be at best overlooked and at worst discarded. Audit coupled with freedom of information in the public sector not only shapes the contours of record series but also the content, as organisations seek to avoid disclosure of sensitive information and interact with communities that they engage.[11] Given that in any organisation it is impossible to retain and manage all the records that might be of interest to an auditor, records management becomes of necessity a question of exposure to risk, which in turn will skew even more the totality of the record.[12] Risk cannot be delegated through an organisation, as those who are fiduciarily accountable for its management have to take responsibility for any failure. Exposure to risk has to be constrained, which requires that information that might result in future liabilities will be destroyed when it is no longer necessary for it to be retained. Although the volume of information within an organisation that may be exposed to external scrutiny is growing, there is information that remains private on such grounds as commercial confidence or national security. Such information, however, has to be considered as intangible assets which will only be 'managed' if it provides competitive advantage or contributes to the bottom line. This is notoriously difficult to measure, but arguably the very act of measurement is reductionist, with all the dangers implicit in the audit culture.

The advance of the audit culture, as Michael Power has argued, represents a failure of trust, but paradoxically the 'spread of audit actually creates the very distrust it is meant to address'.[13] Records managers have sought justification for their profession in 'accountability' without questioning how it is to be discharged.[14] The moral philosopher Onora O'Neill explored this theme in her 2002 Reith lectures entitled 'A Question of Trust'.[15] In her third lecture 'Called to account', she rightly identified that the audit culture requires 'detailed conformity to procedures and protocols, detailed record keeping and provision of information in specified formats and success in reaching targets', but then questioned if the micro-management this represents was as effective as the trust in governance that it displaced. Both Strathern (2000) and O'Neill in her lecture on the Hutton Inquiry into the death of Dr David Kelly[16] extended this argument by drawing a distinction between accountability (satisfying the audit requirements) and responsibility, which has been drawn into sharp focus by the war on Iraq. Government may pass various accountability tests, but that – in the public perception – does not equate to responsibility. Kelly's dilemma, which led to his suicide, had been recognised by Cris Shore and Susan Wright: the 'audit process' 'encourages a form of reflexivity', but 'the reflexive subject is caught within tightly fixed parameters that appear to render opposition futile.'[17] If those who do not conform discount themselves, this will further problematise the record as they seek to avoid inclusion as well as being excluded. Moreover, as Nowotny warns, the very interaction of experts, such as Kelly, with each other and those who make use of or rely on their expertise increases 'vulnerability to contestation' and can act as a deterrent to disclosure.[18]

The records manager in the audit culture, in both the public and private sector, is embedded within the organisational structure with all that that implies. Indeed, they have long argued for an engagement in the process of record creation so as to facilitate their work and to improve 'accountability'.[19] Several studies have identified such involvement as record-keeping systems migrate to the digital. They also illustrate how this process has eroded or even destroyed long-established practices, themselves technologies, which were designed to guarantee the authenticity of the record and to protect those engaged in its creation through a rigorous separation of back- and front-office functions.[20] Some commentators, notably Duranti drawing on her experience of European diplomatic, have restated the enduring importance of the formal structure of documents in the digital order. This is not as straightforward as it may seem, as there is a notorious lack of fixity in the digital world.[21] Attempting to replicate the distinction in a digital environment between the front and back office is more challenging, even where there are powerful compliance drivers. It is expensive, driven by process technology rather than the digital, and there are pressures to abandon it in the name of managerial efficiency.[22] Organisations tend only to act in response to failure, such as Henry Blodget's infamous 'piece of shit' e-mail, but the continuing investigations of Eliot Spitzer, the New York attorney general who discovered it, and the impact of the Sarbanes-Oxley Act should put them on their guard.[23] The outcome will be a proactive approach to records and information management based on an actuarial assessment of the risk of doing nothing or non-compliance, which will only further constrain the record. Iacovino, admittedly from the Australian experience of government corruption and corporate scandals, extends the fiduciary concept of the archive to include monitoring and regulating 'compliance with standards of recordkeeping in government agencies'. This, she argues, 'can only be achieved if the archival authority has investigative powers and a records audit role which includes involvement in recordkeeping systems from the design stage.'[24] It is hard to envisage those responsible for the governance of an organisation delegating such draconian powers to the archives and it begs the question as to who audits the auditors.

There is, however, a distinction between the private and public sector, despite Eastwood's claim that 'the interdependence of institutions across the illusory public and private boundary creates an interdependence among archives and archivists pursuing the ideal of democratic accountability and continuity'.[25] For the private sector to function, risk must be contained that is the burden of limiting corporate liability. Interestingly, in the wake of recent scandals, such protection is no longer enjoyed by non-executive board members, who have to insure themselves against the risk of incurring penalties for non-compliance or failure in their fiduciary duty. Board members would be acting irresponsibly if they knowingly allowed records to be kept beyond the expiry of their retention period, if by so doing they exposed the organisation to future contingent liability. Auditors would also be bound to qualify accounts if they suspected such behaviour. There may be pressures within the public sector to do likewise, but this could be considered in many areas of government to be hardly acting responsibly, particularly where disclosure has been postponed on grounds of national security. This is the nub of the archival function. For an organisation to be seen to act responsibly and to be held to account in the 'court of history', there is an archival imperative, which in turn demands confidence in the authenticity of the record and the transparency of the process used to create it. In the private sector the transfer of records to an archive is a matter of choice. There is rarely any need to demonstrate responsibility over a long period, for example the employment of slave labour during the Nazi regime or the theft of Jewish assets. Some long-established concerns keep archives to protect their reputation, to defend trade marks or to mitigate future risks, such as environmental hazards. With the long arm of legal discovery, records will not be transferred to an archive if the risk of keeping them outweighs the risk of their destruction. Although the record is the constant, it does not follow that management and archiving are flip sides of the same coin.

The problematic ontological status of the records that support the audit culture, compounded by the digital environment, poses serious questions for archivists and their users. If what is recorded is largely a construct of audit and in the public sector is further constrained by transparency delivered through freedom of information, the archive will only provide a very skewed version of events, which may seem to justify the critiques of the poststructuralists and postmodernists, who view all texts as problematic and their interpretation as largely relative. Some archival thinkers, drawing their inspiration from Foucault, believe that this perspective is not only pervasive but also negates the concept of the archive as a trusted repository of 'memory'.[26] Cook is in no doubt that 'there has been a collective shift from a juridical-administrative justification for archives grounded in the concepts of the state, to a socio-cultural justification for archives grounded in wider public policy and public use.'[27] In the view of such thinkers the archive becomes as uncertain and constructed as its contents, resulting in our audit culture not in any release of the archive into a new paradigm but its perversion to serve a self-referential discourse. If, from the optimistic perspective of Fukuyama, the liberal democratic capitalist ideal has triumphed, it may not matter very much as 'history' has ended and accountability will suffice in the wider scheme of things. In her critique of Fukuyama, Gertrude Himmelfarb quotes Lionel Trilling who 'wrote of other historians who prided themselves on taking the "long view", that "the long view" is the falsest historical view of all'; seen from a sufficient distance, 'the corpse and hacked limbs are not so very terrible, and eventually they even begin to compose themselves into a "meaningful pattern".'[28]

In rejecting Fukuyama's contention, Himmelfarb does not surrender to Hayden White's relativist meta-history. Far from it, she argues that, although historians are prepared to admit a 'relativistic' relativism in the interpretation of sources, few are willing so to problematise them that 'truth' becomes unknowable: 'Where modernism tolerates the obstacles in the way of objectivity as a challenge and make strenuous effort to attain as much objectivity and unbiased truth as possible, postmodernism takes the rejection of absolute truth as a deliverance from all truth and from the obligation to maintain any degree of objectivity.'[29] As Deborah Symonds describes in her engaging piece 'Living in the Scottish Record Office', the fact that Agnes Dugald killed her young daughter by the banks of the Clyde in 1768 is unquestionable from the evidence presented at her trial, even if the motive and surrounding circumstances are open to interpretation.[30] Richard Evans, in his penetrating defence of history, emphasises the crucial interplay of fact, current preoccupations and perception and imagination. He concludes emphatically, 'it really happened, and we really can, if we are very scrupulous and careful and self-critical, find out how it happened and reach some tenable though always less than final conclusions about what it all meant.'[31] For such users of archives, the texts they contain are the foundation of their analysis as they have been since the Enlightenment. This is the unambiguous point of departure of the UNESCO project, 'Lost Memory – Libraries and Archives Destroyed in the Twentieth Century': 'Archives are generally considered to form the skeleton of the "Memory of the World", by containing not only factual information but also the information context in which other elements of life, for example paintings and sculptures, wars and discoveries, can be placed and better understood.'[32]

Reassertion of the function of the archive as a trusted repository does not in itself resolve questions about content. A single archive is rarely the panopticon of a user's knowledge. Argument is based on evidence drawn from a variety of archives, some held in recognised repositories, some in private hands, and some drawn from printed (secondary) sources. The multiplicity of sources facilitates corroboration of evidence and provides access to differing modalities of privilege. Critics of the archives, who view it as monolithic and therefore unassailable, often overlook this obvious fact. Jacques Derrida held the view that the archive had 'to be deposited somewhere, on a stable substrata, and at the disposition of a legitimate hermeneutic authority'.[33] This is rarely the experience of historians, who have spent freezing days in attics and cellars where the malign hand of Derrida's archons or Michel Foucault's archivists have never stirred the dust, but this does not mean that the contents are any less *privileged* than those of a recognised repository.[34] The fact that certain records have been stored (archived if you will) is intended even if they are subsequently neglected.[35] The range and depth of sources available to users has been greatly enhanced by exposing catalogues, sometimes surrogates of records and increasingly records themselves, particularly in the public sector, to the Internet. This development, coupled with the migration of much record keeping to the digital, makes the delineation, let alone the defence, of the boundary between archives and libraries much less possible. It was always fuzzy but it is now permeable as the very act of declaring a text or object to the Internet is tantamount to publishing. The text may not come with all the apparatus of a printed book (ISBN or ISSN and copyright library catalogue details), but neither did much 'grey' literature in the print culture. This is just a further development of the technologies of the print culture, which grew out of the technology of writing, making it possible for any number of users to view an 'original' without damaging it or having to travel great distances to see it.[36] The preservation of digital material presents common challenges across the information professions, calling for common facilities and modes of operation, but this does not necessarily imply integration – rather a restatement of the functions of the archives and the library and a greater understanding of their differing practices and procedures.[37] This may or may not result in integration, but it should lead to the active participation of the archival approach in developing information strategies and policies. Interestingly, a report on state records in the United States found that states where the archives were located in 'the state historical society or cultural resources department' were 'less likely to have an information program ...'.[38]

If the archive is to serve as 'memory' then it must be representative of whatever it purports to be the 'memory' of. This will be dynamic as the memorialised subject, itself, changes and the perception of it changes. This can happen long after the subject has ceased, in any meaningful sense, to exist. The 'technology' employed by archivists to construct memory is appraisal, which they jealously guard. Simply appraising the records created to satisfy audit or constrained by freedom of information and the protection of individual rights will not be representative of much except the self-referential world it was constructed to reflect, and much of necessity will be discarded. There will be in Strathern's words no 'loose ends'.[39] Locating loose ends and preserving them in the archive is problematic, as they are unlikely to be found within the records of the subject to be memorialised, even in the public sector with an imperative for responsible behaviour. If they come from elsewhere – and most archives have accepted records that come from outside their organisation and yet reflect on it – this in itself is problematic, as the archive could be considered subversive, holding records that might not only threaten the memorialised subject but also expose it to risk. In the public sector in liberal democracies this is an essential safeguard of the freedom and rights of citizens. The archive does more than memorialise, it protects. This vital fiduciary function has been undermined since 9/11 and the war on terrorism. The protection of the archive from the executive, along with the safeguards it can provide to the executive even in undemocratic societies, comes from an independent judiciary that can prevent unauthorised disclosure and destruction and insist on discovery of pertinent information. Yet, it is this very juridical function that the postmodernist archivist wishes to discard. Such protection, despite Iacovino's plea to the contrary, cannot extend to the private sector unless those in authority are thought to be contravening regulations or statutes.

Searching for loose ends among the maze of information that populates our increasingly digital worlds is forbidding. The Internet superficially encourages the antithesis of the audit culture by allowing everyone to be his or her publisher, the ultimate meta-narratives.[40] Such outpourings may counterpoise the normative, but, as Negroponte is quick to point out, they are entirely self-regarding:

> In the post-information age, we often have an audience the size of one. Everything is made to order, and information is extremely personalized. A widely held assumption is that individualization is the extrapolation of narrowcasting – you go from a large to a small to a smaller group, ultimately to the individual. By the time you have my address, my marital status, my age, my income, my car brand, my purchases, my drinking habits, and my taxes, you have me – a demographic unit of one.
>
> This line of reasoning completely misses the fundamental difference between narrowcasting and being digital. In being digital I am me, not a statistical subset. Me includes information and events that have no demographic or statistical meaning. Where my mother-in-law lives, whom I had dinner with last night, and what time my flight departs for Richmond this afternoon have absolutely no correlation or statistical basis from which to derive suitable narrowcast services.[41]

Such content is so disintermediated that it lacks a 'sense of history – the complex sense of periodisation and cause and effect', 'everything occurs in a consumer present'.[42] If this is the case, then there is no antithesis but a worrying congruity as Negroponte admitted when he postulated the Daily Me, news tailored to an individual's preferences – the ultimate mediation.[43] This is very different from the memorialising evidence of me, as Anthony Giddens puts it, the 'narrative of self', which even if self-regarding has a hermeneutic dynamic.[44] For archivists and their users such personal narratives have provided tangential witness to events they bisect.

Contrary to much of the rhetoric the vast accumulation of information exposed to the Internet is privileged by search engines, but this is very different from the 'privileging' of archivists and librarians as the underlying algorithms are often based on consumer preferences. Those archival thinkers who locate the archive in a public cultural space run the risk of simply gathering loose ends that such, often very sophisticated, heuristics judges to be popular. Such appraisal has a spurious logic that may appeal to paymasters. Although librarians and archivists pretend that consumer preference does not play a part in privileging, only the most reductionist would claim it was the only criterion. Stille, in his book *The Future of the Past*, ends what is otherwise a gloomy prognosis on an optimistic note: 'If people continue to feel that they are losing control of their lives and that they are losing their cultural traditions, they will work to regain control, using technologies in ways that we have not yet imagined.'[45] This may be just a heroic peroration, but there is some evidence to support this perception. Community archive initiatives are predicated on just such assumptions, but they too are in danger of being coeval with a consumer present unless the content is in some way contextualised.

Angela Cheater sets disintermediated personal information collections in a global framework with 'new ways of knowing' that are 'likely to call into question past analytical, theoretical, epistemological, even ontological certitudes'.[46] She defines that context as chaotic and distinct from the order of a Newtonian cosmology, which does appear to subscribe to the poststructuralist agenda where all evidence has equal value and where the past is indeed unknowable as there is no past to know, which is what concerns Stille.[47] Clifford Lynch is excited by the possibility of users joining together the 'granules' of information discovered on the web into their own disintermediated collections, whereas Hur-Li Lee from a library perspective is troubled by the lack of mediation.[48] Stille and Lee's dilemma is compounded, as O'Neill emphasised in her Reith lectures, by the lack of trust in authority, particularly government where every public declaration is thought to be 'spun' either to win support or to comply with the requirements of the audit culture. As she observed echoing Nowotny, 'trust seemingly has receded as transparency has advanced', 'the very technologies that spread information so easily and efficiently are every bit as good at spreading misinformation and disinformation. Some sorts of openness and transparency may be bad for trust.'[49] Such a contention confirms the importance of the capture by the archive of the personal perspective, whether made public over the Internet or entrusted to 'private' reflection. Since much of it will now be in digital form, simply leaving it to be found long after events have taken place is no longer a tenable strategy. Although aware of the problem, Sue McKemmish concluded rather pessimistically in her seminal article 'Evidence of me' that it was difficult to prescribe a solution.[50] Verne Harris deconstructed her premise by pointing out, among other things, that evidence of me was increasingly constrained by compliance, leading to the reflexive discounting Shore and Wright warned of. He questioned whether the remembrance of me was in some way dysfunctional and not representative and went further by interpreting McKemmish's use of 'narrrative' to imply that evidence of and from me was in a postmodern sense fictive.[51] McKemmish and Upward rejected this assertion. While they admitted to an aggregation into evidence of us, by quoting Christopher Koch's novel *Highways to War*, they did not explore this well-trodden path, preferring to concentrate on evidence of me as biography located in a continuum of multi-lane freeways.[52] What they all ignored was the growing mass of evidence of me and us and my and our narratives, which used to be hidden in personal space and is now exposed across the Internet. Stille draws confidence from the fact that 'the Mormons have already placed the names of 400 million dead souls on line – suggesting the desire for finding one's historical roots ranks just after erotic pleasure among humankind's deepest needs.'[53]

This growing body of evidence of me does present the archival community with just the challenges that McKemmish raised in the conclusion of her original paper when she quoted Chris Hurley's plea made in 1995 'to identify and articulate the functional requirements for personal recordkeeping and for socio-historical evidence'.[54] Much of it is difficult to authenticate in any traditional sense, as it lacks any meaningful provenance, reference or fixity of format and has no original order as objects in the digital order enjoy an independence that they do not in the physical. It is unrealistic to expect the providers of such evidence to follow any prescriptive rules to improve the reliability and durability of their evidence, unless they can see some obvious advantage either to themselves or the communities with which they engage. It is just as fanciful to propose that collecting archivists can establish contact with owners except at the margins, as Angelika Menne-Haritz and Adrian Cunningham propose.[55] To discount such evidence because it lacks recognisable phenomenal characteristics would be dereliction, particularly where archives are considered to be 'providers of access to the past so that everyone can investigate it for his own questions'.[56] Developing appraisal and preservation strategies for such a mass of material, which by its very nature 'transgresses the boundaries between specialised knowledge and its multiple, multiple-layered (and often unforeseeable) context of implications'[57] and in the granules in which it resides is in most cases unprivileged, is challenging. However subjective and relative appraisal is, it needs a sense of reference and in many cases hierarchy. Here it is possible to gain something from the postmodern perspective of Mark Greene:

> Contrary to popular conceptions, postmodernism does not seek or result in the annihilation of meaning or value, though it suggests their measure is more localized and contingent than universal and objective. The localized and contingent nature of appraisal is what makes it messy and complex ... Appraisal, I suggest, has always been and always will be not magic, not science, not a mixture of both, but an art. Eugene Delacroix is reported to have said to Baudelaire: 'The visible world is only a shop full of images and signs to which imagination gives relative value and place. It is a kind of pasture-land which imagination should order and transform.'[58]

In quoting Delacroix, Greene is not far removed from the conclusion of Richard Evans's defence of history written from an opposite point of view:

> As [Peter] Novick defines it, the idea of objectivity involves a belief in the 'reality of the past, and [to] truth as correspondence to that reality.' The truth about patterns and linkages of facts in history is in the end discovered not invented, found not made, though as Haskell adds, 'not without a process of imaginative construction that goes so far beyond the intrinsic properties of the raw materials employed that one can speak of their being made' as well. Making such patterns and linkages, casual and otherwise, is by no means the only function of history, which also has a duty to establish the facts and recreate the past in the present, but it is in the end what distinguishes it from the chronicle.[59]

The interaction of contingency and imagination in not only selecting objects for inclusion in the archive but also in their interpretation counterbalances the reductionism of the audit culture. Despite any caveats about the relativity and dysfunctionality of the evidence of me, such an approach should capture the inconsistent and aberrant behaviours that will find partners and contribute to understanding.

The archiving of such objects represents in some senses a paradigm shift as, unlike physical objects, they do not thereby embark on a journey from the private to public space, but from fluidity to permanence. Describing such content will demand ontological and epistemological revisions, as Cheater reminded her readers. The object may lack reference, but it is possible to endow it with at least some attributes by bisection with others to gauge authenticity, even where the author or the author's real intention may never be known with any certainty. This will undoubtedly require interaction with providers, where they can be found, and to a greater extent users familiar with the communities served by such resources. Given the global possibilities of contingencies in the digital environment, content captured locally will present major problems of semiology particularly where there is doubt about its origin. The terminology and taxonomies of description will need to be more clearly defined to avoid confusion, which will lead to convergence within the information professions, but not necessarily loss of identity.[60] Nowotny is optimistic: 'In principle, the experience of participants and of relevant social groups, their attitudes, perceptions and even specific vulnerabilities can all be acknowledged and taken into account.'[61] Those with experience of using controlled vocabularies would not be so sanguine; nevertheless it is incumbent on the information professions to try.

In addressing the complexities of the outcomes of the audit culture and the content of the Internet, the archival community cannot defend the function of the archive without engagement with the wider information landscape. This draws on skills and ideas from disciplines across the sciences with convergent aims and concerns. Technology may enable the audit culture, but it cannot resolve the ethical and moral issues that surround the content. Anthropologists and moral philosophers may raise their voices against the relentless encroachment of that culture, but they cannot resolve how to construct a more 'balanced' record of events or how to persuade governments to distinguish between accounting for their actions and acting responsibly. Librarians may express concern about the lack of mediation in the content of the Internet, but they can only make a difference at the margins. In the end the market will probably determine the outcome. Advancing compliance regimes will prove too expensive and consumers may prefer accepting some risk rather than lower returns and higher prices or taxes. The Internet will become overburdened and resources difficult to discover even with the best search engines, which will force their providers to begin to exploit the potential of metadata applied by archivists and librarians to privilege content.

In joining what are exciting and stimulating debates about the knowledge economy, archivists must be certain what it is they can contribute. A sense of place will continue to be important, because the physical asset will persist. As David Levy commented:

> For some of us, books and libraries symbolize some of the very qualities and modes of being that are threatened in our fast-paced instrumented lives. Books speak of time and depth and attention. They speak of a slower rhythm of life. And in their weighty physicality, they draw us back to our own materiality, and to the materiality of the world. Libraries are places not just where books can be found, but where people can temporarily remove themselves from the speed and busyness of life, where they can read and write and reflect. They are (or can be) shared sacred places in a secular, common world.[62]

The concept of the library as a sanctuary equates with the etymology of the archive as the ark, a secure store where treasures are held fiduciarily on behalf of the community, and those responsible for its care (archivists) are protected by the rule of law. This is the quintessential juridical function, which must be upheld, whatever other roles the archive fulfils. Although this is the classic Jenkinsonian position, it is difficult, given the distrust of the executive and concerns about the culture of audit, to uphold his view that the administration should be solely responsible for appraisal.[63] On the other hand, there are obvious dangers in the post-9/11 world in Schellenberg's concept of the archives as cultural assets, even as a secondary role.[64] As Menne-Haritz puts it, 'the central question is how to achieve the access to a most complete representation of the original information potential that will allow us to construct history out of a network of detectable stories' and it is that outcome that will judge responsible behaviour.[65] Despite everything that has been written about appraisal, this goal of representativeness is problematic, not because of the doubts of the poststructuralists and postmodernists but because of the way in which the records are constrained by the interaction of process, behaviour and technology. Although these interactions are nothing new, they combine in the digital environment in ways that challenge accepted practices and boundaries. Appraisal will inevitably remain messily plural and the archival community must beware of the monopolistic tendencies of digital preservation. It is the plurality of provision that enables the contingency that users seek and which in collecting archives is threatened by suspicion of the subversive. Users must have the continued freedom to reflect on the content in Levy's 'shared sacred places' untroubled by an overbearing executive with powers to know, in the interests of national security, who has consulted what and when. Like any treasury, the archive is central to discourse but can only be protected by the communities it serves and the rules that govern their actions. It is this interaction that the archival sciences are in danger of losing sight of.

Notes

1. See, for example, Cook, T., 'Archival science and postmodernism: new formulations for old concepts', *Archival Science*, 1 (1) 2001, pp. 3–24; Ketelaar, E., 'Tacit narratives: the meanings of archives', *Archival Science*, 1 (2), 2001, pp. 131–41, and Macneil, Heather, 'Trusting records in a postmodern world', *Archivaria*, 51, 2001, pp. 36–47.
2. Eastwood, T., 'Reflections on the goal of archival appraisal in democratic societies', *Archivaria*, 54, 2002, pp. 59–71, and Cox, Richard, 'Archival appraisal alchemy' and response from Mark Greene, 'Not magic, not science, but art: comment on "Archival appraisal alchemy"', *Choices and Challenges, Collecting by Museums and Archives*, 1–3 November 2002, available at *http://www.hfmgv.org/research/publications/symposium2002/papers/* (accessed March 2005).
3. Menne-Haritz, A., 'Access – the reformulation of an archival paradigm', *Archival Science*, 1(1), 2001, pp. 57–82.
4. See *http://www.loc.gov/ead/* (accessed March 2005), *http://www.ica.org/biblio/cds/isad_g_2e.pdf* (accessed March 2005) and Pitti, D. and Duff, Wendy, 'Encoded Archival Description on the Internet', special issue of the *Journal of Internet Cataloguing*, 4 (3–4), 2001.
5. Duranti, Luciana, 'The future of archival scholarship', 1998 (available at *http://www.ucd.ie/archives/html/conferences/cs3.htm*, accessed March 2005).
6. There are many examples from all these disciplines where information (archives) is discussed without any reference except coincidentally to curation; see, for example, Fox-Genovese, Elizabeth and Lasch-Quinn, Elisabeth, *Reconstructing History – The Emergence of a New Historical Society* (New York and London, 1999).
7. An important driver for disclosure in international business is the US Sarbanes-Oxley Act, see *http://www.sarbanes-oxley.com/* (accessed March 2005); Power, Michael, *The Audit Society: Rituals of Verification* (Oxford, 1997).
8. Shore, Cris and Wright, Susan, 'Coercive accountability' in Strathern, Marilyn (ed.), *Audit Cultures – Anthropological Studies in Accountability, Ethics and the Academy* (London, 2000), pp. 57–89.

9. Peis, Peter, 'The trickster's dilemma', in Strathern, op. cit., pp. 150–1 and Williams, Howard, Sullivan, David and Matthews, Gwynn, *Francis Fukuyama and the End of History* (Cardiff, 1997), pp. 1–5.

10. Strathern, Marilyn, 'Abstraction and decontextualisation: an anthropological comment or: e for ethnography', 2000 (available at *http://virtualsociety.sbs .ox.ac.uk/GRpapers/strathern.htm*, accessed March 2005).

11. Nowotny, Helga, 'Dilemma of expertise – democraticising expertise and socially robust knowledge', *Science and Public Policy*, 30 (3), June 2003, pp. 151–6 (available at *http://www.nowotny.ethz.ch/*, accessed March 2005).

12. This is even acknowledged in the public sector; see, for example, *http://www.recordsmanagement.ed.ac.uk/InfoStaff/RMstaff/RMBenefits AndDrivers.htm* (accessed March 2005).

13. Shore and Wright, in Strathern, *Audit Cultures*, op. cit., p. 77 and Power, Michael, *The Audit Explosion* (London, 1994), p. 13.

14. See, for example, Shepherd, Elizabeth and Yeo, Geoffrey, *Managing Records: A Handbook of Principles and Practice* (London, 2003), pp. xi–xiii.

15. O'Neill, Onora (2002) (available at *http://www.bbc.co.uk/radio4/reith2002/ lectures.shtml*, accessed March 2005) and O'Neill, Onora, 'Accuracy, independence, and trust', in Runciman, W.G. (ed.), *Hutton and Butler: Lifting the Lid on the Workings of Power* (Oxford, 2004).

16. O'Neill, ibid.

17. Shore and Wright, in Strathern, *Audit Cultures*, op. cit., p. 78.

18. Nowotny, op. cit., p. 152.

19. See, for example, National Archives of Australia, *Managing Business Information – DIRKS* (available at *http://www.naa.gov.au/recordkeeping/ dirks/summary.html*, accessed March 2005) and *e-Government Policy Framework for Electronic Records Management* (available at *http://www .nationalarchives.gov.uk/electronicrecords/pdf/egov_framework.pdf*, accessed March 2005).

20. See, for example, *Functional Requirements for Electronic Records Management*, University of Pittsburgh, 2000 (available at *http://web.archive .org/web/20000818163633/www.sis.pitt.edu/~nhprc/* (accessed March 2005), and *No Going Back: The Final Report of the Effective Records Management Project*, University of Glasgow, 2001 (available at *http://www.gla.ac.uk/infostrat/ERM/Docs/ERM-Final.pdf*, accessed March 2005).

21. See, for example, Buckland, Michael, 'What is a digital document?', *Document Numérique*, 2 (2), 1998, pp. 221–30, and Allison, Arthur, Currall, James, Moss, Michael and Stuart, Susan, 'Digital identity matters', *Journal of the American Society for Information Science and Technology*, 56 (4), 2004, pp. 364–72.

22. See, for example, Gross, Mitchell, *Bridging the Back-Office/Front-Office Gap* (available at *http://www.kmworld.com/publications/whitepapers/ ECM/gross.htm*, accessed March 2005).

23. See, for example, *http://faculty.baruch.cuny.edu/journalism/msbaruch/ spitzer_transcript.html* (accessed March 2005), Moeller, Robert E., *Sarbanes Oxley Act and the New Internal Auditing Rules* (New York, 2004).

24. RCRG Publication: Iacovino, Livia, 'Reflections on Eastwood's concept of democratic accountability and continuity', 1998 (available at *http://www.sims.monash.edu.au/research/rcrg/publications/la02.html*).

25. Eastwood, Terry, 'Reflections on the development of archives in Canada and Australia', *Papers and Proceedings of the 7th Biennial Conference of the Australian Society of Archivists* (Hobart, 1989), p. 80.

26. Featherston, Mike, 'Archiving cultures', *British Journal of Sociology*, 51 (1), 2000, pp. 161–84, provides a useful discussion.

27. Cook, Terry, 'What is past is prologue: a history of archival ideas since 1898, and the future paradigm shift', *Archivaria*, 43, 1997.

28. Himmelfarb, Gertrude, 'The dark and bloody crossroads: where nationalism and religion meet', *National Interest*, 32 (9), Summer 1993, p. 53, quoting Lionel Trilling, 'Tacitus Now', in *The Liberal Imagination: Essays on Literature and Society* (London, 1951), p. 201.

29. Himmlefarb, Gertrude, 'Postmodernist history', in Fox-Genovese and Lasch-Quinn, op. cit., pp. 74 and 82.

30. In Fox-Genovese and Lasch-Quinn, op. cit., pp. 164–75.

31. Evans, Richard, *In Defence of History* (London, 1997), p. 253.

32. 1996, available at *http://www.unesco.org/webworld/mdm/administ/pdf/LOSTMEMO.PDF* (accessed March 2005), p. 20.

33. Derrida, Jacques, *Archive Fever: A Freudian Impression*, trans. Eric Prenowitz (Chicago, 1996), pp. 2–3.

34. Foucault, Michel, *The Archaeology of Knowledge* (London, 1972), part 3. There is an ambiguity in his writing between an archive as a virtual concept and a place.

35. Currall, James, Moss, Michael and Stuart, Susan, 'Why privileging information is inevitable', *Archives and Manuscripts*, November 2006.

36. Stille, Alexander, *The Future of the Past – How the Information Age Threatens to Destroy Our Cultural Heritage* (London, 2002), pp. 322–4.

37. There is a large literature and many projects concerned with the preservation of digital objects. In the United Kingdom the Digital Curation Centre provides a focus for expertise, *http://www.dcc.ac.uk/*.

38. Irons Walch, Victoria, *Maintaining State Records in an Era of Change – A Report on State Archives and Records Management Programs* (April 1996) (available at *http://www.coshrc.org/reports/1996rpt/1996survey.htm*, accessed March 2005).

39. Strathern, 'Abstraction and decontextualisation', op. cit.

40. Stille, op. cit., p. 338.

41. Negroponte, Nicholas, *Being Digital* (Boston, 1995), p. 164, selection available at *http://archives.obs-us.com/obs/english/books/nn/ch13c01.htm* (accessed March 2005).

42. Stille, op. cit., p. 338.

43. Negroponte, op. cit., p. 153.

44. McKemmish, Sue, 'Evidence of me', *Archivaria*, 29 (1), 2001 (available at *http://www.mybestdocs.com/mckemmish-s-evidofme-ch10.htm*, accessed March 2005) and Giddens, Anthony, *Modernity and Self-identity: Self and Society in the Late Modern Age* (Cambridge, 1991), p. 54.

45. Stille, op. cit., p. 339.

46. Cheater, Angela, 'Globalisation and the new technologies of knowing', in Strathern, Marilyn (ed.), *Shifting Contexts: Transformation in Anthropological Knowledge* (London, 1995), p. 120.

47. Ibid., p. 123.

48. Lee, H.-L., 'What is a collection?', *Journal of the American Society for Information Science*, 51 (12), 2000, and Lynch, C., 'Digital collections, digital libraries and the digitization of cultural heritage information', *First Monday*, 7 (5), 2002.

49. O'Neill (2002), op. cit., lecture 4.

50. McKemmish, op.cit.

51. Harris, Verne, 'On the back of a tiger: deconstructive possibilities in "Evidence of me"', *Archives and Manuscripts*, 29 (1), 2001 (available at *http://www.mybestdocs.com/harris-v-tiger-edited0105.htm*).

52. Upward, Frank and McKemmish, Sue, 'In search of the lost tiger, by way of Sainte-Beauve: reconstructing the possibilities in "Evidence of me ..."', *Archives and Manuscripts*, 29 (1), 2001 (available at *http://www.mybestdocs. com/mckemmish-s-upward-f-ontiger-w.htm*).

53. Stille, op. cit., p. 330.

54. McKemmish, op. cit.

55. Menne-Haritz, op. cit., p. 57, and Cunningham, Adrian, *Collecting Archives in the Next Millennium*, paper presented to the Australian Society of Archivists Annual Conference, Adelaide, July 1997 (available at *http://www.nla.gov.au/nla/staffpaper/acunning7.html*, accessed March 2005).

56. Menne-Haritz, op. cit., p. 59.

57. Nowotny, op. cit., p. 152.

58. Greene, op. cit., and quoting Ben Enwonwu, 'The evolution, history and definition of fine art', *Ijele: Art eJournal of the African World*, 1 (2), 2002, *http://www.ijele.com/ijele/vol1.2/enwonwu2.pdf* (accessed March 2005), p. 3.

59. Evans, op. cit., p. 252.

60. See, for example, Currall, James, Moss, Michael and Stuart, Susan 'What is a collection?', *Archivaria*, 58, 2005, and Currall et al., 'Why privileging information is inevitable', op. cit.

61. Nowotny, op. cit., p. 154.

62. Levy, David M., *Scrolling Forward – Making Sense of Documents in the Digital Age* (New York, 2001).

63. Jenkinson, Hilary, *A Manual of Archive Administration* (London, 1925).

64. Schellenberg, T.R., *Modern Archives: Principles and Techniques* (Melbourne, 1956).

65. Menne-Haritz, op. cit., p. 67.

Bibliography

Allison, Arthur, Currall, James, Moss, Michael and Stuart, Susan, 'Digital identity matters', *Journal of the American Society for Information Science and Technology*, 56 (4), 2004.

Allison, Dik, 'The application of records management disciplines into electronic data management', *Records Management Bulletin*, 103, June 2001.

Anderson, S. and Heery, R., *Digital Repositories Review* (London, 2005).

Ayris, P., *Guidance for Selecting Materials for Digitisation*, Joint RLG and NPO Preservation Conference: Guidelines for Digital Imaging, 28–30 September 1998.

Badendoch, D. et al., 'The value of information', in Feeney, Mary and Grieves, Maureen (eds), *The Value and Impact of Information* (London, 1994).

Baer, Christopher T., 'Strategy, structure, detail, function: four parameters for the appraisal of business records', in O'Toole, James M. (ed.), *Records of American Business* (Chicago, 1997).

Bantin, P., 'Electronic records management – a review of the work of a decade and a reflection on future directions', 2002 (available at *http://www.indiana.edu/~libarch/ER/encycloarticle9.doc*, accessed 3 November 2005).

Barry, R., 'The changing workplace and the nature of the record', unpublished paper presented to Association of Canadian Archivists annual conference, 1995 (available at *http://www.mybestdocs.com/barry-r-aca1995-wkp-rec.htm*, accessed 22 September 2005).

Baxter, T.W., *Archives in a Growing Society* (National Archives of Rhodesia and Nyasaland, Salisbury, 1963).

Bearman, D. and Sochats, K., *Functional Requirements for Evidence in Recordkeeping: The Pittsburgh Project*, n.d. (available at *www.archimuse.com/papers/nhprc/BACartic.html*, accessed 20 June 2005).

Bentley, C., *PRINCE 2: An Outline* (London for Central Computer and Telecommunications Agency, 1997).

Besser, Howard, Hibbard, Sally and Lenert, Deborah (eds), *Introduction to Imaging*, revised edn (Los Angeles, 2003).

Bichard, Sir Michael, *The Bichard Inquiry – An Independent Inquiry Arising from the Soham Murders*, HC 653 (London, June 2004).

Boles, Frank, *Selecting and Appraising Archives and Manuscripts* (Chicago, 2005).

Booms, Hans, 'Society and the formation of a documentary heritage', *Archivaria*, 24, Summer 1987.

Bradley, R., 'Digital authenticity and integrity: digital cultural heritage documents as research resources', *portal: Libraries and the Academy*, 5 (2), 2005.

British Standards Institution, *Information and Documentation – Records Management – Part 1: General*, BS ISO 15489-1 (London, 2001)

British Standards Institution, *Information and Documentation – Records Management – Part 2: Guidelines*, PD ISO/TR 15489-2 (London, 2001).

British Standards Institution, *Code of Practice for the Legal Admissibility and Evidential Weight of Electronic Records*, BIP0008 (London, 2004).

Buckland, Michael, 'What is a digital document?', *Document Numérique*, 2 (2), 1998.

Buneman, P., Khanna, S., Tajima, K. and Tan, W.-C., 'Archiving scientific data', *ACM Transactions on Database Systems*, 29 (1), 2002.

Butler of Brockwell, Lord (Chairman), *Review of Intelligence on Weapons of Mass Destruction*, HCP 898 (London, 2004).

Byres, S., 'Information leakage caused by hidden data in published documents', *IEEE Security and Privacy*, 2 (2), 2004.

Campbell-Kelly, M., 'Railway clearing house and Victorian data processing', in Bud-Frierman, L. (ed.), *Information Acumen. Understanding and Use of Knowledge in Modern Business* (London and New York, 1994).

Canada, Treasury Board of, *Integrated Risk Management Framework* (Ottawa, 2001) (available at *http://www.tbs-sct.gc.ca/pubs_pol/dcgpubs/riskmanagement/rmf-cgr01-1_e.asp*, accessed 15 September 2005).

Cheater, Angela, 'Globalisation and the new technologies of knowing', in Strathern, Marilyn (ed.), *Shifting Contexts Transformation in Anthropological Knowledge* (London, 1995).

Checkland, P. and Holwell, S., *Information, Systems and Information Systems – Making Sense of the Field* (Chichester, 1997).

Colledge, G. and Cliff, M., 'The implications of the Sarbanes-Oxley Act: it's time to take records management seriously', in *KM World*, 12 (8), 2003.

Commission on Preservation and Access and the Research Libraries Group, Preserving Digital Information: *Report of the Task Force on Archiving of Digital Information* (Mountain View, CA, 1996).

Cook, Michael, *The Management of Information from Archives*, 2nd edn (Aldershot, 1999).

Cook, Terry, 'What is past is prologue: a history of archival ideas since 1898, and the future paradigm shift', *Archivaria*, 43, 1997.

Cook, Terry, 'Archival science and postmodernism: new formulations for old concepts', *Archival Science*, 1, 2001.

Cook, Terry, 'Fashionable nonsense or professional rebirth: postmodernism and the practice of archives', *Archivaria*, 51, 2001.

Coppel, Philip, *Information Rights* (London, 2004).

Cordeiro, M.I., 'From rescue to long-term maintenance: preservation as a core function in the management of digital assets', *VINE*, 34 (1), 2004.

Cornwell Consultants, *Model Requirements for Management of Electronic Records* (2002) (available at *http://www.cornwell.co.uk/moreq.html*, accessed 25 November 2005).

Cox, Richard J., 'Access in the digital information age and the archival mission: the United States', *Journal of the Society of Archivists*, 19 (1), 1998.

Cox, Richard J., *Archives and Archivists in the Information Age* (New York, 2005).

Cunningham, A. and Phillips, M., 'Accountability and accessibility: ensuring the evidence of e-governance in Australia', *Aslib Proceedings: New Information Perspectives*, 57 (4), 2005.

Currall, J., *Digital Signatures: Not a Solution, But Simply a Link in the Process Chain*. Paper presented at the DLM Forum, Barcelona (2002) (available at *https://dspace.gla.ac.uk/handle/1905/53*).

Currall, J. and Moss, M., *Process, Policy, Procedure and Practice* (2000) (available at *http://www.gla.ac.uk/infostrat/CapitMMJC.htm*).

Currall, J., Moss, Michael and Stuart, Susan, 'What is a collection?', *Archivaria*, 58, 2005.

Currall, J., Moss, Michael and Stuart, Susan, 'Why privileging information is inevitable', *Archives and Manuscripts*, November 2006.

Currall, J. et al., *No Going Back? Final Report of Effective Records Management Project, Glasgow University* (Glasgow, 2002) (available at *www.gla.ac.uk/InfoStrat/ERM-Final.pdf*, accessed 24 June 2005).

Daniels, Maygene F. and Walch, Timothy, *A Modern Archives Reader, Basic Readings on Archival Theory and Practice* (Washington, DC, 1984).

Davies, A., *A Strategic Approach to Corporate Governance* (Aldershot, 1999).

Day, M., 'Metadata', in Ross, S. (ed.), *DCC Digital Curation Manual* (Glasgow, 2005).

Derrida, Jacques, *Archive Fever A Freudian Impression*, trans. Eric Prenowitz (Chicago, 1996).

DIRKS – Strategic Approach to Managing Business Information, also known as *The DIRKS Manual* (National Archives of Australia, Canberra, 2001) (available at *http://www.naa.gov.au/recordkeeping/dirks/dirksman/dirks.html*, accessed February 2006).

Dollar, Charles, *Archival Preservation of Smithsonian Web Resources: Strategies, Principles, and Best Practices* (Washington, DC, 2001).

Douglas, Janine (ed.), *Total Recall: Managing the Information Environment for Corporate Accountability* (Records Management Association of Australia, WA Branch, Brisbane, 1994).

Duff, Wendy and Johnson, Catherine A., 'Accidentally found on purpose: information seeking behavior of historians in archives', *Library Quarterly*, 72 (4) 2002.

Duff, W., Hofman, H. and Troemel, M., 'Getting what you want, knowing what you have, and keeping what you need', *ERPANET Training Seminar Marburg, Briefing Paper* (Glasgow, 2003).

Duranti, L., 'Concepts and principles ...', *Records Management Journal*, 9 (3), 1999.

Duranti, L. (ed.), *The Long-term Preservation of Authentic Electronic Records: Findings of the InterPARES Project* (Vancouver, 2005).

Eastwood, Terry, 'Reflections on the development of archives in Canada and Australia', *Papers and Proceedings of the 7th Biennial Conference of the Australian Society of Archivists* (Hobart, 1989).

Eastwood, Terry, 'Reflections on the goal of archival appraisal in democratic societies', *Archivaria*, 54, 2002.

Egbuji, A., 'Risk management of organisational records', *Records Management Journal*, 9 (2), August 1999.

ERPANET, *Risk Assessment Tool* (Glasgow, 2006) (available at *http://www.erpanet.org/guidance/docs/ERPANETRiskTool.pdf*, accessed February 2006).

Esanu, J., Davidson J., Ross, S. and Anderson, W., 'Selection, appraisal, and retention of digital scientific data: highlights of an ERPANET/CODATA workshop', *Data Science Journal*, 3, 30 December 2004.

Evans, J., McKemmish, S. and Bhoday, K., 'Create once, use many times: the clever use of recordkeeping metadata for multiple archival purposes', *15th Annual International Congress on Archives* (Vienna, 2004).

Evans, Richard, *In Defence of History* (London, 1997).

Farmer, D. and Venema, W., *Forensic Discovery* (Boston, 2004).

Featherston, Mike, 'Archiving cultures', *British Journal of Sociology*, 51 (1), 2000.

Feeney, Mary and Grieves, Maureen (eds), *The Value and Impact of Information* (London, 1994).

Forde, Helen, 'Access and preservation in the 21st century', *JSA*, 26 (2), 2005.

Foucault, Michel, *The Archaeology of Knowledge* (London, 1972).

Fox-Genovese, Elizabeth and Lasch-Quinn, Elisabeth, *Reconstructing History – The Emergence of a New Historical Society* (New York and London, 1999).

Garmendia, Jone, 'User input in the development of online services: the PRO catalogue', *Journal of the Society of Archivists*, 23 (1), 2002.

Gibbons, P. and Shenton, C., 'Implementing a records management strategy for the UK Parliament: the experience of using Keyword AAA', *Journal of the Society of Archivists*, 24 (2), 2003.

Giddens, Anthony, *Modernity and Self-identity: Self and Society in the Late Modern Age* (Cambridge, 1991).

Greenberg, J., Spurgin, K. and Crystal, A., 'Final report for the AMeGA (Automatic Metadata Generation Applications) Project', *International Journal of Metadata, Semantics and Ontologies*, 1 (1), 2006, pp. 3–20.

Greene, Mark A. and Daniels-Howell, Todd J., 'Documentation with an attitude: a pragmatist's guide to the selection and acquisition of modern business records', in O'Toole, James M. (ed.), *The Records of American Business* (Chicago, 1997).

Gregory, Keith, 'Implementing an electronic records management system – a public sector case study', *Records Management Journal*, 15 (2), 2005.

Hallam Smith, E., 'Customer focus and marketing in archive service delivery: theory and practice', *Journal of the Society of Archivists*, 24 (1), 2003.

Ham, F. Gerald, 'The archival edge', *American Archivist*, 38, January 1975.

Hamilton, C. et al. (eds), *Refiguring the Archive* (Dordrecht and London, 2002).

Harris, Verne, 'On (archival) Odyssey(s)', *Archivaria*, 51, Spring 2001.

Harris, Verne, 'On the back of a tiger: deconstructive possibilities in "Evidence of Me"', *Archives and Manuscripts*, 29 (1), 2001.

Haynes, D., *Metadata for Information Management and Retrieval* (London, 2004).

Hazen, Dan, Horrell, Jeffrey and Merrill-Oldham, Jan, *Selecting Research Collections for Digitization* (Washington, DC, 1998).

Hedstrom, Margaret, 'How do archivists make electronic archives usable and accessible?', *Archives and Manuscripts*, 26 (1), 1998.

Hedstrom, M. et al., *Invest to Save: Report and Recommendations of the NSF-DELOS Working Group on Digital Archiving and Preservation* (Pisa and Washington, DC, 2003).

Henczel, S., *The Information Audit – A Practical Guide* (Munich, 2001).

Heuscher, S., 'Workflow modelling language evaluation for an archival environment', *Archivi e Computer*, XIV (3/04), 2004.

Heuscher, S., Järmann, S., Keller-Marxer, P. and Möhle, F., 'Providing authentic long-term archival access to complex relational data, European Space Agency Symposium', *Ensuring Long-Term Preservation and Adding Value to Scientific and Technical Data* (Frascati, Italy, 2004).

Higgins, S. and Inglis, G., 'Implementing EAD: the experience of the NAHSTE project', *Journal of the Society of Archivists*, 24, 2003.

Himmelfarb, Gertrude, 'The dark and bloody crossroads: where nationalism and religion meet', *The National Interest*, Summer 1993.

HM Stationery Office, *Modernising Government*, Cm. 4310 (London, 1999) (*http://www.archive.official-documents.co.uk/document/cm43/4310/4310.htm*, accessed December 2005).

Hock, D.W., 'Chaordic organization: out of control and into order', *World Business Academy Perspectives*, 9 (1), 1995.

Hofman, H., 'The archive', in McKemmish, S. et al. (eds), *Archives. Recordkeeping in Society* (Wagga Wagga, 2005).

Horsman, P., 'Taming the elephant: an orthodox approach to the principle of provenance', in Abukhanfusa, K. and Sydbeck, J. (eds), *The Principle of Provenance. Report from the First Stockholm Conference on Archival Theory 1993* (Stockholm, 1994).

Horsman, P. 'Dirty hands: a new perspective on the original order', *Archives and Manuscripts*, 27 (1), 1999.

Horsman, P., 'The intelligent management of hybrid systems', *Records Management Bulletin*, 97, June 2000.

Howard, Stephen, 'Hybrid records management – a local government perspective', *Records Management Bulletin*, 110, October 2002.

Hutton, J.B.E. (Baron), *Report of the Inquiry into the Circumstances Surrounding the Death of Dr David Kelly CMG*, HC 247 (London, 2004).

International Records Management Trust, Records Management Project, *Report for the Period April to July 2000 and Project Completion Report*, TAN/YR3/QR4 (2000).

International Standards Organisation, *Documentation – Guidelines for the Establishment and Development of Monolingual Thesauri*, ISO 2788-1986 (Geneva, 1986).

InterPARES Authenticity Task Force, 'Authenticity Task Force Report', in *The Long-term Preservation of Authentic Electronic Records: Findings of the InterPARES Project* (Vancouver, 2002).

Irons Walch, Victoria, *Maintaining State Records in an Era of Change – A Report on State Archives and Records Management Programs* (April 1996).

Jeffrey-Cook, R. 'Developing a fileplan for local government', *Bulletin of the Records Management Society of Great Britain*, 125, 2005.

Jenkinson, Hilary, *A Manual of Archive Administration* (London, 1925).

Johnston, G., 'An alternative model for the design and implementation of records management systems', *Bulletin of the Records Management Society of Great Britain*, 126, June 2005.

Johnston, Gary P. and Bowen, David V., 'The benefits of electronic records management: a general review of published and some unpublished cases', *Records Management Journal*, 15 (13), 2005.

Jones, P.A., *Effective Records Management. Part 3: Performance Management for BS ISO 15489-1*, British Standards Institution, BIP 0025-3:2003 (London 2003).

Kargbo, John A., 'Archives management in Sierra Leone', *Journal of the Society of Archivists*, 26 (2), 2005.

Kenney, Anne R. and Rieger, Oya Y., *Moving Theory into Practice: Digital Imaging for Libraries and Archives* (Mountain View, CA, 2000).

Ketelaar, E., 'Tacit narratives: the meanings of archives', *Archival Science*, 1 (2), 2001.

Koelling, Jill Marie, *Digital Imaging, A Practical Approach* (Walnut Creek, CA, 2004).

Lee, H.-L., 'What is a collection?', *Journal of the American Society for Information Science*, 51 (12), 2000.

Levy, D., *Scrolling Forward. Making Sense of Documents in the Digital Age* (New York, 2001).

Lion, R. and Meertens, R.M., 'Security or opportunity: the influence of risk-taking tendency on risk information preference', *Journal of Risk Research*, 8 (4), June 2005.

Lynch, Clifford, 'Digital collections, digital libraries and the digitization of cultural heritage information', *First Monday*, 7 (5), 2002.

Lynch, Clifford, 'Authenticity in a digital environment: an exploratory analysis of the central role of trust' (Washington, DC, 2000) (available at *http://www.clir.org/pubs/reports/pub92/lynch.html*, accessed February 2006).

MacNeil, Heather, 'Providing grounds for trust: developing conceptual requirements for the long-term preservation of authentic electronic records', *Archivaria*, 50, 2000.

MacNeil, Heather, *Trusting Records* (Dordrecht, 2000).

MacNeil, Heather, 'Trusting records in a postmodern world', *Archivaria*, 51, Spring 2001.

MacNeil, Heather, 'Providing grounds for trust II: the findings of the Authenticity Task Force of InterPARES', *Archivaria*, 54, 2002.

MacQueen, Hector L., 'Reform of archives legislation: a Scots perspective', *Journal of the Society of Archivists*, 26 (2), October 2005.

Maguire, Rachael, 'Lessons learned from implementing an electronic records management system', *Records Management Journal*, 15 (13), 2005.

Malhotra, Y., *Why Knowledge Management Systems Fail? Enablers and Constraints of Knowledge Human Enterprises*, in American Society for Information Science and Technology Monograph Series, 2004.

Managing Business Information – DIRKS (available at *http://naa.gov.au/recordkeeping/dirks/summary.html*, accessed 12 July 2005).

McClure, Charles and Sprehe, Timothy, *Guidelines for Electronic Records Management on State and Federal Agency Websites* (New York and Washington, DC, 1998).

McDonald, J., 'Managing records in the modern office: taming the wild frontier', *Archivaria*, 39, 1995.

McKemmish, S., 'Evidence of me', *Archivaria*, 29 (1), 2001.

McKemmish, S. et al., 'Describing records in context in the continuum: the Australian Recordkeeping Metadata Schema', *Archivaria*, 48, 1999.

McKemmish, S. et al. (eds), *Archives. Recordkeeping in Society* (Wagga Wagga, 2005).

McLeod, J., *Effective Records Management – Part 2: Practical Implementation of BS ISO 15489-1*, British Standards Institution, BIP 0025-2:2002 (London, 2002).

McLeod, J., 'Assessing the impact of ISO 15489 – a preliminary investigation', *Records Management Journal*, 13 (2), 2003.

Mehr, Robert Irwin and Hedges, Bob, *Risk Management: Concepts and Applications* (Homewood, IL, 1974),

Menne-Haritz, A., 'Access – the reformulation of an archival paradigm', *Archival Science*, 1 (1), 2001.

Meulbroek, L., 'The promise and challenge of integrated risk management', *Risk Management and Insurance Review*, 5 (1), 2002.

Miller, F.M., *Arranging and Describing Archives and Manuscripts* (Chicago, 1990).

Moeller, Robert E., *Sarbanes-Oxley Act and the New Internal Auditing Rules* (New York, 2004).

Mommsen, W.J., *The Age of Bureaucracy. Perspectives on Political Sociology of Max Weber* (Oxford, 1974).

Mortimer, Ian, 'Discriminating between readers: the case for a policy of flexibility', *Journal of the Society of Archivists*, 23 (1), 2002.

National Archives, *Guidelines for Management, Appraisal and Preservation of Electronic Records* (1999) (available at *http://www.nationalarchives.gov.uk/electronicrecords/advice/guidelines.htm*, accessed 25 November 2005).

Negroponte, Nicholas, *Being Digital* (Boston, 1995).

NISO, *Understanding Metadata* (Bethesda, MD, 2004).

Norup, T., 'Danish PM's private communications disclosed by MS Word', *The Risks Digest: Forum on Risks to the Public in Computers and Related Systems*, 23 (12), 12 January 2004.

Nowotny, Helga, 'Dilemma of expertise – democraticising expertise and socially robust knowledge', *Science and Public Policy*, 30 (3), June 2003.

Ombati, K., 'Domesticating ISO 15489 and ISAD(G) at the Kenya National Archives and Documentation Service', *ESARBICA Newsletter*, 2004, p. 2.

O'Neill, Onora, 'Accuracy, independence, and trust', in Runciman, W.G. (ed.), *Hutton and Butler: Lifting the Lid on the Workings of Power* (Oxford, 2004).

Park, E., 'Understanding authenticity in records and information management: analyzing practitioner constructs', *American Archivist*, 64 (2), 2001.

Pavuza, F., Strodl, S. and Rauber, A., 'Evaluating preservation strategies for audio and video files', *Proceedings of the DELOS Workshop on Digital Repositories: Interoperability and Common Service* (Crete, 2005).

Pearce-Moses, Richard, *A Glossary of Archival and Records Terminology* (Chicago, 2005) (available at *http://www.archivists.org/glossary/index.asp*, accessed February 2006).

Pederson, Ann, 'Professing archives – a very human enterprise', in McKemmish, S. et al. (eds), *Archives. Recordkeeping in Society* (Wagga Wagga, 2005).

Peis, Peter, 'The trickster's dilemma', in Strathern, Marilyn (ed.), *Audit Cultures – Anthropological Studies in Accountability, Ethics and the Academy* (London, 2000).

Perer, A., Shneiderman, B. and Oard, D.W., *Using Rhythms of Relationships to Understand Email Archives* (n.d. but probably 2005).

Phillips, John T., 'The challenge of web site records preservation', *Information Management Journal*, 37 (1), 2003.

Pitti, D. and Duff, Wendy, 'Encoded Archival Description on the Internet', special issue of *Journal of Internet Cataloguing*, 4, 2001.

Power, Michael, *The Audit Explosion* (London, 1994).

Power, Michael, *The Audit Society: Rituals of Verification* (Oxford, 1997).

PREMIS Working Group, *Implementing Preservation Repositories for Digital Materials* (Dublin, OH, and Mountain View, CA, 2004).

Puglia, Steven, 'The costs of digital imaging projects', *RLG DigiNews*, 3 (5), 15 October 1999.

Radner, R., 'Hierarchy: the economics of managing', *Journal of Economics Literature*, 30 September 1992.

Rankin, Frank, *Scottish Postgraduate Training Project Report* (Glasgow, 2002) (available at *http://www.archives.gla.ac.uk/hostsite/spat.pdf*, accessed February 2006).

Rauber, A. et al., 'DELOS DPC testbed: a framework for documenting the behaviour and functionality of digital objects and preservation strategies', in Thanos, C. (ed.), *Delos Research Activities 2005* (Pisa, 2005).

Rauch, C. and Rauber, A., 'Preserving digital media: towards a preservation solution evaluation metric', *Proceedings of the International Conference on Asian Digital Libraries* (Shanghai, 2004).

Records Continuum Group, *Prototyping of Integrated Systems Environment Supporting Automated Recordkeeping Metadata Capture and Re-use* (Monash, 2005) (available at *http://www.sims. monash.edu.au/research/rcrg/research/crm/firstiteration.html*, accessed 12 July 2005).

Reed, B., 'Metadata: core record or core business?', *Archives and Manuscripts*, 25 (2), 1997.

Richmond, Lesley, 'The memory of society: businesses', *COMMA*, 1–2, 2002.

Roberts, D., 'Defining electronic records, documents and data', *Archives and Manuscripts*, 22, May 1994.

Rosenthal, D.S.H., Robertson, T., Lipkis, T., Reich, V. and Morabito, S., 'Requirements for digital preservation systems', *D-Lib Magazine*, 11 (11), 2005.

Ross, S., 'Strategies for selecting resources for digitization: Source-Orientated, User-Driven, Asset-Aware Model (SOUDAAM)', in Coppock, Terry (ed.), *Making Information Available in Digital Format: Perspectives from Practitioners* (Edinburgh, 1999).

Ross, S., *Changing Trains at Wigan: Digital Preservation and the Future of Scholarship* (London, 2000).

Ross, S., 'Position paper on integrity and authenticity of digital cultural heritage objects', *Integrity and Authenticity of Digital Cultural Heritage Objects,* Thematic Issue, 1, 2002.

Ross, S., *Digital Library Development Review, National Library of New Zealand* (Wellington, 2003).

Ross, S., 'Reflections on the impact of the Lund Principles on European approaches to digitisation', in *Strategies for a European Area of Digital Cultural Resources: Towards a Continuum of Digital Heritage* (The Hague, 2004).

Ross, S., 'Strategie per la conservazione digitale: descrizione e risultati dei primi studi di casi di ERPANET', *Archivi e Computer*, XIV/3.04, 2004.

Ross, S., *Commentary on Pittsburgh University Recordkeeping Requirements Project*, paper to Society of American Archivists Annual Meeting, 1995 (available at *http://eprints.erpanet.org/archive/ 00000060/01/SR_commentary_SAA1995.htm*, accessed 3 November 2005).

Ross, S. and Day, M. (eds), *DCC Digital Curation Manual* (Glasgow, 2005 onwards).

Ross, S. and Gow, A., *Digital Archaeology? Rescuing Neglected or Damaged Data Resources* (London, 1999).

Ross, S. and Hedstrom M., 'Preservation research and sustainable digital libraries', *International Journal of Digital Libraries*, 5 (4), 2005.

Ross, S. and Higgs, E. (eds), *Electronic Information Resources and Historians: European Perspectives* (St Katharinen, 1993).

Ross, S. and Kim, Y., 'Digital preservation automated ingest and appraisal metadata', in Thanos, C. (ed.), *DELOS Research Activities* (Pisa, 2005).

Ross, S. and McHugh, A., 'Audit and certification: creating a mandate for the digital curation centre', *Diginews*, 9 (5), 2005.

Ross, S., Greenan, M. and McKinney, P., 'Digital preservation strategies: the initial outcomes of the ERPANET case studies', in *Preservation of*

Electronic Records: New Knowledge and Decision-making (Ottawa, 2004).

Ross, S. et al., *ERPANET Case Studies in Digital Preservation* (Glasgow, 2006).

Ryan, David, 'The future of managing electronic records', *Records Management Journal*, 15 (3), 2005.

Sampson, K.L., *Value Added Records Management: Protecting Corporate Assets, Reducing Business Risks*, 2nd edn (Westport, CT, 1992).

Samuel, J., 'Electronic mail', in Higgs, E. (ed.), *History and Electronic Artefacts* (Oxford, 1998).

Sanett, Shelby, 'Toward developing a framework of cost elements for preserving authentic electronic records into perpetuity', *College and Research Libraries*, 63 (5), 2002.

Schellenberg, T.R., *Modern Archives: Principles and Techniques* (Melbourne, 1956).

Shepherd, E. and Yeo, G., *Managing Records. A Handbook of Principles and Practice* (London, 2003).

Shore, Cris and Wright, Susan, 'Coercive accountability', in Strathern, Marilyn (ed.), *Audit Cultures – Anthropological Studies in Accountability, Ethics and the Academy* (London, 2000).

Simons, R., 'How risky is your company?', *Harvard Business Review*, 7 (3), May/June 1999.

Skjekkeland, Atle, 'Email mismanagement: a looming disaster', *M-iD*, 2005.

Smith, Abby, *Why Digitize?* (Washington, DC, 1999).

Smyth, Zoe A., 'Implementing EDRM: has it provided the benefits expected', *Records Management Journal*, 15 (3), 2005.

Standards Australia, *Records Management* (AS 4390.1 – 1996 to AS 4390.6 – 1996) (Sydney, 1996).

State Records of South Australia, *Keyword AAA. A Thesaurus of General Terms* (Sydney, revised edn 1998, reprinted 2001).

Stephens, David O., 'The Sarbanes-Oxley Act records management implications', *Record Management Journal*, 15 (2), 2005.

Stille, Alexander, *The Future of the Past – How the Information Age Threatens to Destroy Our Cultural Heritage* (London, 2002).

Strathern, Marilyn, 'Virtual society? Get real!' (2000) (available at *http://virtualsociety.sbs.ox.ac.uk/Grpapers/strathern.htm*, accessed 12 July 2005).

Thanos C. (ed.), *Delos Research Activities 2005* (Pisa, 2005).

Tharlet, Eve, *The Elves of Cologne* (Zurich, 2005).

Thompson, D., 'Risk management: a brief history', *Journal of Banking and Financial Services*, 117 (3), June–July 2003.

Tibbo, H.R., 'On the nature and importance of archiving in the digital age', *Advances in Computers*, 57, 2003.

Tibbo, H.R., 'Primarily history: how US historians search for primary sources at the dawn of the digital age', *American Archivist*, 66 (1), Spring/Summer 2003.

Todd, M., *Recordkeeping* (London, Winter 2005) (available at *http://www.nationalarchives.gov.uk/services/pdf/winter2005.pdf*, accessed February 2006).

Tombs, K., 'Knowledge management is dead: long live records management', *Records Management Journal*, 14 (2), 2004.

Tough, A.G., 'Records management standards and the good governance agenda in Commonwealth Africa', *Archives and Manuscripts*, 32 (2), November 2004.

Tough, A.G., 'The post-custodial/pro-custodial argument from a Records Management perspective', *Journal of the Society of Archivists*, 25 (1), 2004.

Tough, A. and Moss, M., 'Metadata, controlled vocabularies and directories …', *Records Management Journal*, 13 (1), 2003.

Trimble, G.R., 'Emulation of the IBM system/360 on a microprogrammable computer', International Symposium on Microarchitecture, Conference record of the 7th annual workshop on Microprogramming, Palo Alto, CA, 1974.

Turner, J.M., 'The MetaMap: a tool for learning about metadata standards, sets, and initiatives', in Bischoff, F.M., Hofman, H. and Ross, S. (eds), *Metadata in Preservation: Selected Papers from an ERPANET Seminar at the Archives School Marburg*, in *Veröffentlichungen der Archivschule Marburg, Institut für Archivwissenschaft*, 40, 2003.

Tyacke, Sarah, 'Archives in a wider world: the culture and politics of archives', *Archivaria*, 52, Fall 2001.

Tyler, J.R., Wilkinson, D.M. and Huberman, B.A., 'Email as spectroscopy: automated discovery of community structure within organizations', *Communities and Technologies*, 2003.

United States of America, Department of Defense, *Design Criteria Standard for Electronic Records Management Software Applications*, DoD 5015.2-STD (Washington, DC, 2002).

Upward, F., 'Structuring the records continuum, part two: structuration theory and recordkeeping', *Archives and Manuscripts*, 25 (1), May 1997.

Upward, F., 'Modelling the continuum as paradigm shift in recordkeeping and archiving processes, and beyond – a personal reflection', *Records Management Journal*, 10 (3), 2000.

Upward, F., 'Records continuum', in McKemmish, S. et al. (eds), *Archives. Recordkeeping in Society* (Wagga Wagga, 2005).

Upward, F. and McKemmish, Sue, 'In search of the lost tiger, by way of Sainte-Beauve: Reconstructing the possibilities in "Evidence of me ..."', *Archives and Manuscripts*, 29 (1), 2001.

Usherwood, B., *Perception of Archives, Libraries and Museums in Modern Britain* (Sheffield, 2005).

van Ballegooie, M. and Duff, W., 'Archival metadata', in Ross, S. and Day, M. (eds), *DCC Digital Curation Manual* (Glasgow, 2006).

Walker, F. and Thoma, G., 'A web-based paradigm for file migration', *Proceedings of IS&T's Archiving Conference* (San Antonio, CA, April 2004).

Wallace, D.A., 'Recordkeeping and electronic pail policy: the state of thought and the state of the practice', *Society of American Archivists* (Orlando, FL, 1998).

Wheatley, P., 'Migration – CAMiLEON discussion paper', *Ariadne*, 2001.

White-Dollman, Mary M., 'ISO 15489: a tool for records management in mergers', *Information Management*, 38 (5), September/October 2004.

Wiggins, Bob, 'Making the case for electronic records management: a Churchillian viewpoint', *Records Management Bulletin*, 110, October 2002.

Williams, David J., 'EDRM implementation at the National Weights and Measure Laboratory', *Records Management Journal*, 15 (3), 2005.

Williams, Howard, Sullivan, David and Matthews, Gwynn, *Francis Fukuyama and the End of History* (Cardiff, 1997).

Willis, Anthony, 'Corporate governance and management of information and records', *Records Management Journal*, 15 (2), 2005.

Wilson, John, 'Ten questions to ask vendors of EDM systems', *Records Management Bulletin*, 93, October 1999, p. 3.

Wodehouse, P.G., *Leave it to Psmith* (London, 1924).

Yusof, Zawiyah M. and Chell, Robert W., 'Towards a theoretical construct for records management', *Records Management Journal*, 12 (2), 2002.

Unpublished papers

Bedford, S., 'Records classification systems', unpublished paper at Records Management Association of Australasia Conference, 2005.

Currall, J., 'What's wrong with archivists and records managers?', unpublished paper for Society of Archivists Conference, Glasgow, 2 September 2004.

Donath, J., 'Visualizing email archives' – draft, 2004.

McDonald, J., 'The wild frontier ... isn't so wild anymore', unpublished paper for Annual Conference of the Records Management Society of Great Britain, Cardiff, 15 April 2002.

Index

Preserving Access to Digital
Information (PADI), 144*n*
PRINCE (project management
methodology), 15
processes – *see* business processes
professional bodies, 103–4
professionalism, 102–5
PROFS – *see* litigation: *Armstrong* v.
Executive Office of the President
project management, 15, 42
PRONOM, 58, 67*n*
provenance, xi, 131–2, 152*n*,
159–60, 168–9, 182, 186
public authorities:
digital curation in, 115–16
legislation affecting – *see* access to
environmental information
legislation; freedom of
information legislation;
Regulation of Investigatory
Powers Act 2000; Reuse of
Public Sector Information
Regulations 2005
and private authorities, 230–1
Public Company Accounting Reform
and Investor Protection Act
2002 – *see* Sarbanes-Oxley Act
2002 (SOX)
Public Service Quality Group
(PSQG), 206

quality control, 38–9, 41

Radner, Roy, 75
Rankin, Frank, 87
Rasmussen, Anders Fogh, 148*n*
RCRG – *see* Records Continuum
Research Group
record keeping – *see also* DIRKS
(Design and Implementation of
Record Keeping Systems)

as academic discipline, ix–x
in Australia, xi
in Canada, xi
contingent nature of, 237–8, 240
impact of technology on, 1, 7
metadata, 12–15
models, 2–6
in South Africa, xi
traditions, 1–2
in United Kingdom, xii
records – *see also* accuracy;
appraisal; authenticity;
confidentiality; context;
destruction; integrity; life cycle
model; metadata; provenance;
retention; retrieval; security
capture of, 28–30
continuum, 3–5, 93–4, 136, 160,
181, 186, 193–4, 199, 201
creation and creators of, 17, 21,
86, 94–5, 157–8, 183–4, 194
duplication of, 30
as evidence, 17, 21, 158, 182, 194,
234, 236
of higher education, 182, 185–7
– *see also* Gateway to the
Archives of Scottish Higher
Education (GASHE)
as memory, 157, 231–3
original order of, 185, 217
personal records, 135–6, 236
surveys, 10, 194–9
vital records, 34, 77
Records Continuum Research Group
(RCRG), 21
records management – *see also*
business classification schemes;
DIRKS (Design and
Implementation of Record
Keeping Systems); electronic
document and records